RELIGION IN ANCIENT MESOPOTAMIA

RELIGION IN ANCIENT
Mesopotamia

Jean Bottéro

Translated by Teresa Lavender Fagan

The University of Chicago Press
Chicago and London

Jean Bottéro is emeritus director of l'École Pratique des Hautes Études, quatrième section, Paris. He is the author of *Mesopotamia: Writing, Reasoning, and the Gods* and coauthor of *Ancestor of the West: Writing, Reasoning, and Religion in the Ancient Near East,* both published by the University of Chicago Press.

The University of Chicago Press, Chicago 60637
The University of Chicago Press, Ltd., London
© 2001 by The University of Chicago
All rights reserved. Published 2001
Printed in the United States of America
10 09 08 07 06 05 04 03 02 01   5 4 3 2 1

ISBN (cloth): 0-226-06717-3

Originally published as *La plus vieille religion: En Mésopotamie,*
© Éditions Gallimard, 1998.

The University of Chicago Press gratefully acknowledges a subvention from the government of France, through the French Ministry of Culture, Centre National du Livre, in support of the costs of translating this volume.

Library of Congress Cataloging-in-Publication Data

Bottéro, Jean.
   [Plus vieille religion en Mésopotamie. English]
   Religion in ancient Mesopotamia / Jean Bottéro ; translated by Teresa Lavender Fagan.
      p.   cm.
   Translation of: La plus vieille religion en Mésopotamie.
   Includes bibliographical references and index.
   ISBN 0-226-06717-3 (alk. paper)
   1. Iraq—Religion.   I. Title.
BL2350.I7 B6713   2001
299'.21—dc21

                                         00-011052

CONTENTS

Preface   vii
Translator's Note   xi

1   **Religion and Religions**   1

2   **Mesopotamia and Its History**   7
     Prehistory   7
     History   11
     Historical Overview   18

3   **The Sources: What We Can Expect
     from Them**   21

4   **Religious Sentiment**   29
     Sources   29
     Reverence   36
     Henotheism?   40

5   **Religious Representations**   44
     The Gods   44
     The Mythology of the Divine   58
     The Mythology of the World   77
     The Mythology of Man   95

6   **Religious Behavior**   114
     The Theocentric Cult   114
     The "Sacramental" Cult   170

7   **Influence and Survivals**   203
     Influence   203
     Survivals   208

     Conclusion   219

     Notes   225
     Bibliography   233
     Index   237

PREFACE

Mesopotamian Religion:
The Oldest of All Known Religions

The oldest religion we are aware of, one that is explicitly revealed to us through excavated sites and prodigious numbers of images and objects used in religious services and above all through a huge amount of written material—hundreds of thousands of often quite detailed local documents—is the religious system of ancient Mesopotamia, dating from the fourth millennium B.C. to shortly before the birth of Christ. Beyond simply making us aware of this religion, ancient artifacts offer another advantage, which only those of ancient Egypt might rival: they enable us to trace the development of Mesopotamian religion over three full millennia—up to the time of its demise.

This dual advantage allows us to visit a monumental, partially reconstructed edifice, which so far we have sought for in vain elsewhere, and introduces us to the daily life, the hearts and minds, of those ancient, vanished Mesopotamians, whom we have ultimately come to recognize as our most ancient ancestors, those discernable and accessible in our most distant past, the first builders of the civilization that continues to sustain us and that has spread widely throughout the world. It should also provide us with unhoped-for enlightenment that might help to clarify many of the problems still posed by the existence, evolution, and knowledge, not only of our own and other religions, but of the religious phenomenon itself.

Written at the publisher's request,[1] the present work is in fact a revision of a small text written in 1948 and published in 1952 by Presses Universitaires de France under the title *La religion babylonienne*, which has been out of print for several years. It is perhaps not irrelevant to reissue it: in the last half-century a great deal of water has flowed under the bridges of Assyriology; much of what we knew before has been better studied and digested; a great many discoveries have been made; many uncertainties have been resolved and errors corrected. Furthermore, the basic issues themselves have been reformulated on more than one occasion: thus the question of the fundamentally Semitic character of Mesopotamian religion, which to me had once seemed rather pressing and worthy of demonstration, should at present no longer meet with any serious disagreement, and I have stressed that issue much less (and in other ways) here.

While essentially maintaining the general structure of my earlier book, I have preferred to rewrite it in large part, even if I have at times reproduced entire passages from it. I have augmented the text with many more translations of original documents, especially in the realms of the imagination and emotions, which necessarily go hand in hand in all religions, and nothing takes the place of reading original documents in order to analyze and fully understand ideas. Such contact is much better than simply working with more detailed, more scholarly, and more abstract explanations, those already digested by *us*. To further stress that this is after all a revised work, along the lines of my *Mésopotamie: L'écriture, la raison et les dieux (Mesopotamia: Writing, Reasoning, and the Gods)*, I have replaced "Babylon" in the title with "Mesopotamia," in order thus to emphasize the most original and the most remarkable fact that has recently been brought to light concerning this religious system: its exceptional antiquity and its very long life, commensurate with that of a venerable land.

I trust I will not be criticized if, in order to do the subject justice by explaining it as best as I can, I have set aside all scholarly discourse, beginning with a supercilious chronology, which would be too off-putting for nonprofessional readers, who have, even more than others, a right to this book. If I have (rather discreetly!) here and there referred to more technical works, going beyond the citing of original texts, the most honest means of verifying information, it is not to point nonspecialist readers in those directions, readers who do not regularly have anything to do with those heavy, inaccessible tomes, but rather to justify myself, as is fitting, in the eyes of my colleagues, or in those of members of the "Secret Society" of Assyriologists.

To reflect the very nature of the subject in question, my plan should be logical and clear. I must begin by defining and explaining the specific object of the research undertaken here: *religion,* the essential components of which govern the organization of what I have to say about it. Then I must sketch the historical framework in which this system was born and developed before asking the question: to what degree and within what limits can a religion so distant in time, and extinct for two millennia, still be the object of an indirect, sufficiently supported *knowledge*. I must give some critical idea of the *sources* available to us, especially documentary sources, composed and written down by the religion's adherents and in which something of their religious experience has remained for us to discover. Only then, in more lengthy presentations, will it be easier, and more fruitful, to enter through the monumental doors of *religious feeling, religious representations,* and *religious behavior,* into the vast and dusty sanctuary of "the most ancient of all religions." And we must finally investigate the degree to which that religion influenced the world around it, and whether anything survived from it.

Transcription and Other Conventions

Names of people and of places are generally rendered in their usual transcription (Ḫammurabi, Aššurbanipal, Nineveh), except where it seemed better to show their component parts for one reason or another (Âṣu-šu-namir, Atra-ḫasîs). The same applies to names of gods and goddesses (Marduk, Utu, Ninḫursag).

Sumerian nouns are transcribed in Roman type, and the elements of compound words are always separated by periods (dam.kar). Akkadian nouns are in italics, and their syllabic division in the writing is expressed by hyphens *(tam-ka-ru).*

For both languages most of the consonants and vowels used in the transcriptions are pronounced as in English. The following points should be noted:

> *â* is always pronounced *a* as in *father*
> *ê* is pronounced *a* as in *ace*
> *î* is pronounced *ee* as in *beet*
> *û* is always pronounced *oo* as in *boot* (Uruk = Oorook)
> all the consonants are articulated (Ningirsu = Nin-gir-soo; *ng* is never pronounced as in the English ending *-ing*)
> all the consonants are voiced, or hard (Ningirsu = Nin-gir-soo; *g* is always pronounced as in English *go*)
> ḫ corresponds to a sound close to the *j* in Spanish *jota*
> š denotes English *sh*
> ṣ, ṭ, and q indicate so-called emphatic values that are unknown in our phonetic system

Acute and grave accents and subscript numbers that are found with certain syllables in Sumerian (e.g., šá, šà, u₄, unuₓ) have no phonetic significance whatsoever and only distinguish the cuneiform signs that correspond to different Sumerian words.[2]

A superscript Roman lowercase letter before a word reflects the use in the cuneiform writing system of a "determinative," which indicates the semantic category to which the word that follows belongs. Thus the superscript *d* in *dŠamaš* is used to indicate that Šamaš is the name of a god (*d* is the abbreviation for "deus" or "dingir," the Latin and Sumerian words for "god").

The numbers at the left of a translated passage or inserted within the translated text refer to the number of the line or the verse in the entire work.

Capital Roman numerals refer to the tablet of a work that consists of more than one tablet in the original cuneiform version. The lowercase Roman numerals refer to the column if there is more than one on the tablet. The line or verse numbers are preceded by a colon; R. indicates the reverse of the tablet. Thus *Epic of Gilgameš* I/iv, R.:8–15 is to be understood as verses 8–15 of the fourth column of the reverse of the first tablet of the *Epic of Gilgameš*.

Unless otherwise indicated, all dates are to be read B.C.

TRANSLATOR'S NOTE

Whenever possible, I have used published English-language versions of the original texts Mr. Bottéro cites in his work. In this regard, I would like to extend my continued thanks to my friend Professor Matthew Stolper of the University of Chicago's Oriental Institute for his invaluable help in locating the appropriate English translations. When English editions could not be found, or if the translations were badly outdated, I translated directly from Mr. Bottéro's French versions.

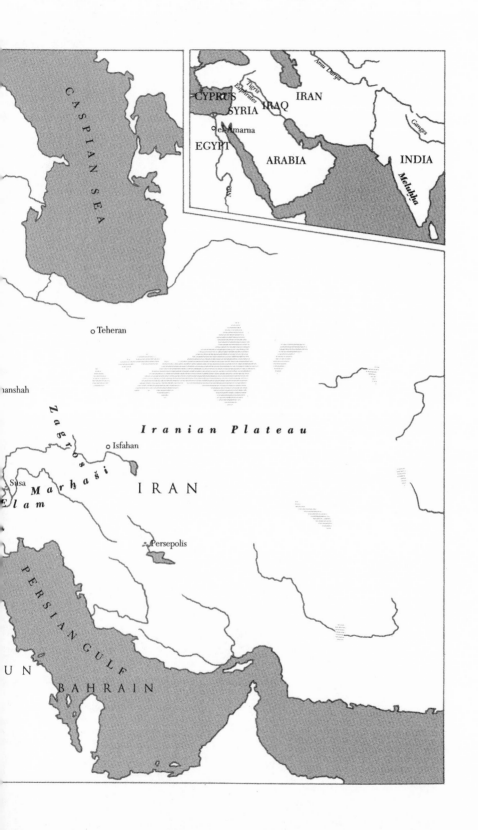

CHAPTER ONE

Religion and Religions

No one can undertake a thorough study of the economy of Meso-potamia, Greece, China, or anywhere else without at least first hav-ing a clear idea of what is implied by the term "economy" itself. It would be just as frivolous, just as risky, to delve even slightly seri-ously into any religion whatsoever without first reflecting on the constituent elements that can be expected to make up a given reli-gion—in other words, one must start with a rather clear vision of what the phenomenon "religion" itself actually means.

Obviously, this is not the place to initiate a philosophical or psy-chological discussion (have such discussions ever achieved their goals?), especially since it is not to our advantage—we others, simple historians and those who are curious about ancient artifacts—to contemplate things on that ethereal level. Before drowning in an ocean of detail, without bottom or shores, in our goal to uncover, to describe, and, insofar as possible, to put those details in order, as we attempt to understand the religion of the ancient Mesopotamians, it is advisable to establish how the structure of that religion is simi-lar to those of other religions. Thus can we find in an order (a natu-rally *logical* order, not a *chronological* one, at this stage of our under-taking) and within a system the essential facts that indeed make it a religion, which we will then have to classify and ponder using such a huge amount of material. Before beginning, it is always bet-ter at least to know where one wishes to go.

What is immediately obvious to anyone who hopes to understand a religious system—or religion itself—is its social nature. Religion above all affects its faithful in their lives within a group, imposing upon them a certain number of feelings, conceptions, and practices to which they would not have been led had they not been together. In studying a religion, therefore, one might focus on this collective aspect. (Such an approach is, moreover, taken almost obligatorily ever since the advent of sociology, which discovered and learned how to make use of its value. And who could deny that such a concern is useful and even indispensable?)

But to stress the collective nature of religion from the outset is to forget that the only *real* and *primary* elements of any society—the only true sources and subjects of social, religious, and other constraints, the only beings who uphold the essential explanation of such obligations and who can show their authentic and complete functioning in a clear way—are the *individuals* who make up that society and without whom it would not exist. Were the old Scholastics, who had much better sense than is usually attributed to them by those who do not understand them, wrong to say, using their own jargon, that "an assembly of people, disregarding the assembled individuals, is a portrait of the mind/spirit" (multitudo sine multis non est, nisi in ratione)? Thus, no religion is truly real—identifiable and analyzable—except through and within the individuals who practice it, individuals who, alone, using the mechanism of their minds and their hearts, hold the secrets of it, even if they are unaware that they do so. And it is primarily this mechanism, conscious or not, that we must isolate, in order to understand its functioning within a given system.

Considered in this way, any religion, let us say, religion as a whole, would be incomprehensible if it did not have a specific and primary object that governs a more or less spontaneous mental attitude, one common to all its followers (the fact that, I will say it again, its individual adherents only rarely, or never, have a full or even vague awareness of it is of little importance). The same is true, moreover, with many other dispositions of our nature, which intervene just as powerfully in all of our lives.

We can understand this better if, like using indirect lighting, we take a look at another of our specific inclinations—love, for example. Innate and irrational, it irresistibly pushes each one of us toward "another," someone within our reach, in whom we obscurely sense a sort of enrichment indispensable to our lives, a necessary complement to our selves, whom we must seek out and obtain regardless of all opposition. What similarly legitimizes and justifies religion is found, not on our level, on our, shall we say, "horizontal" plane, but in a sense "vertically," above us. It is the unthinking and intimate attraction, all the stronger in that it is instinctive and imprecise, that directs us toward something inaccessible that reaches far beyond us: the vague apprehension, the obscure feeling that there exists, much higher "up," much greater than we, an undefined order of things, absolutely superior to us and to all that we know here on earth, but to which we are in a certain way impulsively inclined to submit and toward which we feel compelled to turn if we wish to be fully complete. This "order of things" (as I am calling it, since it first appears to us as ontologically indeterminate; neither personalized nor impersonal) is what, for lack of a better term, we call *the supernatural,* but also *the sacred, the numinous, the divine*—the primary object of religion, without which it would not exist, having no reason for being.

That which—still within a logical and not chronological order—directs us toward "It" is *religiosity,* or *a religious sentiment,* the root of all religion, which alone justifies, infuses, and governs it, whether that sentiment is positive or negative, centripetal or centrifugal. For we can feel respectful, or even fearful, in the face of the supernatural, of what is completely beyond us, and whose formidable presentiment is enough to make us want to flee; but we can also feel oddly attracted to it, if it promises a prodigious richness of being and life. This dual, contradictory movement covers the field of what we call the *religious sentiment,* which colors, permeates, and defines a given religion—either as a "religion of fear" or as a "mystical religion."

We are spontaneously driven to clarify the supernatural, toward which the basic impulse of our hearts immediately leads us, in the dark night, to define it, to portray it more vividly than in the light and shade in which from the beginning we only sensed its existence: for "it is in our nature always to seek to know" (Aristotle). Again using the comparison with love, is not love's first characteristic curiosity, that ardent search for the image and the secrets of its object? Religion follows the same path. Depending on its fantasy and its scale of values, depending on its tastes and its revulsions, depending on its imagination and phantasms, each culture in which a religion has been born and taken root has sought to portray the divine, the sacred, which is its soul, as either one or more material realities; or as an "order of things," an imprecise "force," but one with noticeable effects; or as one, or several, personalities whose image would be more or less familiar to us. We then speak, depending on the case, of "fetishism," of "pantheism," of "anthropomorphism," of "polytheism," or of "monotheism."

Such *representations,* which each religion necessarily constructs for the supernatural, proliferate throughout time; curiosity and reflection are rarely lacking in this realm, one open, perhaps even more than others, to perplexity, rumination, inquiry, and imagination. Such representations arrange themselves at random, in agreement or in divergence. With the unique reinforcement of fantasy, the only possible recourse in the circumstances, they easily make up an entire *mythological system* that is more or less polychromatic; and when a certain logic triumphs over this imaginative foundation, we can even speak of *theology*.

Furthermore—and again like love, which endlessly pushes lovers to "do something" to benefit the object of their attachment, to bend as much as possible to his or her wishes, needs, assumed desires—a religious spirit also feels compelled to see the divine as one of the goals, if not the very center, of his life, the receiver of his goods, the master of his spirit. This is the realm of *religious behavior* (which is also commonly called *worship*), whose content and program vary depending on the sentimental ties that attach believers to the supernatural, as well as on the image that they have created of it.

It is clear that the result of all the purely religious activity of a *representation of the divine* and of one's *attitude toward it*, which are dependent on and animated by each other, each in its own way, through the *religiosity* that penetrates them (the images that we create of the divine and of that which touches it, as well as the rules we impose upon ourselves to follow it) are exclusively and completely the products only of our creative and fanciful ingenuity and activities—our *imagination*. By definition, none of us has ever seen or will ever see, perceive, hear, or touch, in any way, that object of our religiosity, an imperceptible and shadowy object whose existence, let us repeat, is only suggested by a powerful, but blind, feeling. Everything we propose about it and its demands is pure conjecture and the creation of our imagination and derives from that curiosity and imaginativeness alone, made up of "calculated imagination," following a certain dialectic, which, in the strict sense of the word, we call *mythology*.[1] Religion is mythological, and every religion is mythological. This in no way dissuades us from strenuously pursuing its objects, as if we knew that they existed, or from "believing in it," more or less firmly or casually, and from conforming to its precepts and routines, with fervor or half-heartedly.

We must also consider a completely different aspect of religions in order to classify, characterize, and understand them: *their origins*.

For most religions, especially the most ancient and, as we say, "primitive," it is impossible to know anything of their beginnings: they are lost in the deep night of prehistory or in the impenetrable fog of "parahistory," of which we have no accounts or documents to orient ourselves. Every religion of this type is ultimately only a reflection of the culture out of which it developed. And every culture, all of which have a particular scale of values, a concept of social life, a type of social organization, a concern for others, a collection of tastes and aversions, of preferences and fears, necessarily includes a determinative attitude toward the divine: a religious dimension, a religion, born within that culture and developed through imperceptible stages. This is what we call a *prehistoric* or *traditional religion,* or, if we wish, a *popular* or *primitive* religion.

Like everything in a given culture, such religions were transmitted from parents to children, in the endless succession of generations, without any specific authority watching over them, without further constraints than those presiding, for example, over alimentary habits or over the laws of kinship. Every prehistoric religion was a rich body of hereditary customs, received and practiced without question, *because it has always been thus* and because everyone was plunged into it at birth, and it never entered anyone's mind to escape it, or to change it, any more than one would change one's way of life.

But it happens that at a historical moment, in other words, a moment identifiable by us in space and in time, there arrives a figure, equally identifiable by us, who comes to interrupt the course of a traditional religion, on his own, by himself creating and diffusing *his* own religion: *his* emotional attitude with regard to the sacred, *his* personal conception of the sacred and of the duties it imposes. Such religions are what we call *historical religions* (or *revealed religions*), which demand of individuals, at least when the religions have not yet been implanted and passed into the common culture, a "conversion," that is, a voluntary abandonment of the traditional system to blend into the new one. Each historical religion is in fact only a more or less radical reform of the prehistoric system in which its founder was born and first lived.

There are not many of these types of religions, but (without discussing localized phenomena such as Mormonism, launched in the United States some two centuries ago by Joseph Smith) several have been attractive enough or have had enough success, spontaneously or through force, to conquer large parts of the world: in the West, Judaism (created by Moses around 1250), Christianity (by Jesus Christ, at the beginning of our era), and Islam (six centuries later, by Muhammad); and in the East, Buddhism (by Siddhartha Gautama, around A.D. 500). The essence and structure of those religions were contemplated and developed by the great religious "inventors" who were first inspired by them and who were ardent enough to convert disciples, then by believers, and then by authors, by themselves or with their entourage and successors, whose "holy writings" aimed to establish and propagate everywhere and forever the letter, the framework, and the essential obligations of their new religious system. Because of the way they are constituted, historical religions could not in fact exist except via a strict and everlasting tie to such written documents, which reveal the thought of their founders. And they always demand a complete conformity of thought *(orthodoxy)* and behavior *(orthopraxy)* to the original doctrine set down in writing. Each such religion, in its own way, in order to ensure this monolithic cohesion, has provided itself with an official body responsible for remembering and enforcing it; each such religion tends toward intolerance of all that is outside it.

Putting the subject of the present work, Mesopotamian religion, in the context of what has just been presented, let us say that its *religiosity* was made up above all of a "centrifugal" feeling of fear, respect, and servility with regard to the divine; that the divine was portrayed on the human model *(anthropomorphism)* and was spread out over a whole society of supernatural beings, gods *(polytheism)*, whose needs people were expected to fulfill and whose orders were to be carried out with all the devotion, submission, but also generosity and ostentation that were thought to be expected by such lofty figures. Furthermore, it was resolutely and exclusively a prehistoric religion without holy scriptures, religious authorities, dogmas, orthodoxy, orthopraxy, or fanaticism, and it evolved sporadically, depending upon the culture of which it was only the reflection and on the time and events.

CHAPTER TWO

Mesopotamia and Its History

If a prehistoric religion such as that of Mesopotamia is in fact only the local culture's self-extension into the supernatural, it can be fully understood only in the context of the development and history of that culture and of the world in which it flourished.

Prehistory

In geological terms, Mesopotamia, whose territory covered approximately that of present-day Iraq, is not truly an old land. With the formidable barrier of the Caucasus to the north, the glacis of the Iranian plateau to the east, the Persian Gulf to the south, and the uncrossable Syro-Arabian desert to the west, Mesopotamia began to emerge only a few millennia after the end of the final European glaciations, perhaps some twelve thousand years ago. By drastically reducing precipitation and the amount of humidity in the air, glaciation had repercussions in the Middle East. A vast expanse of alluvial land that until then had formed the enormous bed of only a single river was uncovered. The much narrower remnants of that river are the Tigris and the Euphrates.

The first inhabitants of the land that was thus gradually revealed in the sixth millennium at the latest probably came from the surrounding highlands to the northwest, the north, and the east, and they were undoubtedly ethnically and culturally diverse. We know nothing about them but the paltry vestiges of their lives that archeologists have uncovered here and there. These poor fragments, in their varied and voluminous heaps, are naturally unable to reveal the inhabitants' religion and what it might have inspired in them in terms of thought and action, except with the help of our imagination and conjectures. As they came to settle on scattered plots of land on a still new earth, the settlers necessarily imported not only their rudimentary tools and ways of life but also their plants and their domesticated animals. As time passed, we can imagine them, each group in its own way, plodding along, slowly progressing, and spreading out or disappearing. We can be fairly sure that they must have left quite a bit of themselves in the future Mesopotamia, but we have no sure knowledge of what these influences were or which groups were responsible.

Following centuries of stagnation, changes can be discerned beginning in the fourth millennium, if not a few centuries earlier: for lack of available details, we can only speak, especially here, in rather broad chronological terms. Two events, the details of which are inaccessible to us but of which we are nevertheless able to note the effects, gave impetus to the actual history of the land.

First was the invention of methods to artificially irrigate fields. There was little (primarily winter) precipitation in Mesopotamia, and its two rivers had few and weak tributaries. The soil was devoted to raising sheep and large-scale grain crops. The inhabitants realized one fine day that they could expand the territory watered by the rivers, and thereby increase productivity, by digging canals branching off from existing sources of water.

Such an undertaking eventually created a much better nourished workforce and made it indispensable to have some organization and above all a centralized, energetic, and disciplined management, one that brought together, at least for the irrigation work, villages that until then had been independent. This does indeed seem to have been the opportunity for the still small and isolated groups to band together into larger political units, each under the rule of a single chief. Depending on how it was occupied, no doubt usually by small and scattered groups, the land gradually adapted to that type of regime, forming what we call *city-states* (or *urban states*), groups of villages that were henceforth associated around and under the orders of a more powerful concentration of strength, the seat of authority. It was out of that setting that the indestructible monarchic tradition of the land, the creation of cities, and high urban culture began its rise.

The other highly significant event that is believed to have occurred around the same time was the arrival of the Sumerians. We are still unable, and there is very little chance that we ever will be able, to satisfactorily identify this population, whose origins are so murky, or to link it to an ethnic, cultural, or linguistic branch of any kind.

Some scholars see the Sumerians as descendants of one of the groups that had inhabited the land for varying amounts of time. That hypothesis, however, seems to collide above all with the famous legendary or mythical tradition of the Seven Sages, according to which the southern population, which was still rough-hewn and wild, had been "initiated into all that constituted civilized life" by strange beings who "came from the sea." [1] We can easily be persuaded—since myths often arise out of ancient, thinly disguised memories—that the legend describes some form of immigration, apparently peaceful (?), which must have introduced a culturally superior population who, due to their superiority, greatly raised the level of life there. It is thus easier to imagine them arriving from, or through, the maritime region, perhaps by following the Iranian shores of the Persian Gulf. They would then have settled near the water in Lower Mesopotamia, which would later be called the "Land of Sumer"—thus explaining their name. But where did they come from? This we will never know.

In the same old documents, the other half of the land, farther north, up to the indistinct border of the Hamrin Mountains (the Jebel Hamrin), is given the name Land of Akkad. By "Akkadian" we mean members of a Semitic population, most certainly the most ancient of that stock known to have inhabited the land. Their language was related to other Semitic languages that developed later.

The Semites represent a venerable culture connected to a linguistic family whose members, known for close to five thousand years, still flourish, especially in the Middle East. During the course of the two millennia before our era, Akkadian, Eblaite, Canaanite, Aramaic, South Arabian, and Arabic, along with all their dialects, emerged from the same tree. Whatever the most ancient history of these peoples might have been, a history beyond our grasp but which appears to have occurred within Arabia even before its desertification, everything leads us to believe that beginning in the fourth millennium at the latest considerable numbers of them resided in the territory that is today Syria, on the northern edges of the great Syro-Arabian desert, where, since they raised sheep, they were seminomadic, searching out the best grazing lands along with their herds. Later, fully in the historical era, at the end of the third millennium, we see bands of them, tempted by the gentler and more gratifying life of the Mesopotamians, moving in large or small groups to join them, traveling along the banks of the Euphrates, sooner or later settling down to a sedentary existence among them, more or less consumed and absorbed by that opulent civilization.

This was apparently the initial situation of those whom by convention we call the "Akkadians"—"those from the Land of Akkad." When did they arrive there? It is impossible to know, especially since their arrival probably occurred in successive waves over greater or lesser intervals of time. And it is generally agreed that they were already established even before the arrival of the Sumerians and were subsequently acculturated and educated by them, as is suggested in the *Myth of the Seven Sages.*[2]

Whatever the facts of that hazy ancient history might be, of which we can only note the obvious results, but whose complete origins escape us irretrievably, here we have before us, right in the fourth millennium if we are to believe an ancient local tradition, Lower Mesopotamia: broadly, from the Jebel Hamrin to the sea, populated in the north, in the Land of Akkad, by the most ancient Semites we are aware of; and in the south, in the Land of Sumer, by the Sumerians.

Both populations most likely included representatives from other ethnic groups and cultures that were older than or external to them, but their simultaneous presence in the land is nevertheless beyond argument: the traditional use of two radically different languages in the first centuries of the third millennium has been amply and lastingly attested to on site; this indicates very strongly the presence of two populations that spoke those languages and two cultures that enveloped them and which they represented.

Everything began there, in Mesopotamia. For, leaving aside what its other inhabitants, more ancient or not, might have contributed, it was above all the encounter between and the more or less lengthy symbiosis of the Sumerians and the Akkadians that gave birth to a mixed, original, complex, and very high culture. Thus we can indeed give it the title, exceptional at that time, of *civilization,* one that would continue to grow and would exert great influence for three millennia.

Made rich both through the surplus of its agriculture and its herds and through the ingeniousness of its inhabitants, Mesopotamia very quickly, through commerce and its armed campaigns—raids or warfare—turned toward the various lands surrounding it, certainly in order to obtain the indispensable materials it was lacking (wood, stone, minerals) and most probably at the same time exchanging more than one cultural trait, which were adopted and adapted by both sides. But above all, throughout the centuries Mesopotamia never ceased to disseminate the treasures of its thinking and its experience: its discoveries, its technical knowledge, the products of its imagination, its representations.

In our complete ignorance of the original ancestry and "mentality" of the Sumerians and our almost complete ignorance of those of the most ancient Semites, except for what we learn from accounts derived elsewhere and much later, whose points of view are possibly slanted by some conceivable Mesopotamian influence, it is almost impossible to separate what that civilization owes to the Sumerians from what it owes to the Akkadians. Perhaps we will be able to detect here a few, less problematical traits.

Not only is it probable a priori that the Akkadians contributed their share of Semitic influence, but it is documented by Sumerian vocabulary, which includes terms borrowed (the word with the thing!) from the Semitic language. Later, when focusing on the religious realm, we will see even better the quality and the importance of the Akkadians' contribution. What jumps out at us, on the other hand, is the indisputable cultural preeminence of the Sumerians: in Akkadian vocabulary, to be sure, but also in all the traces remaining of those early times and, in particular, in many aspects of the religion. The *Myth of the Seven Sages* is most certainly accurate in explaining the degree to which "those who came from the sea," faced with those rough Akkadians, who were still more or less nomadic and evoked well by Enkidu in the *Epic of Gilgameš,* were able to educate them, "teaching them everything that made up civilized life."[3] And looking at the oldest documents, one is necessarily impressed by the obvious preeminence of the Sumerians during the first third of Mesopotamian history, even if, through the fog that veils things at such a great distance, it is safe to assume that, at the end of the fourth millennium at the latest, the two cultural groups were already sufficiently blended and mutually acculturated and we can speak, with circumspection, of a "Mesopotamian civilization."[4]

History

Mesopotamia's stroke of genius, which occurred scarcely a few centuries after the establishment of Mesopotamia, was the invention of

writing: a prodigious invention that would gradually be universaliz-
ing, revolutionizing our minds and increasing our intellectual possi-
bilities a hundredfold. It was born without fanfare (around 3200, as
archeologists today believe) as a simple mnemonic device, an aid to
an already age-old accounting practice in that fertile land, where it
was obviously urgent to master the multiple and apparently complicated circulation of goods.[5]

It took only a century or two for the users of those thousand or so
original signs, which were picto-ideographic and at first able only to
suggest or represent *things,* to recognize that each sign had the ability also to evoke the *names* of those things, which immediately connected them to the spoken language. In less than half a millennium,
still strangely complicated to be sure, and necessarily reserved for
professionals, "cuneiform" writing, as we call it because its charac-
ters seem to be made by pressing "wedges" and "nails" into clay tablets (Latin *cuneus,* "wedge"), progressively became a perfected and
supple instrument, able to precisely record, transmit, and diffuse all
the products of the mind, the heart, and the speech of humans in
all imaginable fields. For us such writings were initially significant
as accounts concerning the authors and the time in which they lived
—as *documents,* which finally introduced us into the era of *history.*
Later we will note, at least as concerns religion, the irreplaceable
value of those documents as sources of knowledge of those ancient,
long-forgotten times.

Even if the oldest forms of that writing, created using the nascent
graphic system, which was still only a memory-jogger, are practically
impenetrable to us in the current state of our knowledge and do not
teach us very much, we have some reason to attribute the ingenious
and unprecedented discovery of writing to the Sumerian cultural
contingent of the Mesopotamian population, those who were the
most active, the most creative, the most fertile: for a very long time
to come, writing would almost exclusively serve to represent the Sumerian language, at that time the only official language of the land.

This situation continued for close to a millennium. Then, things
changed. The Akkadians had constant reinforcements through the
arrival of new Semitic kin and therefore became more numerous
than the Sumerians. Since their arrival in the land, the Sumerians
never seem to have received the smallest drop of fresh blood from
the related peoples they must have left behind, we know not where.

They were destined to disappear, inevitably swallowed up by the burgeoning population of Semitic stock.

Our documentation, which has increased throughout the centuries, allows us to note that starting from the final days of the third millennium, although the written language as a general rule remained Sumerian, Akkadian gradually became the single official spoken language. And yet, as sparkling testimony to the indelible mark that since the beginning of their history the Sumerians had made everywhere on the civilization of the land, the educated, those who could write, to the very end, not far from the beginning of our era, remained faithful to the Sumerian language, which had then become dead in common usage but remained a sacred instrument of the culture—just as Latin remained for us until the Renaissance.

At the end of the third millennium there was virtually no longer any strictly Sumerian population in Mesopotamia. The Semitic Akkadians had long ago been educated and trained by the Sumerians and were henceforth the lone inheritors, the sole promoters and bearers, of that old mixed civilization. This was a decisive turning point in the long cultural history of the land.

Another considerable innovation dating from the same key period, this time in the political arena, is revealed to us in our documentation, and it probably precipitated many changes. Around 2300 Sargon the Great, the energetic and powerful ruler of the city of Akkad (archeologists are still unable to pinpoint the exact location of this capital), in the Land of Akkad, through a series of wars, annexations, and conquests, put an end to the ancient regime of the city-states. Up to that time they had prospered side by side in their own territories, each occupying a patch of land approximately one-third the size of a French *département* (roughly equivalent to the area of a county in a U.S. state), which, except for a variable amount of "steppe," was almost entirely reserved for pastureland and small peasant villages centered on the capital. There, along with the corps of sedentary occupations, one found the palace, the seat of the monarchic authority, who in most instances was some petty prince or king. Such division on a political level—this must be stressed—had virtually no effect on the cultural unity of the land: all the city-states shared the same way of life and the same religion, from the divine personnel of which each city-state, probably since the time of autonomous villages, chose a particular god with his own divine court as its patron and supernatural chief. Sargon wiped out that political mosaic with a single blow: he assembled all those principalities under his iron fist around his own capital, Akkad, which became the capital of the entire land. Pushing his ambition and his control even farther, he incorporated all the surrounding lands from western Iran to Asia Minor into a huge empire, no doubt the first, and the only one that the ancient Near East had ever seen. Fragile indeed due to its enormity and its disparate ethnic, political, and cultural groups, that huge edifice would not last two centuries before falling into gigantic ruin.

But it introduced considerable changes into the land. People acquired the taste, and almost the need, for unification on a large scale, for huge and powerful political constructions. The sought-after ideal was no longer the weak city-state but the vast, powerful, organized kingdom, which was in every way more wonderful than those juxtaposed miniprincipalities of the past. Suddenly, the image of the prince was to be presented in a completely different light: he would no longer be that good-natured and easily accessible petty king, but the proud and haughty chief at the head of a huge region, of a large collection of people, henceforth existing well above the masses, governing them all from above in his quasi-supernatural majesty, and simultaneously evoking admiration, prostration, and fear. The scale of political greatness, and of greatness itself, had changed.

The final century of the third millennium saw the appearance, on the ruins of the empire of Sargon, of a kingdom that was much smaller, most certainly, but solidly built and even glorious, centered on rulers of the southern city of Ur, who still kept Sumerian as their official and literary language, the final homage rendered to those old and unforgettable ancestors.

But, to direct our attention back to the henceforth Semitic predominance, there then appeared here and there in the land, and first as a hostile and threatening force, the first representatives of a new wave of immigrants, more recent relatives of the ancient Akkadians, who like them arrived from the northwest and who were called "Westerners" (Martu in Sumerian, and *Amurrû* in Akkadian; we now call them Amorites). They spoke a language that was related to Akkadian. We call it "Canaanite," and it was that language that later developed into Ugaritic, Hebrew, and Hebrew's close relatives. Alone, in families, or in bands, they spread out over the land for several centuries. But they very quickly allowed themselves to be tempted and subjugated by the civilization they found around them, which was in full strength and was much more brilliant and accomplished than the one into which their Akkadian predecessors had been introduced. They brought with them a new verve and fresh blood, like a ripening, like a new beginning: we can see this right away simply by reading two or three masterpieces of the literature and thought that were then being composed regularly in the Akkadian language.[6]

It is perhaps in part the disturbance and the disorder provoked by some of the incidents relating to the arrival of the Amorites, as well as the hostilities of their neighbors to the southeast, the Elamites, that first brought about not only the ruin of the kingdom of Ur but, for one or two centuries, a sort of return to the fragmentation of the ancient city-states.

Around 1800 the intelligent, capable, and vigorous ruler of Babylon (one of the city-states that up until then had been pretty much ignored and without glory), Ḥammurabi, of Amorite descent, reorganized the land into a kingdom, as he, too, was obsessed with that political yearning for cohesion and for grandeur that had infected old Sargon of Akkad. He therefore put all his energy into regrouping and coalescing around his capital not only Lower Mesopotamia—the "Land of Sumer" and the "Land of Akkad," the theater of the birth and the centuries-long progress of the local civilization—but several areas on its periphery, beginning with the north, beyond Jebel Hamrin. This area, "Assyria," had been under Semitic influence for a long time but no doubt beyond civilizing contact with the Sumerians. Once in the cultural orbit of southern Mesopotamia, it began to be noticed. From that time, the political cohesion of the kingdom formed by Ḥammurabi would never again fall into oblivion: whatever its vicissitudes, Babylon and its surroundings (i.e., "Babylonia") remained the heart, the cultural center, of the land and even, in its own eyes, of the world.

And yet, less than a century after its establishment, that grandiose and "immortal" political construction, undermined by internal dissent and enemy assaults, fell like a ripe fruit into the hands of the Kassites, rough mountain dwellers who came down from the Zagros and about whom we know very little. They took hold of the region and controlled it for a long time, although we do not know very well, aside from that control, what precise political role they might have played there. At the very least, it would seem that they in no way halted or even slowed down economic activity, in no way changed or impeded progress, literary creativity, or the exercise of intelligence and thought, being content, it seems, to leave the land in a sort of political and military lethargy that was, after all, perhaps favorable to its development, its maturation.

During this centuries-old sleep, interrupted by a few brief and ephemeral outbreaks and terminated by a local, independent, and more active dynasty, new elements appeared that were to govern the future evolution of the land. On the one hand, Assyria to the north, in the face of this torpor and Babylonia's inability to react, raised its head, rediscovered its former independence, and formed itself into a rival kingdom centered on Aššur, its principal capital (replaced by Kalḫu/Nimrud shortly before 850, then by Nineveh beginning around 700). Henceforth Mesopotamia was politically divided: Babylonia to the south and Assyria to the north. The two kingdoms until the end maintained ambiguous, if not openly hostile, relationships. But although most often Assyria was the stronger, that advantage, even when glaring, never tarnished the still uncontested glory and prestige of Babylon, which was held, at least by the Babylonians, to be a sort of sacred and almost supernatural city on a somewhat cosmic level: the Metropolis of the entire land.

On the other hand, a thousand years after the arrival of the Amorites, other Semites descended in turn from the northwest in a lengthy process and came, like their predecessors, to settle in the land. Their language, Aramaic, had recently formed within the large Semitic language family. "Aramean" is the generic name that we have attributed to them, even if their populations, having existed for a long time, bore several specific and tribal names, in particular that—little known in itself—of *Chaldeans.* They brought a treasure with them: the *alphabet,* which was invented in Syria-Palestine, probably around 1500, and greatly simplified writing, but which the Mesopotamian scholars always despised, even if the future belonged to it. The Arameans, moreover, neither imposed nor even proposed the alphabet; far from allowing themselves to be easily seduced and absorbed, as their Amorite predecessors had, by the brilliant local civilization, they did not immerse themselves in it right away; their tribes (since they maintained that type of organization for a long time) preferred, as was their custom, to camp on the steppes, even at the city gates. Sometimes, they did not hide their ill intentions or predatory designs from the inhabitants of the towns and attacked and raided them, provoking great and lasting disorder and carnage, upsetting life and prosperity, above all in Babylonia (Assyria appears to have remained less affected). They ultimately integrated into the population, but with more hesitation and delay than their Amorite predecessors, and finally settled more or less in various chosen territories. But their presence and influence would underlie the evolution of the land during part of the next millennium.

The first centuries of that final millennium were above all filled with the glory and the all-powerfulness of the Assyrian kingdom, which was endowed with a few energetic, strong, and lucky monarchs: the Sargonids, between 720 and 609. From Iran to Asia Minor, to the kingdom of Israel (we know this well from the Bible!), as far as Egypt, they made all peoples tremble through their ruthless annual campaigns of conquest and pillage. But the most "eternal" states are no less fragile for all that: twenty years after the death of its most famous monarch, Aššurbanipal (668–627), everything fell apart in Assyria at the first shock wave from Babylon, which, ever since its liberation from the Kassites (around 1150), made steady progress, with a few setbacks, in slowly regaining its strength, in part, thanks to the integration of Aramean and Chaldean elements. Nineveh fell in 609, and suddenly Assyria found itself forever erased from history.

But in spite of the efforts and the success of rulers of the caliber of Nebuchadnezzar II (604–562), the brief Chaldean dynasty (as it is called) did not last a century in Babylon. The erasing of the Babylonian domination was inevitable in the face of the new power that was rising up in the east, in Iran: the Persian Achaemenid dynasty. Its first ruler, Cyrus the Great (550–530), easily made himself master of Mesopotamia, immediately incorporating it as the richest and the most glorious province (satrapy) in his immense empire. It was not a custom, and even less in the interest of the Persians, to demolish in order to reign: thus they did everything they could to maintain the life and economic prosperity in that old land and venerable culture, whose prestige, success, and brilliance they admired so much. But Mesopotamia was no longer independent, and it was thus more difficult for it to sustain its ancient and rich cultural treasure by itself. It even began to lose its traditional language: Cyrus preferred Aramaic, even over his own language, Old Persian, and made it the linguistic link in his empire. In Mesopotamia, Aramaic began slowly but steadily and patiently to encroach on Akkadian, which, in a few centuries, underwent the fate that it had itself once imposed on Sumerian: not only did Akkadian speakers borrow cultural terms, which they then Akkadianized, from the Arameans, but in economic documents and other "business papers"—authentic accounts of daily life—personal names began to be written in alphabetic Aramaic in the margins, next to names written in cuneiform script.

Only two centuries after Cyrus, in 330, Alexander the Great conquered the entire land, which was incorporated after his death into the kingdom of the Seleucids, of which Babylon was no longer even the capital.

Mesopotamia quietly subsided to its demise. It almost forgot its Akkadian, replaced, as was to be expected, by Aramaic in common usage; and Greek, the eminent language of culture, was superimposed, at least within the cultivated classes, over popular Aramaic. Ancient Akkadian, and its inseparable Sumerian, were no longer understood or written except by a few select groups of old scholars who became increasingly secret and withdrawn and who alone appreciated and preserved their magnificent three-thousand-year-old heritage of reflection, invention, order, and intelligence. Political events must have in no way affected those recluses, not even the destruction of Babylon by the Parthians, victorious and conquering, which in 127 marked the final annihilation of that incomparable capital. From that time it would be only a fabulous memory, its history and its glory, increasingly distant and hazy, fallen, in just a few centuries, into a two-thousand-year oblivion.

The most recent cuneiform document, the very last link in that long chain, dates from the year A.D. 74; it is an abstruse and austere astronomical almanac. When its author died, that entire venerable and magnificent civilization closed its eyes with him, remembered perhaps for a short while (for how long?) through translations, possibly into Aramaic, of a few great selections of its literature and by transcription of fragments of its knowledge into Greek letters.

Perhaps we will nevertheless learn here that on the religious level a little bit of that civilization did in fact survive.

Historical Overview

Unless otherwise indicated, all dates presented in this book refer to the period before the Christian era. Before the fifteenth century these dates are subject to a degree of error that becomes larger as the dates become more distant.

Prehistoric Era

Sixth millennium

The region emerges little by little from north to south as a great lowland between the Tigris and the Euphrates. It was populated by unknown ethnic groups who had come from the piedmonts of the north and the east. There is no doubt that those groups included Semites from the northern edges of the Syro-Arabian desert.

Fourth millennium (at the latest)

After the arrival of the Sumerians (most probably from the southeast), a process of interaction and exchange began to form the first major civilization in the area. An urban society soon arose through the unification of more or less autonomous primitive villages.

Historical Era

Ca. 3200

Early Dynastic Period: invention of writing.

2900–2330

First Dynasty of Ur (Ur I), the dynasty of Lagaš: time of independent city-states.

2330–2100

Old Akkadian Period: the first Semitic empire founded by Sargon the Great (Akkadian dynasty); invasion of the Guti and the time of "Anarchy."

2100–2000

The kingdom of Ur (Third Dynasty of Ur, Ur III): first arrivals of new Semitic tribes, the Amorites.

2000–1750

Rival kingdoms: the dynasties of Isin, Larsa, Ešnun, Mari, etc.

Old Assyrian Period: first rulers of Assyria.

Old Babylonian Period (begins in 1894): First Dynasty of Babylon (Babylon I).

1750–1600

Hegemony of Babylon. Ḥammurabi (1792–1750) reunites the country in a kingdom centered on Babylon, which his five successors would maintain.

1600–1100

Middle Babylonian Period: invasion and control by the Kassites, who draw the country into a political torpor, which favors a vigorous cultural development.

Middle Assyrian Period: ca. 1300, Assyria (capitals: first Aššur, later Kalḫu, and then Nineveh) gains its independence.

1100–1000

First infiltrations of new Semitic tribes: the Arameans. Second Dynasty of Isin: ca. 1100, Babylonian revival. Battle for hegemony between Assyria and Babylonia. Even when

	the latter was politically dominated, it maintained its cultural supremacy.
1000–609	Neo-Assyrian Period: Assyrian dominance, time of the Sargonids (Esarhaddon, Aššurbanipal).
609–539	Neo-Babylonian Period and Chaldean dynasty: Babylon takes control of Assyria in 609; Aramaization continues.
539–330	Persian Period: in 539 Babylon falls to the Achaemenid Cyrus, and Mesopotamia is incorporated into the Persian Empire; Aramaization intensifies.
330–130	Seleucid Period: in 330 Alexander conquers and takes over from the Persians and brings the entire Near East into the Hellenistic cultural orbit; his successors, the Seleucid rulers, maintained their hold over Mesopotamia.
130–	Arsacid Period: in 127 Mesopotamia passes into the hands of the Parthians, under the Arsacid dynasty. The land lost not only all autonomy but all contemporary political and cultural significance. Another era begins.

CHAPTER THREE

The Sources: What We Can
Expect from Them

Those who participated in that three-thousand-year adventure, like their contemporaries everywhere around them, were still far from having "disenchanted their world." Because their entire existence was infused by their religiosity, just about everything they have passed on to us can be used as a source of knowledge about their religion.

The most telling and the most impressive remnants are the concrete remains of human industry: the countless sites and monuments (these include everything that people made, altered, or used) that archeologists have extracted, either amazingly intact or too often badly damaged, from that ancient earth during the hundred and fifty years they have joyfully been digging in it. The sacred nature of images, utensils, other objects, buildings, and sites is sometimes quite obvious.

But exactly what these unearthed objects have to tell us is never obvious, and by the nature of things, they are always reticent, hazy, ambiguous, if not misleading, never giving a clear overview of the facts. The most beautiful statue, one that has emerged undamaged, might be able to tell us where the sculptor went to obtain the diorite from which it was sculpted, and even may allow us to imagine an entire assiduous commerce with those who controlled the deposit. But it will never by itself respond to the question of all questions: Whom does it represent and why that particular representation? Archeological vestiges illustrate what we learn elsewhere rather than inform us directly, although they have the advantage of being able to restore our information to three dimensions.

The only primary, indisputable, detailed, and indispensable sources of information that we can hope is complete are *documents:* written materials that convey their authors' own representations and the muted echo of their voices beyond the grave. Most often written on clay tablets, later dried or baked (these were the "paper" of Mesopotamia), simultaneously resilient and crumbly, these documents have been extracted, often in quite lamentable condition but in an astonishing quantity, from the depths of the earth where they lay hidden for so long. No one to my knowledge has ever made an exact count of the tablets found; but at first glance, and without too much exaggeration, we can indeed suggest the respectable round number of half a million pieces, of all sizes, that have been distributed among large and small museums around the world—without counting, of course, those that in their deep graves are patiently waiting to be brought to light.

In just about all of these documents, even those dealing with the most down-to-earth subjects, we can find at least an indirect reference to the supernatural world, if not some teaching concerning it. For example, the name of the divine recipient of food provisions; an allusion to some prerogative of a divinity as regards, let's say, the protection of sheep or matters of justice; reference to a monthly feast; or even simply the name of a person, the expression of a feeling that linked the bearer of that name to his "patron" on high. Historians of religion in Mesopotamia must therefore neglect nothing in this ocean of writing, even if what they derive in information is too often of mediocre weight, trivial and known from other sources. Certainly, if we take into account the universal religious impregnation of the entire culture and life at that time, only a certain percentage of the texts are of a formally and explicitly religious nature.

These are the sorts of testimonials that make up the documentation that will be brought into play here; they represent countless pieces and their presentations vary greatly: in Sumerian or in Akkadian; in prose or in verse; and in almost all the "literary genres" known and used at that time.

Without claiming that they are univocal—for things, especially in this realm, are never cut and dried—some of these documents above all illustrate *the religious sentiment:* [1] countless prayers, both official and private, and hymns and songs, either choral or solos, were addressed to representatives of the supernatural order of things, not only to the divinities themselves but also to their images, the objects of their cult, and their residences, to which the gods conveyed something of their sublimeness. Other sources primarily explain the *representations* that were made of those sacred figures—of their behavior, their powers, their positions as creators, administrators, and protectors of the world and of human beings. The most telling texts on the subject, which are often quite loquacious, are the many myths that have come down to us, deliberately written as such or sometimes only suggested. A separate, totally unexpected category, but one completely in keeping with the Mesopotamian genius, comprises the lists and catalogs of divine names, lists that are sometimes interminable and whose arrangements easily translate true "theological" flights of fancy. Other writings, each in its own way, seek to pose and resolve specific issues regarding the gods' relationship to humans: the destinies of things and beings, or problems concerning evil and misfortune. Finally, on the level of *religious practice,* the formalism and the minutiae of those people, no less than their universal use of writing, have endowed us with an entire, complete literature not only of advice and manuals of good behavior but of rituals, in which we find the many ceremonies and routines governed by the liturgy meticulously written down and divided up into successive moments.

Let us reiterate that the present work is only a sketch. The entire panorama is much more rich, subtle, alive, and unexpected. Each one of these literary categories might easily hold unlooked-for testimony, quite different from what we at first would expect: a ceremony might unveil a certain mythological particularity, and a song to the glory of a certain god or a myth might reveal a liturgy that was reserved for it.

The pieces of this generous documentation come from just about every age in the history of the land and its religion. Aside from a few personal names from the beginning of the third millennium, the oldest date from around 2600—fragments of religious songs and prayers, myths, rituals, words of wisdom—all in the Sumerian language, whose notation in writing was still imperfect, which makes our understanding of them uncertain, if not impossible. We are dealing here with a corpus of some four or five hundred tablets and fragments extracted from the sites of Fâra (formerly known as Šuruppak) and of Tell Abû Şalābīkh in southern Mesopotamia, which make up the oldest literary collection known in the land and throughout the world. At the other end of the spectrum, the last cuneiform texts are from around the beginning of our era and are most often copies or new editions of older works or scholarly texts. Accounts come not only from all eras but also from all locations, from Mesopotamia itself and from adjacent territories: there is no excavated site (with the exception of those that go back to prehistory, before writing) that has not continuously—though haphazardly—yielded tablets and other cuneiform inscriptions.

However impressive it might be, such an abundance of documents, if we think about it, is obviously not all that plentiful compared to everything that was ever written down in that land in the course of its long history, both inconsequential scribblings and venerable texts—and we are speaking now only of the realm of religious affairs—and even less so compared to all that was ever done, thought, or *said* there, since the written tradition was paralleled by an oral tradition, one much richer and more prolific and much more ancient. And regarding only what was written down, not only do we not possess *everything*—far from it—but what has reached us has passed through three filters: that of recording, for they did not write *everything* down on tablets, and we can assume that much important information that everybody knew was never, probably for that very reason, put down in writing; that of the preservation of the written tablets (how many of them, as the centuries went by, locked up in their tombs, crumbled into dust?); and that of discovery, for the ground of the Near East is still riddled with unimaginable wealth, and the slightest blow of a pickaxe can reveal new, unexpected, and even sometimes revolutionary information. Our documentation is constantly being enriched, sometimes through the discovery of entire archives: fifteen or sixteen thousand tablets were uncovered at once at Ebla a few decades ago, and an equal number were found at Mari after 1933 during a few archeological digs.

Our information is therefore still incomplete and partial. A mass of potentially essential data, from all times and all places, remains hidden from us, in particular relating to everything dealing with "origins." Many fundamental facts relating to the religion of that innovative land, in which writing was used prodigiously, predate writing. Writing, moreover, did not supplant the spoken word, which was always richer than writing. Myths and rituals have centuries of oral tradition behind them—and beside them—a tacit, untouchable tradition about which we will never know a thing. Over the centuries institutions and belief systems change, but many of the milestones of that evolution are still sorely lacking. We lack sufficient information to even imagine and support reasonable hypotheses to compensate for our deficiencies, and we are too often reduced to idleness, powerlessness, and perplexity before a text that does not wish to speak, and even less tell us everything.

Although a general chronology of Mesopotamian history has been established with some certainty, a chronology of the religious system is impossible to determine. For example, we are unable to establish the composition date of certain documents that were not dated —or even those that were—by their authors: regarding the *tablet* in our hands, it might be relatively easy to date it by examining the writing, the paleography, the language, and the vocabulary; but exactly when, how, by whom, and why was the *work,* transcribed in a certain way and usually anonymously, *composed?* This is what so often escapes us, to the detriment of a more exact knowledge of the stages, the moments, and the turning points in the development of ideas and things. And this is also what makes it impossible to form a true chronological sequence, an authentic history, I will not even say of Mesopotamian religion, but of just about everything that makes it up.

Finally, the last barrier, the most impassable one that truly bars our way from entering into that ancient citadel, is precisely, in spite of the historical guides and the huge amount of information available to us, the enormous hiatus that the centuries have imposed between those ancient ancestors and ourselves. Religion in particular is deeply connected through infinite visceral ties to the entire culture, to the mentality, the vision, and the sentiments that those elements bring about, to the collective memories, the imagination, the system of values, the infinite details of the daily lives of its followers, all of which is not, or no longer, inherently our own, even if we cannot help recognizing some of its characteristics at the origins of our own religion. What struck and attracted the Mesopotamians long ago, what moved them, what leapt to their attention, no longer immediately affects us, no longer speaks to us as it did to them, and can even go right by us unnoticed. We read the same texts, the same sentences, the same words, incapable of reacting to them initially as they did, except by contemplating them for a greater or lesser time, and by surrounding them with heavy and scholarly commentaries, which, there is every reason to believe, cannot provide us with everything that the Mesopotamians immediately and effortlessly found in the texts. Whoever is familiar with a foreign language, especially one that is quite different from his native language, knows that no poetry, indeed no work of prose, is truly and totally translatable; serious historians should always remember the limits of what they have learned, especially when it does not concern banalities or truisms.

What ultimately, then, is the point of these vigorous, justifiable reservations presented here as a counterbalance to the abundance of our documentation? To remind us that any knowledge of the Other in general and, more specifically under the circumstances, of the Other in the past, if it claims to be profound, intimate, alive, and complete, is only a chimera. We must not confuse *historical knowledge* with *immediate knowledge.* Not only do we not have what we need to know everything about the past, but we are completely incapable of "actualizing" what we do learn of it, given the distance in time, spirit, culture, language, and thought, as did those for whom it was the present: we necessarily put too much of ourselves into it! There is always, necessarily, a more or less extensive, uncrossable gap in time between them and us, for which we compensate as well as we can using the means available to us. We can see them in the distance, with binoculars, as if they were on the other side of a wide river, but it is impossible to approach them, to touch them, to breathe them in. This is what is forgotten by authors—so-called philosophers, anthropologists, psychologists—of more or less abstruse systems devised to explain the "mentalities" of today as well as those of yesterday and the days before. They construct them and propagate them, rather obscurely, moreover, which does not help matters, and in complete speculation and without the slightest feeling of the obligatory hiatus that comes between people and between the centuries, without the slightest historical sense. They are wonderful utopianists!

No less so are those who, from the opposite perspective, take advantage of those gaps and conditions—which are obvious but which should be an obstacle only for a too ambitious and chimerical project—to declare that "a systematic presentation of Mesopotamian religion cannot and should not be written," as Leo Oppenheim wrote in 1964.[2] He was tilting at windmills: no one with common sense and seeing things as they are could ever attempt, in any seriousness, such a project of rediscovery. And in fact, the same might be safely said about any religion, ancient and forgotten or contemporary and living, beginning with our own. At the end of the present volume, if readers push on that far, they will be able to decide if we truly must give up the notion of obtaining an idea as *historians* and not as *witnesses* of that ancient religion.

Since, not to mention the reduced space assigned to this little book, when a large volume would scarcely be enough for an appropriately full treatment, we must equally take into account the astonishing wealth of our sources as well as their incomparable gaps and obscurities, it would be unreasonable to expect here anything other than a general presentation of the Mesopotamian religious system and a look above all into the *spirit* that animated it, taking into account only a few noteworthy traits and turns in its very long trajectory. Should we dwell on a certain social or cultural category: the "official religion," the "private religion," the religion of the "educated" (the only ones, after all, who are known to us directly, through all that was written down in the land), the religion of the "people" (the obscure peasants and shepherds in the hinterland or other groups?)? Should we emphasize a certain city or province: Ebla, Mari, Assyria? Should we concentrate on a certain period in time: the Seleucid, the Achaemenid, the Chaldean, the Neo-Assyrian, the Kassite, the Old Babylonian, the Neo-Sumerian, or the Old Akkadian Period? Since, contrary to what some would imprudently lead us to believe, there were no distinct religions but only successive states of the same religious system—just as throughout our childhood, adolescence, maturity, and decline we remain truly the same person, only enriched or diminished—such an approach would be excessive, even pointless.

For example, if words have a meaning, a "Sumerian religion" is not even envisionable except through rhetoric or exaggeration, not only when, as in my own case, one is not truly a Sumerologist but in and of itself! Completely isolated on every level, primarily cultural and linguistic, unlike the Semites, we encounter the Sumerians only in Mesopotamia in the middle of the fourth millennium. They were already quite likely in direct contact with unknown nonnatives, and especially with the Semitic Akkadians, all in the process together, through a sort of mutual osmosis, of developing that high hybrid civilization that was to become the glory of them all. To claim to be able to identify and expose, with a minimum of rigor, the religious system particular to the Sumerians is as naive a proposal as is claiming to do the same with the Akkadians of that time, who were equally subject to the same acculturation process, and consequently the same cultural alteration, as were the other Semites. We can at best timidly gather and label the scattered fragments of so-called cultural Sumerisms (as well as, moreover, Akkadianisms or even Semitisms), like so much scattered debris of a broken ancient statue. All that we can modestly hope to attempt with regard to Mesopotamian culture and religion as we know them—as they were already formed or in the process of being so—is to reveal the traits that might emerge from what we think we know about Semitic and Akkadian religiosity and, through conjecture, to attribute to the Sumerians those traits that are too divergent and appear to belong to them, such as the richness of the pantheon and the importance of the liturgical ritual.

It thus seems much less presumptuous and much more reasonable when dealing with the realm of religion, as with all others, to take as our primary objective here what I would call the spirit and the broad outlines of Mesopotamian religion as it was, once it was culturally formed and launched into history. Mesopotamia constructed an original, great civilization and its own unique religion: it is exactly that religion, with its great parameters and its structure, that we must attempt, to the best of our abilities and through intelligent study, to rediscover and to understand by using what is left of it and by trying to reduce as much as possible, through sympathy and a certain affinity, the vast distance that separates us from those very old deceased members of our family.

CHAPTER FOUR

Religious Sentiment

Sources

Religious sentiment, the first element in the logical sequence of an analysis of a religion, permeates a religion and governs it and confers upon it an identity distinguishing it from other religions. Before entering that enormous ancient temple, we must obtain this indispensable key if we do not wish to go astray in its labyrinthine structure.

The ancient Mesopotamians did not specify or define their unique religiosity anywhere in what they left behind. We must deduce it, soaking it up wherever it might surface, and principally in the writings, prayers, and songs of praise or of celebration through which its followers expressed their emotions most distinctly in the face of the supernatural objects closest to them. Here, then, are a few samples of these devotions (we will have occasion to look at many others), taken at random from the vast local liturgy.

If readers have not yet been initiated into much of the concrete data of this ancient and exotic religion, they will do well not to let themselves be discouraged by the details (in particular, divine names and titles), which might for now be enigmatic, and they should settle for cultivating an empathy, always indispensable when studying human history, for the feelings that are primarily conveyed by these entreaties and praises. Once readers are better informed, if they wish to reread the texts, they will find more meaning in them.

By virtue of their very orientation and nature, all are poetic. Yet the Mesopotamians of old, with very few exceptions, were never considered to be great lyricists and were rather placid in temperament, inclined toward formalism in their words, their phrases, their images, and their repetitions of attributes. Even through these clichés, this heaviness, and this difficulty in rising from the ground, we will nevertheless easily recognize that which, in the presence of the beings from On High, the objects of their religiosity, caused their souls to resonate.

To the God Anu

First, here is an address to Anu, the sovereign god, the father and founder of the divine dynasty. It is bilingual: the text in Sumerian alternates with its Akkadian translation. It was to be recited during a celebration in honor of that very lofty figure. The beginning and the end of the text have been lost. It dates from the second millennium.

>   1   . . . It is You who possess royal insignia,
>   Prince of the gods!
>   Your word holds authority
>   In the council of the greatest gods!
>   5   O Lord of the brilliant Tiara,
>   Endowed with marvelous brilliance,
>   You straddle the great Cyclones,
>   Standing like a prince on the noble royal Dais!
>   10   The celestial gods listen
>   To Your sovereign words,
>   And all the infernal gods
>   Approach You trembling!
>   At Your voice all gods bow down
>   Like reeds in a storm!
>   15   If Your word carries away everything, like the Wind,
>   It also causes pastureland and watering holes to flourish!
>   At Your voice, even in anger,
>   The gods return to their homes!
>   May all the gods approach You
>   20   From Heaven and Earth,
>   R.1 With their gifts, their offerings!
>   May all kings bring You their heavy tributes!
>   May all people,
>   Standing, every day, before You,
>   5   Offer You their oblations,
>   Their adoration, their prayers! . . .[1]

To Enlil

Composed at the latest around the end of the third millennium, in Sumerian, here we have a short passage from a liturgical hymn addressed to the ruler of the gods and of men.

1   Enlil! his authority is far-reaching;
     his word is sublime and holy.
     His decisions are unalterable;
     he decides fates forever!
5   His eyes scrutinize the entire world!
     When the honorable Enlil sits down in majesty
     on his sacred and sublime throne,
     when he exercises with perfection
     his power as Lord and King,
     spontaneously the other gods prostrate [themselves]
        before him
     and obey his orders without protest!
10   He is the great and powerful ruler
     who dominates Heaven and Earth,
     Who knows all and understands all![2]

To Enki

The opening of a Sumerian myth, dating probably from the end of
the third millennium and explaining how the world had been organized by Enki (whom the Akkadians called Éa), celebrates that
most ingenious and most active of gods:

1   The Sublime lord of heaven and earth, the one respected for
        himself,
     Father Enki, whom a bull has begotten, whom a wild bull
        caused to be born,
     The tenderly cared for one of Enlil, the great mountain, the
        beloved one of the holy An,
     O king, who planted the *mes*-tree planted in the Absû, who is
        elevated in all the lands,
5   The great dragon, who stands in Eridu,
     Whose shadow covers heaven and earth,
     An orchard full of fruit trees stretched over the Land,
     Enki, lord of prosperity, (lord) of the Anunna gods,
     Nudimmud, the KI.A GAL of the Ekur, the strong one of
        heaven and earth
     . . . .
20   Their [of all men—trans.] king in their [house?] you are . . .[3]

To Marduk

At the end of the second millennium, the god Marduk took the
place of Enlil in the Mesopotamian pantheon as head of the uni-

verse. The following text, in Akkadian, dates from the second half of the second millennium.

6   Lo[rd En]lil [that is, Marduk as supreme god], prince surpass-
      ing of perception.
      Battle formation and warfare are in the hand of the sage of
      the gods, Marduk,
      He at whose warfare the heavens quake,
      At whose cry the depths are roiled,
10   At whose blade edge the gods retreat.
      There was none came forth against his furious onslaught.
      Awe-inspiring lord,
      none like whom has arisen among the gods,
      Stately is his progress through the shining firmament,
      Heavy his responsibilities in Ekur, the cherished dwelling.
15   In the ill wind his weapons are flashing,
      Tortuous mountains are destroyed by his flame,
      The surging (?) ocean tosses up its waves.[4]

To Sîn

The same sentiments were revealed when people addressed divinities of lesser importance. Here is a fragment from a prayer to the
moon god, Sîn (whom the Sumerians called Nanna or Nannar). The
bilingual text may go back to the second millennium.

1   O Lord, chief of the gods, who in heaven and on earth alone
      is supreme!
      Father Nannar, lord of increase, chief of the gods!
      Father Nannar, lord of heaven, great one, chief of the gods!
      Father Nannar, lord of the moon, chief of the gods!
      Father Nannar, lord of Ur, chief of the gods!
      Father Nannar, lord of E-gis-sir-gal, chief of the gods!
15   Father Nannar, lord of the moon-disk, brilliant one, chief of
      the gods!
      Father Nannar, who rules with pomp, chief of the gods!
      Father Nannar, who goes about in princely garb, chief of
      the gods!
20   O strong bull, with terrible horns, well-developed muscles,
      with a flowing beard of the colour of lapis lazuli, full of
      vigour and life!
      O fruit, which grows of itself, developed in appearance, beau-
      tiful to look upon, but whose luxuriance does not produce
      fruit!
25   O merciful one, begetter of everything, who has taken up his
      illustrious abode among living creatures!

O merciful and forgiving father, who holds in his hand the
   life of the whole country!
29 O Lord, thy divinity is full of fear, like the far-off heavens
   and the broad sea!
O ruler (?) of the land, founder of shrines, proclaimer of
   their name!
O Father, begetter of gods and men, builder of dwellings,
   establisher of offerings!
35 Who proclaims sovereignty, bestows sceptre and who determines destinies for far-off days!
O mighty leader, whose large heart no god understands!
O fiery one (?), whose knees do not grow weary, who opens
   up the road (?) for the gods his companions!
. . . who from the horizon to the zenith . . . who opens the
   doors of heaven, establishes his light (?)
· · · · · · · · · · · · · · · · ·
O Father, begetter of everything . . .
47 O Lord, who determines the decisions of heaven and earth,
   whose command no one [can set aside]!
O thou who holdest fire and water, who rulest over all creatures! What god can attain thy position?
In heaven who is exalted? Thou alone art exalted!
On earth who is exalted? Thou alone art exalted![5]

To Šamaš

Šamaš (Utu in Sumerian) was, among other things, the patron god
of the sun and of justice. He is the object of a very long hymn (two
hundred lines) in Akkadian known from tablets dating from the beginning of the first millennium. The poem may go back a few centuries more and is a masterpiece of powerful poetry, more literary
than liturgical. Here are a few excerpts, taken from the first part of
the poem:

1   Illuminator of all, the whole of heaven,
    Who makes light the d[arkness for mankind] above and
      below,[6]
    Shamash, illuminator of all, the whole of heaven,
    Who makes light the dark[ness for mankind a]bove and
      below,
5   Your radiance [spre]ads out like a net [over the world],
    You brighten the g[loo]m of the distant mountains.
    Gods and netherworld gods rejoiced when you appeared,
    All the Igigi-gods rejoice in you.
    Your beams are ever mastering secrets,

At the brightness of your light,
10   humankind's footprints become vis[ible].
Your dazzle is always seeking out . . . ,
The four world regions [you set alight] like fire.
You open wide the gate of all [sanctuaries],
You . . . the food offerings of the Igigi-gods.
15 O Shamash, mankind kneels to your rising,
All countries. . . .
Illuminator of darkness, opener of heaven's bosom,
Hastener of the morning breeze (for?) the grain field,
     life of the land,
Your splendor envelops the distant mountains,
20 Your glare has filled all the lands.
Leaning over the mountains, you inspect the earth,
You balance the disk of the world in the midst of heaven
     (for) the circle of the lands.
You make the people of all lands your charge,
All those king Ea, the counsellor,
     has created are entrusted to you.
25 You shepherd all living creatures together,
You are their herdsman, above and below.
You cross regularly through the heavens,
Every day you traverse the vast earth.
High seas, mountains, earth, and sky,
30 You traverse them regularly, every day, like a . . .
In the lower regions you take charge of the netherworld gods,
    the demons, the (netherworld) Anunna-gods,
In the upper regions you administer all the inhabited world.
Shepherd of the lower regions, herdsman of the upper
    regions,
You, Shamash, are regulator of the light for all.
35 You cross time and again the vast expanse of the seas,
[Whose] depths not even the Igigi-gods know.
[O Sham]ash, your radiance has gone down to the deep,
[The hairy hero-m]an of the ocean can see your light.
[O Shamash], you tighten like a noose, you shroud like a mist,
40 Your [bro]ad protection is cast over the lands.
Though you darken each day, your face is not eclipsed,
For by night you traverse [the below?].
To far-off regions unknown and for uncoun[ted] leagues
You have persevered, O Shamash,
     what you went by day you returned by night.
Among all the Igigi-gods there is none who does such
45   wearisome toil but you,
Nor among the sum total of the gods one
     who does so much as you!
At your rising the gods of the land assembled,

Your fierce glare covered the land.
Of all the lands of different tongues,
50 [You] know their intentions, you see their footprints.
All humankind kneels before you,
[O Sha]mash, everyone longs for your light, . . .[7]

To Nergal

Nergal, ruler of the Netherworld, received similar praise. Here is a portion of a hymn, in Akkadian, known from tablets dating from the beginning of the first millennium, but whose text is certainly older.

1   O warrior, splendid one, offspring of Nun[amnir] [Enlil],
    Let me sound your [praises], O lordly one,
            arrayed in awesomeness.
    O bearer of pointed horns, clad with frightening sheen,
            first born son of Kutumshar,
    Monitor of the lower world, overseer of the Six Hundred,
            let me always praise your greatness!
5   You are supreme in strength, overwhelming all disobedient,
            forcing the . . . to submit.
    O tireless mighty one, who gladdens Enlil's heart,
    Mighty of arms, broad of chest,
            perfect one without rival among all the gods,
    Who grasps the pitiless deluge-weapon,
            who massacres (?) the enemy,
    Lion clad in splendor,
            at the flaring-up of whose fierce brilliance
10 The gods of the inhabited world took to secret places,
            evildoer and wicked have found their way into crevices.[8]

To Inanna/Ištar

Naturally, goddesses were not excluded from such glorification. Here is how the most famous of them, Ištar (Inanna, and sometimes Irnini, in Sumerian), was celebrated in a long address (of which I am citing only excerpts), in Akkadian, which possibly goes back to the second third of the second millennium at the latest.

1   I implore you, lady of ladies, goddess of goddesses,
    Ishtar, queen of all the inhabited world,
            who governs the peoples,
    Irnini, you are noble, the greatest of the Igigi-gods,
    You are powerful, you are queen, exalted is your name.

5   You are the luminary of heaven and earth,
         the valiant daughter of Sîn,
     Who brandishes weapons, who prepares for battle,
     Who gathers to herself all rites, who dons the lordly tiara.
     O Mistress, splendid is your greatness, exalted over all
         the gods
.   .   .   .

15   Where is not your name, where are not your rites?
     Where are your designs not put into effect,
         where are your daises not set up?
     Where are you not great, where are you not exalted?
     Anu, Enlil, and Ea have lifted you high, they have made
         your authority greatest among the gods,
     They have given you the highest rank among all the
         Igigi-gods,
             they have made your (heavenly) station highest of all.
20   At the thought of your name, heaven and netherworld quake,
     The gods totter, the Anunna-gods tremble.
     Mankind extols your awe-inspiring name,
     You are the great one, the exalted one
.   .   .   .

31   O splendid lioness of the Igigi-gods,
         who renders furious gods submissive,
     Most capable of all sovereigns,
         who grasps the leadrope of kings,
.   .   .   .

35   Shining torch of heaven and earth,
         brilliance of all inhabited lands.
.   .   .   .

43   Look upon me, mistress, accept my entreaty!
     Look steadfastly upon me, hear my prayer!
.   .   .   .

103 "Ishtar is pre-eminent, Ishtar is queen,
     "The lady is pre-eminent, the lady is queen,
     "Irnini, the valiant daughter of Sîn, has no rival."[9]

These few documents, and those that we will see later, reflect the
general tone of the devotional literature of Mesopotamia and enable
us to come to two conclusions concerning them.

Reverence

First, in spite of an agreed-upon style—a constant reuse of images,
some of which, like Homeric epithets, are true clichés (the "luminous sheen," the insignia of sovereign power, the domination of the
universe, the mastery of other gods, etc.)—and in spite of the om-

nipresent, all-too-apparent official tone, we sense an authentic religious emotion in these texts. More than one passage might be included among those "numinous hymns" that R. Otto has brought
to light:[10] in them the supernatural is not the object of a coldly reasoned glorification, but in truth we see extreme reverence, profound
devotion, the unarguable emotion that the supernatural evoked in
the hearts of those ancient believers.

This religious sentiment was obviously of the "centrifugal" and
"fearful" type, with no trace of exaltation or "Dionysian" elements,
and it was diametrically opposed to our own form of religiosity. In
other words, the divine, in its multiple, personalized presentations,
was above all considered to be something grandiose, inaccessible,
dominating, and to be feared. Before it, even "the gods" were believed "to bend like reeds in a storm."

From the outset the divine frightened and paralyzed. In the *Epic
of Gilgameš* the hero, on his way to the Cedar Forest, has a night-
mare that causes him to awaken with a start, terrified. He then questions his companion, Enkidu, who had not fallen asleep: "Why am
I so disturbed? Did a god pass by? Why are my muscles trembling?"[11]
The word "god" here might in fact imply "ghost," but it nevertheless refers to something superhuman and terrifying; and the imagined closeness alone of the supernatural thus had the effect of par-
alyzing Gilgameš with fear.

The divinity was never the object of an anxious, enthusiastic pursuit: "to seek out *(šê'û)* a god," as was sometimes said, was out of a
need for his protection, his assistance. It was not inspired by a desire to be close to him, to be in his presence, to have the peace or
happiness of finding oneself in his company. Hymns professing a
bottomless desire for a god's presence indicate admiration (as in the
case of the moon god, the splendid lamp of the night) and not an
impatience to get closer to him. The divine did not attract in the
manner of a desirable thing, of a presence apt to enchant the heart
—as in a true form of love.

There was absolutely nothing "mystical" about Mesopotamian religion. Its gods were considered to be very high "authorities" (we
will return to this fundamental metaphor of power), upon whom
one depended in complete humility, obligated to serve them: they
were distant and haughty "bosses," masters and rulers, and above all
not friends! One submitted to them, one feared them, one bowed
down and trembled before them: one did not "love" or "like" them.

The verb "to like/to love" (*râmu*/ág) appeared only sporadically with the name of a divinity as its object; and in those rare cases it never conveyed the sense of an impetuous and tender pursuit, even less of a need, a passionate desire, but only the inclination that a modest and self-effacing servant might feel toward an omnipotent and sublime "lord and master" *(bêlu)*. "Honor your god! Connect yourself to Him!" (literally, "Love Him"): in this exordium in a religious song,[12] the first couplet suggests the true importance of the second. The gods were too highly placed, vertiginous, transcendent, to evoke the thirsts, the flames of captivation: their powers, like their nature, were much too far beyond the human grasp, much too crushing and formidable to unleash in human hearts anything other than a fearful reverence, an admiring respect, a humble adoration.

This "centrifugal" sentiment inspired by the gods stands out in even greater relief when we look at certain representations that were made of them and attributes that were recognized in them. For example, to depict, if not to define, what was particular to the gods' nature, people had for a long time imagined a sort of eruption or terror which they believed emanated from the gods, as well as an extraordinary density of being; this they based on the model of a prodigious luminosity residing in the gods, or which the gods wore, like a cloak of light, or placed on their bodies or their heads like a sparkling jewel, which shone around them, lighting and enchanting everything with a "supernatural shine," marvelous as well as terrible—like all that is fascinating.[13] People used the word *melammu* (from the Sumerian compound m e, "power," and lám, "incandescent") for that source of both marvel and fear that primarily distinguished the gods: they were simultaneously admirable, by virtue of their splendor, and apt to repel humans by forcing them to kneel before such a strong ray of light, such a source of energy, which they emitted, proportional to their ontological density, as if light and luminosity in that land served as ideograms for what we call "the being." This flamboyant aspect of the gods' divine nature (some half-dozen synonyms of it were commonly used: *rašubbatu, namrirru, šarûru,* and even *puluḫtu,* literally, "fear," "horror," all simultaneously evoking the same mixture of brilliance and fear) could, moreover, be granted by the gods, throughout time and in a more diminished form, to others—sovereign people or sacred objects—which then at least reflected the appearance of the "divinity." In short, *melammu* was simply the mythological translation of the fundamental religious sentiment, composed simultaneously of brilliance and of terror, both of which were evoked by the gods.

Therefore, one did not hesitate—this is rather clear in the texts cited above—to apply qualifiers to the gods that were borrowed from everything that appeared here on Earth as formidable, admirable, and fearful, from natural phenomena ("Deluge," "Tempest," "Flood," "Mountain," and so on), to the most imposing and feared animals ("Wild Ox," "Lion," "Dragon"), no less than the most alarming products of human industry (weapons, notably, were easily "deified").

This tone of the Mesopotamian religious sentiment can even be seen in onomastics. In Mesopotamia people's personal names were usually short phrases, declarative or placatory, based on the name of a divinity, thereby conveying the relationship to that god held by the bearer of the name. We have found thousands of such names from all periods, from the beginning of the third millennium on, first in Sumerian, then in Akkadian. They constitute a source of knowledge about religious thought and sentiment, a source all the richer and more suggestive in that unlike so many writings, it allows us to enter into the religiosity of *everyone,* even the huge number of illiterates in the land.

In those names we find the "luminous burst," the "majesty," the "authority," and the "sovereignty" of the gods, as well as the reverence, the respect, the fear, and the adoration evoked among humans by so much sublimity and strength: *Sîn-nawir,* "Sîn is sparkling"; *Sîn-apir-agâ-šu,* "Sîn wears his crown (of light)"; *Nabû-nebi-ana-ilî,* "Nabû sparkles before the gods"; *Ina-šamê-šarrat,* "She [Ištar] is the queen of Heaven"; *Enlil-nûr-šamê-irṣitim,* "Enlil is the light of Heaven and of Earth"; *Rabât-amat-Sîn,* "Imposing is the word of Sîn."

Of course—and this completes the tableau—we also often encounter terms that express an easier attitude toward the divine. In them the divine appears to hold an authentic potential for goodness, for gracious condescension, for indulgence toward humans. For it was inevitable that since nothing inherently forced humans to suspect the gods of being particularly mean and cruel, humans found it natural to expect help, good deeds, and favors from the gods (until the contrary was proved!), just as one might naturally expect the same from the politically powerful of this world. The hymns and prayers cited above mention a certain number of traits that manifested not only the authority, loftiness, and power of the gods but also their good-natured and helpful side: Sîn was a "merciful and forgiving father," and Šamaš took "care for all the peoples of the lands," whereas one could implore Ištar, "lady of ladies, goddess of goddesses," and expect a favorable response to entreaties and prayers.

The personal names of people abundantly echo the same sentiments: *Ili-naplisam,* "My god, cast your eyes on me!" *Rêmêni-Marduk,* "Marduk, have compassion on me"; *Sîn-abi-enši,* "Sîn is the father of the wretched"; *Šamaš-ḫatin,* "Šamaš is protector"; *Šamaš-epiri,* "Šamaš takes care of me."

From this angle we understand better the use of kinship terms in personal names, which also highlights the attention and the interest with which the gods were credited, and which referred to their protection but not to tenderness: *Marduk-abi,* "Marduk is my father"; *Ištar-ummi,* "Ištar is my mother"; *Bêl-mušallim-apli-šu,* "Bêl, takes care of [me], his son." Such names reflect a certain confidence that tempered the fear of the gods.

But looking at that fear closely, it always outweighed everything else, and the solicitude recognized in divine beings and associated with the gracious condescension that was hoped for and anticipated from very high level figures could not turn the basic disquiet that was felt upon approaching the gods into an attraction or enthusiasm. The gods were above all "lords and masters" *(bêlu)* who might show kindness but always remained enveloped in majesty, distant and fearsome, isolated in their own sphere, inaccessible to everything but their own kind. This is what we call *transcendence,* a sentiment that is certainly familiar to the Semites and is prominent in all of their religions, with its apogee in the Bible, but which, in any case, was strongly rooted in Mesopotamia.

Reverence, admiration, and self-effacement with respect to the gods dominate in the texts. I know of no text that represents another side of religious sentiment: the tendency to get closer to the divine, to seek it out as a possible source of happiness, a strictly "mystical" attitude. Anything that might come close to this "mystical" sense—and there are hardly any instances of it—is open to contextual interpretation that leads it back to fear and to the "sentiment of distance" maintained constantly between humans and the gods.

Furthermore, no document reveals a sense of the presence of the divinity within a person. The gods, as we will later see, "resided" in Heaven, on Earth, under Earth, in their temples, and in their statues but never in the heart or spirit of a person, which was, more over, logical, since too entirely anthropomorphic—the gods were not and could never truly be "immaterial."

Henotheism?

A second important conclusion can be drawn. In reading the above texts we will have certainly noticed that in each address to a given divinity that divinity was exalted above all the others, was reputed to be the primary one of all, the most important one. Anu was "the prince of the gods," but so was Sîn. The "Word" of each god was "preponderant" and "was to be taken above those of the other gods," who were subjected to it, "trembling." Each god was "the ruler of Heaven and Earth," "sublime throughout the universe," supreme and "unequaled." Ištar "dons the lordly tiara" and "gathers to herself all rites," all powers, the m e, a term whose importance we will look at more closely later but which, in any case, marked an ability, unique to the gods, to intervene in the composition and the workings of the world. All of these superlatives were attributed not only to the gods who were traditionally recognized as being above all the others, such as An(u), Enlil, Enki/Éa, Marduk, Inanna/Ištar, Aššur, but also to Adad, Šamaš, Sîn, Ninurta, Zababa, and others, who were always of lesser importance, in spite of their popularity. The Assyrian king Adad-nirari III (810–793) even went so far as to proclaim in one of his inscriptions, engraved on a statue of the god Nabû: "Whoever you are, after (me), trust in the god Nabû! Do not trust in another god!"[14]

On this subject as well, Mesopotamian onomastics provides a great deal of information. A certain number of gods are frequently qualified as "above all others" (ašarîdu), as "lord and master" (bêlu), as "king" (šarru), and even, to use the strongest term, as "Enlil of the gods," the paragon of supreme and absolute power, something like "god of the gods" (Enlil-ilî): Adad-šar-ilî, "Adad is the king of the gods"; Ninurta-ašarîd-ilî, "It is Ninurta, the first of the gods"; Šamaš-Enlil-ilî, "Šamaš is the god of gods"; and so on. Many others show the same thing, in a different formulation, in particular with rhetorical questions, which one also finds, notably, in hymns and prayers: Mannu-kî-Aššur, "Who is like Aššur?" Mannu-šânin-Šamaš, "Who can rival Šamaš?" Mannu-kîma-Adad-rabû, "Who is as great as Adad?"

True monotheism, completely unknown in Mesopotamia, as we will soon see, is an exceptional and unique fact in our past—even if, once it was "discovered," comparatively late in human history, it spread everywhere and won over the multitudes. Religious sentiment is not necessarily monotheistically inclined: religious sentiment needs only to address a sufficiently imprecise and mysterious Order-of-Things, and the question of the divinity's personalization can remain in the shadows, in one's mind and heart. But there can be no question that such a sentiment is more easily satisfied when that sacred Order-of-Things is in fact represented by a single subject and partner: the religious spirit more easily relates to *one* "being opposite," even one that is hazy and indistinct, than to a whole group of figures, a plurality, an uncertain mixture or a vague Force.

This is what explains henotheism—which, unlike monotheism, admits the plurality of the gods but is interested in and attached, at least *hic et nunc*, to only one of them. It is, in a certain way, a higher form of polytheism and has been detected here and there in Mesopotamia.

Therefore, in light of the information we have, it seems that in Mesopotamia at least, since it alone concerns us here, a profound tendency toward religiosity pushed the faithful in a certain way to encapsulate all sacred potential into the particular divine personality whom they were addressing at a given moment. Their tradition proposed innumerable divinities to them, and their reasoning rejected none of them; but in the actual practice of their religiosity, their reverence and adoration could be directed spontaneously onto *one* divine personality, in whom they concentrated, for a moment, all that was divine and sacred.

Many documents illustrate this phenomenon, which comes under the heading of religious psychology. It is certainly that phenomenon, in part, that clarifies the existence of "personal gods" (*il rêši:* literally, the "god of the head" of someone, his individual divinity), each of whom with regard to his faithful seemed to play the role of all the gods with regard to all humans: "Thou art my god, thou art my lord, / Thou art my judge, thou art my helper, / Thou art my avenger,"[15] as the exorcist recited while invoking the god of fire, whom he called upon to help him. And it is also here that the "familial names" applied to the gods derived all their meaning.

We might consider such an attitude as only a too-human example of that *captatio benevolentiae* that underlies almost obligatorily all requests for service: flatter the one from whom one seeks to obtain a favor, to ensure his positive response. But it is clear that we must see more than that; there is a true necessity in the religious sentiment not to disperse one's energies over a multitude of objects but to project oneself entirely onto one single personality, not in principle, but in fact.

Such an emotional and religious propensity toward henotheism is at the root of the ideological efforts of Mesopotamian theologians to organize their pantheon in an increasingly monarchical and concentrated fashion.

CHAPTER FIVE

Religious Representations

The Gods

In Mesopotamia, as elsewhere, if religious sentiment had once been simply suggested and was defined in only a few words, everything changed with the pressing need to "know": to represent using one's imagination the supernatural order of things which was first and foremost the product of that imagination. Not only did an infinite number of questions arise concerning that mysterious universe, sensed and apparently wide open to investigation, but the fantasies of people were already inexhaustible. It is therefore going to take many pages now to delve into this, even if we necessarily confine ourselves here only to the main features of an exuberant system.

Resolutely polytheistic and anthropomorphist from the beginning, and well before writing and history, the ancient Mesopotamians, in order to dispel the innumerable secrets behind things of this world, were inclined to place many figures behind those things, imaginary figures based on their own models, although obviously well above them, like an amplified projection of themselves. Each figure was believed to be responsible for certain natural phenomena and for certain human concepts to explain the regular functioning and the hazards of this world, like a driving force or a director. In other words, the ancient Mesopotamians doubled their universe with a parallel universe of supernatural personalities whose names reflected their roles: An was Heaven, and the god who presided over Heaven; Utu/Šamaš was the sun and the sun god; Ašnan was grain and the goddess who watched over it; Namtar was not only "decisions" (this is the meaning of that Sumerian term), presiding over the turning points in our "destiny" *(item),* but also the god who governed them; Mîšaru was justice and the divinity who was in charge of it—not to mention other entities and "forces" of all kinds, including human, upon whom people felt compelled to confer, we do not know when, who, or how, a supernatural personality. Thus was born a huge multitude of supernatural beings whose names (archaic or borrowed), we must indeed admit, often no longer mean anything to us.

The Ranks of the Gods

We describe that imaginary community of gods as a "pantheon." The word for "god" was dingir in Sumerian and *ilu* in Akkadian and referred to a particular class of beings. Their status was highlighted in writing by the placement of the cuneiform "determinative" sign for "Heaven" directly in front of the name of each god. It indicated the "lofty," or supernatural, nature of the figure; and we now commonly transcribe it with a superscript lowercase "d" (for dingir), as in ᵈMarduk, or sometimes in parentheses, (d)Marduk.

What is at first surprising is the strange collection of beings bearing this sign who made up the pantheon. I do not believe anyone has yet attempted an exact count of them; but even in round numbers we reach figures that appear totally unbelievable. The most complete count that was ever done in the second millennium by Babylonian scholars came up with almost two thousand names. In his *Pantheon babylonicum* of 1914, A. Deimel counts three thousand three hundred names; and the inventory of K. Tallqvist, *Akkadische Götterepitheta*, compiled in 1938 on stricter criteria, includes around two thousand four hundred! I know of no more recent listing, but the list was not, and still is not, complete: new documents, as they are discovered, continue to present us with names of deities that were hitherto unknown.

We must not conclude, however, that the Mesopotamians adored each of these supernatural figures with the same feeling and on equal footing. That would be above all to forget those three thousand years of history during which many things happened, on the religious level as well as on all others, beginning with the progressive and centuries-long transfer, between the fourth and the third millennium, of the Sumerian legacy to the Semitic Akkadians. With a few exceptions the great majority of names of ancient divinities are in the Sumerian language, as the Sumerians more than others obviously must have had the idea of doubling the visible world by an entire invisible, explicative, and directive world and must have been responsible for the recognition and "discovery" of such a multitude of gods, which they transmitted with their culture to the Akkadians, who were apparently less imaginative and more moderate on this subject, at least insofar as we can determine.

Such a situation seems to have caused the Akkadians to decide first to accept the mass of Sumerian gods as they were and then, whenever possible, to gradually indulge in *syncretism,* by comparing, indeed by identifying, with their own those divinities that were at first foreign to them. When they did not find anyone in their own much less exuberant pantheon to take the place of an analogous Sumerian figure, they kept that figure's Sumerian name, either in its original form, unchanged (e.g., this is the case with Enlil, "Lord Air," the ruler of the gods and the world), or by adapting the name to their own language (thus An, "the god of Heaven," was Akkadianized to Anu through the addition of a final -*u,* designating the nominative case). Sometimes such gods changed names completely: thus Nanna, the Sumerian moon god, and Utu, the sun god, rather quickly gave way to their Akkadian equivalents: Sîn (also written Su'en) and Šamaš. The great Sumerian god Enki (whose name, to our eyes, seems not to have any obvious original meaning) was adopted by the Akkadians, first under his original designation, which was replaced rather quickly by that of a Semitic god whom we do not know very well and who must have been called something like Ia; the name was then spelled Éa.[1]

This process continued for a long time, and more than one divinity who was at first autonomous found itself in the course of time and depending on the religious vision (without our always being able to follow the vicissitudes of the process) more or less connected to, even absorbed by, another divinity, sometimes one with quite different attributes. For example, the Sumerian god Ninurta, "Lord of the Arable Land," was the object of very strong devotion at the end of the third millennium and was proportionately associated at times with the names and prerogatives of some half-dozen other ancient members of the Sumerian pantheon: Uraš, Zababa, Papsukkal, Lugalbanda, Ningirsu, etc. And there was above all the famous Sumerian goddess of "free love" (Inanna, "Lady of Heaven"—for Ninanna, which has that meaning in Sumerian), to whom the Akkadians conferred the name of one of their own divinities: Ištar. She gradually received, most certainly beginning quite early and because of her superabundant and exceptional personality, so many supernatural roles that were first reserved for other goddesses that at the beginning of the second millennium her Akkadian name was even used to designate "the feminine form of the divine." The word *ištaru* meant, ultimately, "a goddess."

Such combinations and connections were never the result of any official decision, since this religion was governed only by usage, which changed depending on the time, the place, and the devotion, making the divinities, to us, rather hazy. If we take into account all that shifting around and all those connections and syncretisms between divinities, we will certainly be less impressed by the excessive multiplicity of divine names, since a great many of them ultimately designated a single figure.

Moreover, many of those denominations, insofar as we can understand them, were, in fact, and no doubt already in the time of their Sumerian creators, only *epithets* for the same figure, a bit like the names Notre-Dame de Lourdes, Notre-Dame de La Salette, the Black Virgin, and so on, are for us, all referring to the mother of Christ, in her various sanctuaries. The Sumerians thus used such names to translate their ancient vision of the world as doubled by a superhuman group of figures who governed all its workings. They called them "kings" (Lugal-) or "lords/ladies" (En-/Nin-) of those phenomena: *Lugal-a-ab-ba*, "King of the Sea"; *En-amaš*, "Lord of Livestock Pens"; *Nin-kilim*, "Lady of the Small Wild Animals"; and so on. The Akkadians, not very attracted by this supernatural system of universal explanation, kept only a small number of them: for example, *Bêlit-ṣêri*, "Lady of the Steppe"; and above all the very imposing *Bêlit-ilî*, "Lady of the Gods." Various other appellations were similarly merely ways of designating by some prerogative or particularity gods who were otherwise known by their names. Thus Kurgal, "Great Mountain," was used to evoke the imposing majesty of Enlil; Nudimmud, "Manufacturer-Producer," for Enki/Éa, the great one responsible for the existence of things; Ašimbabbar, "Brilliant Rise" for Nanna/Sîn, the moon god. And further, Bêl, "The Lord," was understood above all to be first Enlil, then Marduk, his "successor" as ruler of the world. The conclusion of the *Epic of Creation* lists and explains, one by one, the "fifty names" of Marduk that had been conferred upon him, through common devotion and probably above all by "theologians."[2] Some names were quite well known (Asalluḫi, Tutu, Enbilulu, etc.); others were little used. Following the well-established conviction in that land which *identified* the name with the thing it named, each one of those designations implied a "destiny": a prerogative or a particular merit of the god, the accumulation of which, on the level of grandeur and omnipotence, made him "an exceptional figure"[3] in the eyes of his followers.

These many divine epithets not only incline us to view the onomastics of so many gods as rather blurry and fluctuating but substantially decrease the number of divine personnel hidden behind so many names, reducing the actual number in the ancient pantheon to some few hundred, at most.

We see clearly at the same time that their numbers must have diminished through the centuries. The gods were countless and teeming in the time of their Sumerian creators; but the Akkadians, less at ease before so many supernatural beings, apparently gradually introduced many fewer of them from their own pantheon (in the oldest catalogs, from around 2600, we still count only three Akkadian gods out of more than five hundred; and the overall total, a few centuries later, was never more than thirty!). It was as if, faced with that Sumerian legacy, the Akkadians preferred to elevate the dignity and power of their gods as they were simultaneously reducing the number of them.

From the Group to a System

Thus the few hundred divinities, the majority of Sumerian origin, made up quite a large, more or less disordered and confused group. All the efforts of the religious thinkers of that land from the first part of the third millennium were focused on turning that group into a *system:* to impose a rational, hierarchical order upon it. We can measure the results of this effort by local theologians in the various successive catalogs of divine names, which reflect the classificatory genius of those people and which were composed throughout the centuries, probably beginning quite early.

The most ancient accounts, unearthed at Fâra (Šuruppak) and Tell Abû Ṣalābīkh, date from around 2600; but they may record an even older tradition. At the very beginning of a list of some 560 names of divinities we read the following sequence, at the top of the first column:

> An
> Enlil

Inanna
Enki
Nanna
Utu[4]

We know, moreover, that from that time until the beginning of our era that sequence of names was always affixed to the systematic listings of divinities, thereby representing the highest-ranking gods at the head of the entire divine world—a rather good demonstration of the Mesopotamian interest in classification. In the above list we see, in descending order of importance, first of all An, the founder and chief of the divine ruling dynasty (we will later discuss his predecessors); then his son, Enlil, the current ruler of the gods and the world; then a goddess, subsequently long associated with those "authorities" to represent the feminine and maternal element among them. She had other more universal designations, in particular that of *Bêlit-ilî,* "Lady [and Mother] of the Gods." The name Inanna, which is listed here, was most likely a sort of ideogram for her, for it is not easily equated here, as it subsequently was on an almost regular basis, with the true Sumerian Inanna (she whom the Akkadians later called Ištar), goddess of love and discord.[5] After her there was Enki, traditionally included in that tetrad—or triad when the feminine element was omitted—in his role as grand vizier, responsible for ensuring the fruitful exercise of the sovereign power held by the king. Then followed Nanna, the Sumerian moon god, and Utu, the sun god.

Later, another tetrad was permanently constructed in conjunction with the first, the second of lesser authority and importance, more or less based upon the first. In addition to the moon god and the sun god, it included the weather/storm god (Iškur/Adad) and the true Inanna/Ištar. Only two of the gods of this second tetrad are listed here (perhaps the tetrad had not yet been fully developed or disseminated).

The Šuruppak text then goes on to list divinities, almost all Sumerian, whose names mean absolutely nothing to us, and about whose formation and organization we cannot derive very much. Here and there we find gods and goddesses who appear in later sources, such as Nisaba, "Lady of the Grain" and, later, of surveying and writing; Ninurta, god of agriculture, but also a warrior god; Ninegal, "Lady of the Palace" (later, in Akkadian, *Bêlit-ekallim*); and so forth. But all these names seem, perhaps wrongly, to be randomly scattered, and we are unable to discern the organizing principle that the authors of the list most likely followed. Thus, very early on, the ancient Mesopotamians attempted to impose order onto the mass of gods: even if the ordering principle in the ancient list of Šuruppak escapes us, the placement of the most important group at the head of the list suggests a further ordering of all the gods.

Of the analogous listings, more recent than those of Šuruppak, the most extensive is about a thousand years younger. It is referred to, according to custom, by its first words: *An:* ᵈ*Anu(m),* "An (is) Anu."[6] It includes no fewer than two thousand divine names spread over seven tablets. Many of the names are ancient, almost all Sumerian, and already figured here and there in the earlier listings of names; only a small number of them are new, and these are of Akkadian origin. The names are arranged in two parallel columns, in the style of "lexical" lists, so typical of Mesopotamian scholarly literature and thought: on the left is the name; on the right, its explanation. For example, concerning the great mother goddess (I:25ff.), there is this excerpt:

ᵈ*Nin(= Bêlit)-ilî*   *dam Annake* ([She is] the first wife of Anu)
ᵈ*Nin-ur-salla*   *dam-bànda Annake* ([She is] the second wife of Anu)
ᵈ*Nammu*   *ama* ᵈ*Enkigake* ([She is] the mother of Enki)

Each name is placed in a predetermined, perfectly organized position according to a perspective that is easily perceived even by just glancing through the entire work. We find the two tetrads that opened the list of Šuruppak: Anum,[7] Enlil, Inanna/Bêlit-ilî, and Enki/Éa; then Sîn, Šamaš, Adad, and Ištar. But instead of being grouped together in that order, at the head or elsewhere, these names are scattered, each followed by a more or less lengthy list of divine figures placed in a relationship of kinship with or dependence on it. Anum's group covers tablet I, lines 1–95; Enlil's, I:96–370; Bêlit-ilî's, II:1–128; Éa's, II:129–422; Sîn's, III:1–96; Šamaš's, III:97–205; Adad's, III:206–284; and Ištar's, IV:1–296. A few divinities of lesser importance (such as Ninurta and Nergal) are also listed, and the seventh and final tablet appears to be a supplement dedicated to Marduk, whose elevation was recent at that time.

The multitude of gods was divided into larger or smaller groups, and each was attached to a principal divinity upon whom it more or less depended. The whole formed something like a layered "pyramid of powers," a *system.* To illustrate the links imagined between the gods, here is a summary of the "chapter" devoted to Anum and his entourage (I:1–95). After his name is mentioned, ten couples are listed, his "fathers and mothers"—in other words, his ancestors through ten generations (we will return to this). Then his eight "wives" are listed, beginning with the first wife. Then his close entourage is recorded, beginning with his *sukkal,* or "lieutenant," followed by the *sukkal*'s "wife," his "fourteen children," "two valets," and the "seat-bearing" officer. We are presented next with Anum's seven "valets," his "sword-bearer" and his wife, the three great "head chefs," the two "head shepherds," the "gardener," and the two "advisers."

Among the "personnel" of the other principal divinities, we again note the close relatives: "ancestors," "wives," "sons," and "daughters." Titles and names of subordinate functionaries are also given: "vizier" (even "grand vizier"), "agent," "ambassador," "aide-de-camp," "bodyguard," "steward," "secretary," "interpreter," "hairdresser" (both masculine and feminine), "bailiff," "gatekeeper," "sentinel," and a few others. Our translations are necessarily approximate, since we are unable to ascertain all the nuances pertaining to the time during which the text was written. Those offices, and their grouping around an individual of high station or a representative of power, were in no way capricious, invented only for the subject at hand. For as we can easily attest, if we only look carefully at the secular documentation of the time, all were borrowed from the organization of the state and the royal palace.

In this way, the ancient Mesopotamians organized the huge mass of gods from ancient tradition and placed them into a rational and "realistic" framework, mythologically transposed from the common political order in the land, as is eloquently conveyed by all those titles and names of functions. The innumerable gods and their initially disorganized world were transformed into a supernatural reflection of earthly political authority. Like that authority, the world of the gods had its supreme representative, a king and his ancestors. The initial head of the pantheon, Anu, was supplanted by Enlil (a highly unusual situation on earth, but imaginable, all the same) but was still honored for his experience and wisdom and was surrounded by his wives, his children, and the rest of his "house." His eldest son, Enlil, assumed the role of the practicing monarch, surrounded, too, by his wives and children and an entire court of high dignitaries and functionaries—so many positions occupied by the gods, chosen by virtue of criteria that for the most part escape us. And each god, in turn connected through blood to the supreme chief, was also at the head of an analogous corps of personnel, whose activities overlapped those of other divinities.

The first group of gods, all born out of archaic and fortuitous circumstances, about which we no longer have the slightest idea, who were at first a simple incoherent gathering, had thus become, through centuries of evolution, mythological reflections and calculations, a true organization of supernatural power, rational, logical, and rigorous (perhaps even a bit too much so, for the man on the street . . .), which dominated people as the structured earthly royal authority dominated its subjects. The whole formed a "pyramid of powers."

We can follow the development and the major vicissitudes of this system, at least in broad strokes, through documents and reasonable conjectures, throughout the religious history of the land. We are naturally inclined to use our imaginations, as we know almost nothing at all about the "original" religion, the one before writing, or about its divine personnel. There is some likelihood that in all of the first villages, which were isolated and weak, people also worshiped divine personalities who exercised their supernatural authority from On High, as the political authorities exercised theirs on Earth. A number of divinities, including those whose names, prerogatives, and myths appear later, must have originated in those distant times. The Sumerians, whose arrival in the land occurred perhaps even before their entrance onto the historical scene, had already sketched out their own pantheon in its broad strokes; and, once settled, they were able to absorb through syncretism and to more or less remodel and "name" a certain number of native archaic divinities, about whom we speculate in vain.

Following the association and the fusion of those villages into larger political entities, under the rule of chiefs who were more vigorous and capable of planning and carrying out the great work of digging canals and of preparing more land for agriculture, there had to have been a coming together, a blending, even syncretisms, among the members of the respective divine personnel, which had until that time been locked in their respective villages. Larger and more composite pantheons were created, most likely already more or less hierarchized on the model of the civil authorities and connected by ties of kinship or dependency. No doubt, a sort of "national" pantheon was drawn, at least in its earliest stage, by transposing the common culture that was developing onto the religious level. But how can we determine the progress, composition, and dissemination of that religion? We can, with some reservations, go so far as to conjecture that among the old mythological constructions dating from those times was the supreme tetrad.

When the political organization of the land had developed into the regime of the city-states, this religious framework, which was embedded in the shared, common culture, was compatible with reduced pantheons, reflections of those city-states, each of which might have had reason to prefer and choose particular divinities either from its own ancient local stock or from the common pantheon and to assemble them depending on their specific form of devotion. It is possible that worship of particular divinities was influenced by religious centers, whose prehistory, famous or exemplary, rendered them even more influential. In particular, there was Eridu, where the venerable and famous Enki, traditionally considered to be responsible for the origins of "culture," reigned; and there was Nippur, headquarters of the great Enlil, who was the sacred king of the gods, of the land, and of the world, until he was supplanted by Marduk, who would in turn confer a particular religious authority on Babylon.

As a result, beginning in the second quarter of the third millennium, each city-state had one of the great divinities of the "national" pantheon as its supernatural chief: Enki in Eridu; Enlil in Nippur; An (and Inanna, his inseparable hierodule) in Uruk; Nanna in Ur; Utu in Larsa and in Sippar. And each god in his temple, the high place of the "capital" and of the region, was surrounded by his family and his court. For example, in Lagaš, the sovereign gods were Ningirsu (the local name of the son of Enlil, Ninurta, "the Lord of Girsu," one of the principal cities near Lagaš) and his wife Bawa. In their court and family there were notably the god Lugalsisa, as "adviser"; the goddess Nanše, daughter of Enki and sister of Ningirsu; her husband, Nindare; Ningizzida, the personal god of Prince Gudea; Geštinanna, Ningizzida's wife; and the mother goddess Gatumdug. Nothing prevented their faithful from also devoutly turning to the greater and lesser divinities of the common pantheon: An, Enlil, Enki, Inanna, Nanna (also called by his Akkadian name Su'en, the Sumerian version of Sîn), Nisaba (the goddess of grain), Utu, and so forth.

As noted above, as the Sumerian cultural dominance weakened, not only did the number of "active" gods decrease, but the power, majesty, and importance of their personae increased, thus reflecting the rulers of the land, who, notably after Sargon of Akkad, were no longer the weak petty kings of tiny city-states but vigorous and omnipotent chiefs of great political organizations: the empire of Sargon, at the end of the third millennium, the empire of Babylon under Ḥammurabi (1792–1750), and of Aššur under Šamši-Adad (1813–1781). The gods' turf remained intact, organized and systematized in the eyes of the theologians, but the ordinary person was interested, in fact, in only a reduced number of gods. Ḥammurabi, in the opening of his law code, exalts Marduk, a god who was until then without great fame and without glory beyond his realm, and pronounces him the supernatural chief of the city of Babylon:

> When the lofty Anu, king of the Anunnaki, and Enlil, lord of heaven and earth, he who determines the destiny of the land, committed the rule of all mankind to Marduk, the eldest son of Éa; when they made him great among the gods. . . .[8]

Throughout the entire law code, along with Marduk, his wife Zarpanitu, and their son, Nabû, only some thirty deities are mentioned: Adad, Aya (wife of Šamaš), Anu, Dagan (the great West Semitic god, imported by the Amorites), Éa, Damgal-nunna (Éa's wife, the mother of Marduk), Enlil and his spouse Ninlil, Gula (a healing goddess), Ištar, Mamma/i (one of the designations of the great mother goddess, a member of the supreme tetrad), Nâru (the patron god of running water), Nergal (the ruler of the Netherworld), Ninazu (the physician god), Nintu (the "Lady of Childbirth," a synonym for Mamma), Ninurta, Sîn, Šamaš, Tišpak (patron god of the city of Ešnunna; of unknown foreign origin), and Zababa (ancient Sumerian warrior god), and so on. This list sufficiently represents the pantheon that was familiar to the common people at the beginning of the second millennium. Only the theologians and the clerics were more concerned, when the opportunity arose, with the others, whose names always filled the columns of the "lists" of the gods. It is quite likely that most average Mesopotamians, not to mention the rural farmers and the illiterate, whose religiosity was assuredly very unrefined (and, in any case, essentially unknown to us), while maintaining some vague notion of a great number of divinities, were in truth preoccupied only with their own immediate relationship with their "personal god," who they imagined had the destiny of his protégé well in hand. People's personal names illustrate this: the number of divine names used is small.

Further emphasizing the weak interest that was paid to "the crowd of gods," people had developed, beginning in the third millennium, collective terms to evoke the gods as a whole: "the great gods," to denote the most important among them, the most "cosmic"; "the gods of Heaven and Earth"; "the gods of the land." The *Epic of Creation* offers the round number of "six hundred" gods and, showing a concern for symmetry, distributes one-half "On High" and one-half "Below"—on and above Earth, and below it.[9]

Texts also speak of the Anunnaku, or Anunnaki (in Sumerian, A.nun.na[k], "Offspring of the Prince," most likely, An, Enlil, or Enki —the mythological allusion is obscure), and of the Igigi/Igigu (of uncertain origin). The first of these terms appears initially to have referred to the "gods On High," "of Heaven," the most powerful, the most eminent, and, in some way, the upper class and the "chiefs" of the others. At the very beginning of the poem *Atraḫasîs,* these high-level gods make the others work, and they themselves, like the good holders of power they were, remain without anything to do. Those who worked were the Igigi. Later (we are not sure when or why), the situation was reversed, and the latter represented the celestial gods, whereas the Anunnaku became the gods who resided in the Netherworld.

Henotheistic Tendencies

In the years that followed the first part of the second millennium, this divine system was maintained, though its details scarcely interested the common person. However, a few innovations came into play, especially in practice, and we must at least point out the most important of them, which, in one way or another, had repercussions for the entire religious realm and must even have reached more or less all the faithful.

One innovation concerns the divine figure who was traditionally honored as the lord of the gods and of the entire world. Enlil, a member of the great tetrad, assumed this honor. Later, Marduk,[10] the chief god, patron, and lord of Babylon, became increasingly popular when Babylon asserted its predominance over the entire land, not only through its political and military might but also through intellectual and religious primacy. From the middle of the second millennium, the number of personal names in which Marduk's name appears grew considerably, with attributes that were increasingly distinguished and heavy with religiosity: *Marduk-muballit,* "It is Marduk who gives life"; *Ilî-Marduk,* "My god is Marduk"; *Pâni-Marduk-lûmur,* "Let me contemplate the face of Marduk"; and so on, into the hundreds.

Babylon then entered a long period of sluggishness and political insignificance. Shortly before 1100, Babylon recovered its former independence and glory. Babylon's grandiose and famous sanctuary of Marduk, the Ésagil (from the Sumerian é.sag.íl, "the temple with the sublime pediment"), became in some sense the religious high place of the entire country. Babylon's clergy, faced with the growing swell of devotion to their god, decided to elevate him to "Lord of the Gods and of the World," successor to Enlil, just as Enlil, long ago, must have replaced An(u)—an image of the successive sequence of earthly rulers.

Hoping to impose and justify such a goal, the unknown authors, undoubtedly priests serving at the Esagil, wrote (in Akkadian) and distributed the famous *Epic of Creation,* as we call it (in Mesopotamia it was cited by its *incipit: Enûma eliš,* "When On High . . ."), a magisterial "treatise" of mythological apologetics proclaiming and defending the extraordinary promotion of their great divine patron.[11] Their argument was persuasive: Marduk was to be crowned king of the entire divine population by the unanimous decision of the Council of Gods because he had saved them from the great original mother goddess (here called "Sea," Tiamat), who had been irritated and had decided to destroy him. He *had to be* the sacred king of the world because he had imagined and built it from the remains of Tiamat, whom he had conquered and sacrificed; and he *had to be* the sacred king of humans, because he had conceived the idea of them and had created them. This work, of lofty and stiff poetry, a bit gloomy, it is true, but not without grandeur, overflows with a grave enthusiasm for the god who is its hero, who is endowed with "fifty" names/destinies/privileges and is exalted as "an exceptional figure" among the gods, that is, a god superior to all others.

From that time and after that "charter," even though it is above all literary and evidently had no "doctrinal" authority, Marduk truly became, through the popular devotion that was encouraged in it, what the clergy of the city wanted him to be. Granted, in that land where they had no taste for revolutions and where they clearly preferred to accumulate rather than to replace, Enlil more or less continued to appear in his ancient place, in the middle of the great triad, which had succeeded the first tetrad. It nevertheless happened, in time, in the first millennium at least, that Enlil was occasionally considered a *deus otiosus* and was even imagined, like a man, to be "deceased"—withdrawn from his responsibilities and assigned, like humans but undoubtedly magnificently, to that final infernal refuge where the inactive and sluggish dead were imagined to reside.

However, Marduk, "the lord" (*bêlu, bêl,* a title up until then reserved for Enlil), was increasingly celebrated as the greatest of all gods, something like the "god of gods." Here is how he was addressed and presented on certain occasions:

> 3 Sîn is your divinity, Anu your sovereignty,
> Dagan is your lordship, Enlil your kingship,
> 5 Adad is your might, wise Ea your perception,
> Nabû, holder of the tablet stylus, is your skill.
> Your leadership (in battle) is Ninurta, your might Nergal,
> Your counsel is Nus[ku], your superb [minister,]
> Your judgeship is radiant Shamash, who arouses [no]
> dispute.[12]

And a new list of gods explained:

> 3 Marduk is Ninurta, the god of agriculture;
> He is Nergal, the god of battles;
> 5 Zababa, the god of war;
> Nabû, the god of accountants;
> Enlil, the god of governing;
> Sîn, the god who lights the night;
> Šamaš, the god of justice;
> 10 And Adad, the god of rain . . .[13]

We would be wrong to take these pious assertions more literally than we did the exclusivist sentiments recorded and commented on above, which appeared to distance all the other gods from the divine prerogatives of the one who was being addressed at the moment. We still have here only the fleeting demonstrations of a vague *henotheism,* all the more ambiguous in that, especially in the first millennium, a few other divinities, Nabû and Šamaš in particular, as well as Aššur in Assyria, of which he was the "national god,"[14] were

the objects of the same sentimental superexaltations, without truly
changing the order of things that had been admitted for such a long
time and was still universally maintained, which held to the systematized plurality of the gods and to their traditional hierarchy.
Contrary to what has sometimes been believed, indeed advanced
from time to time, a true monotheism could scarcely be born out of
this religion, which assuredly never ceased to intelligently rational-
ize and organize its polytheism, and which, in truth, as everything
indicates, never departed from it.

The Mythology of the Divine

The subject has already been broached, since *polytheism*—the very
existence of the gods, their number, and their hierarchized distribution—necessarily arose from that "rational imagination" which
sought to represent the supernatural with a certain coherence, and
which we call mythology. It remains to be discussed how divine beings were represented in that mythology, before examining the
gods' relationships to the world and to humans.

The Notion of "Divinity," of "Divine Nature"

The notion of divinity was never explicitly defined in Mesopotamia,
but only described, as it were, by a diverse plurality of particulari-
ties and prerogatives. This, moreover, was the case with all generic
and even specific abstractions in a culture that very well recognized the concept of "man" *(awîlu)* and even of "all men" *(awîlûtu)*
but was never concerned with isolating and defining a concept of
"humanity."

Even the word "god" (dingir in Sumerian; *ilu* in Akkadian) in no
way explains its original meaning, since in neither language do we
have the slightest sure etymology of it. It is only on the graphic
level, in its ideogram (which also served as a determinative), that we
find some semantic aid. It is shaped like a star, ✳ → ⋈⊦, and also
signified "Heaven," everything that, by its position or its nature,
was "above," "elevated," "superior." Thus "the god" was first imagined via his *superiority*—his superiority over everything else, but especially over humans, since in the anthropomorphic regime of the
local religion, the divine was represented in an exalted and superior
form based on the human model. Every god was thus perceived as

having been formed in our image but was believed to be superior to us in everything, both positively and negatively.

To obtain an idea of the extraordinary range of advantages and powers that were recognized in the gods, we need only once again take a look at the texts presented above to illustrate religious sentiment. Enki is the "Sublime Lord of Heaven and Earth, the one respected for himself"; he is "the strong one of Heaven and Earth"; his "shadow covers Heaven and Earth." Marduk destroys "tortuous mountains," "at whose warfare the heavens quake / At whose cry the depths are roiled." Šamaš's "radiance [spre]ads out like a net [over the world]"; he is "illuminator of all, the whole of heaven/ Who makes light the d[arkness for mankind] above and below"; he "brightens the g[loo]m of the distant mountains"; he "balances the disk of the world in the midst of heaven (for) the circle of the lands"; and he makes "the people of all lands [his]charge": "Among all the Igigi-gods there is none who does such wearisome toil but [him],/Nor among the sum total of the gods one who does so much as [him]!" Sîn is "chief of the gods, who in heaven and on earth alone is supreme" and "holds in his hand the life of the whole country," whereas his "divinity is full of fear, like the far-off heavens and the broad sea." And Ištar, "powerful . . . queen, exalted is [her] name," is the "luminary of heaven and earth": the greatest gods "have lifted [her] high, they have made [her] authority greatest among the gods . . . they have made [her] (heavenly) station highest of all," whereas "at the thought of [her] name, heaven and netherworld quake, / The gods totter, the Anunna-gods tremble" —she, alone, is "the great one, the exalted one."

The other gods are not exempt from this exaltation of their person, their sublimity, their omnipotence. To see this, one needs only to glean here and there the qualifiers that are constantly applied to them: they are "powerful" *(dannu; gašru),* even "all-powerful" *(dandannu; kaškaššu);* "great" *(rabû)* and "very great" *(šurbû);* "very highly placed" *(šûturu);* "majestic" *(šagapûru);* "glorious" *(šûpû);* "sublime" *(nâ'idu; ṣîru);* "perfect" *(gitmalu);* "unsurpassable" *(lâ maḫar);* and so on. These descriptions clearly derive from the gods' superiority over humans and were recognized everywhere, as we can note by simply glancing at a list of personal names: *Sîn-rabi,* "Sîn is great"; *Nabû-nâ'id,* "Nabû is sublime"; and so forth.

The poets' verve is unleashed whenever they wish to have us share their endless admiration for one of their divinities. This is seen, for example, in the hymn to Šamaš cited above. And here is how their enthusiasm presents Marduk, just recently brought into the world and still a little baby:

> 85 He suckled at the breasts of goddesses,
>   The attendant who raised him endowed him well with glories.
>   His body was magnificent, fiery his glance
>   · · · · · · · · · · · · · · · · · ·
>   When Anu his grandfather saw him,
>   He was happy, he beamed, his heart was filled with joy.
>   He perfected him, so that his divinity was strange,
>   He was much greater, he surpassed them in every way.
>   His members were fashioned with cunning beyond
>   comprehension,
>   Impossible to conceive, too difficult to visualize:
>   · · · · · · · · · · · · · · · · · ·
> 99 He was tallest of the gods, surpassing in form,
>   His limbs enormous, he was surpassing at birth.[15]

Regarding the keenness of the gods' vision, their perception of things, the liveliness of their minds, their intelligence, it is difficult to find words and images lofty enough for them: they are "intelligent" *(ḫasîsu)*; "wise" *(le'û)* and "very wise" *(tele'û)*; "aware" *(muntalku)*; "clever" *(rapaš uzni; itpêšu)*. And concerning Marduk, at his birth Anu notes that he has twice the capacity for knowledge (the eyes) and for perception (the ears, organs for intellectual ability) of the other divinities:

> 97 Formidable his fourfold perception,
>   And his eyes, in like number, saw in every direction.[16]

We are often reminded that the thoughts, designs, paths, intentions, plans, and will of the gods are inaccessible, incomprehensible to humans. Thus, the author of the *Theodicy* writes:

> 82 The plans of the god . . . like the centre of heaven,
>   The decrees of the goddess are not . . .
>   To understand properly
>   · · · · · · · · · · · · · · · · · ·
> 256 The divine mind, like the centre of the heavens, is remote;
>   Knowledge of it is difficult; the masses do not know it.[17]

And the author of *Ludlul,* despairing of ever knowing why the gods have assigned such a cruel fate to him, goes so far as to imagine a complete inversion of words and meanings between us and them:

33   I wish I knew that these things were pleasing to one's god!
     What is proper to oneself is an offense to one's god,
     What in one's own heart seems despicable is proper to
         one's god.
     Who knows the will of the gods in heaven?
     Who understands the plans of the underworld gods?
     Where have mortals learnt the way of a god?[18]

The *transcendence* of the divine over the human is one of the fundamental truths of Mesopotamian religious thought. We find this idea just about everywhere among the ancient Semites, and because it is associated with monotheism and is thus absolute, its role is essential in the Bible.

At the same time another attribute was used to emphasize the ontological superiority of the gods, *melammu,* that terrifying "supernatural brilliance," that fulgurating "divine splendor," fascinating and terrible at the same time, which we have recognized as a projection of the religious sentiment. Marduk, at the time of his birth, already

102   wore (on his body) the auras of ten gods,
      had (them) wrapped around his head too. . . .[19]

This was a way of saying that he was ten, even fifty, times "more god" than the others.

Assuredly the disadvantage of mortality separated humans most obviously from the gods. Gods could not die a natural death, exhausted by the prolongation of existence and aging. And they were less frequently the victims of those accidents and illnesses that weaken us and ultimately close our eyes.

The death of a god, of which we find only a few documented examples, was always violent and intentional. In *Atraḫasîs* the (minor) god Wê is deliberately immolated by his peers in order to allow a "superior" element to be introduced into human nature.[20] And the same is true of the rebellious god Qingu in the *Epic of Creation.*[21] But "death" could also be of only analogous importance. Like "deceased" humans *(de-functi),* that is, those who have become inactive once their "function" in life on earth had been accomplished, the gods to whom religious vicissitude had ceased to attribute an active role (a bit like our old saints, picturesque and outdated) were imagined to have been assigned, like us, to an infernal retirement. They were withdrawn from their interventions, which were then transferred to

other members of the divine personnel, and were "dead" to the
devotion of humans, even if, unlike the latter, they sluggishly conserved their supernatural prerogatives, ready to come back to life if
only their adorers would need them once again. Even "dead," the
gods maintained their superiority over humans.

Just as one might speak of the death of a few gods, so endless life
was sometimes granted to a few humans, as we see in the *Epic of Gilgameš,* in which the survivors of the Flood, Utanapištim and his wife,
were made immortal by the gods and existed all alone until the end
of the world.[22] Gilgameš clearly counts on the communicability of
that privilege to escape his own death. He is disabused of his hope,
but (we do not know why or how) he finds himself all the same,
very soon after his death, not only immortalized but "divinized," in
the company of a few figures as archaic and famous as himself: notably Dumuzi and Lugalbanda, kings of Uruk, like himself.[23] Lugalbanda was Gilgameš's father, and his wife was a goddess (or a divinized mortal woman?), Ninsuna, the "Lady of Wild Cattle." The
divinization of these old rulers and the presence in the pantheon of
the semidivine couple Ninsuna and Lugalbanda as well as (the result
of their "mixed" marriage) their son—"Two-thirds of him is god;
one-third of him is human"[24]—would lead us to believe that at least
in very ancient times, and undoubtedly from the time of Sumerian
domination, a small portion of the pantheon could be composed of
very ancient "divinized" mortals and that the notion of "divinity"
was somewhat "elastic." The fact is that until around the beginning
of the second millennium we encounter more than one ruler whose
name is sometimes preceded by the divine determinative of the
"star": Narâm-Sîn (2254–2218) and Šar-kali-šarri (2217–2193), for
example. This seems to be the last echo of an archaic belief, perhaps
attributable to the Sumerians, whose disordered polytheism and the
great number of their divinities might have favored a vision of the
divine that was less rigorous than the sentiment of "transcendence"
and the strict isolation of the gods in their own sphere found later
among the Semites (Akkadians and others), and thus admitted an
easier passage from the human order to the divine.

The situation is not completely the same when it is a matter of the
supernatural character of a few other entities inhabiting the universe
of the ancient Mesopotamians. The most visible of the heavenly
bodies—the Moon, the Sun, the planet Venus—were often more or
less identified with the divinities who represented and ruled over

them (in the hymn to Šamaš, that god is glorified by all the prerogatives of the star). Even the least eminent stars and constellations
derived something from the nature and the privileges of the divinities who were believed to animate and govern them. They were also
believed to have supernatural powers, and people prayed to them.
But a true divinization of the stars, making them equal to the gods,
never seems to have been formally recognized: the stars' names
were not written out in full in the lists of gods and were never regularly preceded by the divine determinative, but only by the sign *mul*,
"star," the determinative for stars.

We must certainly also consider other palpable "realities" superior
to humans but inferior to the gods themselves, which were endowed
with a supernatural character, that is, with superhuman powers: for
example, the mountains, imposing, crushing, sublime, which approached Heaven and its inhabitants. Above all (these were introduced into the lists of divinities) bodies of water (*Nâru/Íd*) were
endowed with divine prerogatives: "creative," purifying, and even
judicial. A judge incapable of settling a case for lack of evidence submitted those concerned to the Ordeal, which in that land normally
was accomplished through recourse to the discriminating power of
a river. Fire was mysterious, dangerous, and helpful, purifying and
destructive. The fertile powers of nature, for example, the growth of
sheep *(Laḫar)* and the growth of grain *(Ašnan)*, were great, secret, impenetrable, and irresistible. These phenomena were integrated into
the pantheon, providing it with additional personalities, of a second
order, of course, and quite far from the "great gods," but to which
one willingly turned.

The case of "demons," as we call them, is a bit different. Such a
collective term for these entities existed in neither Sumerian nor Akkadian, which included only words specific to harmful and dangerous beings or "forces." These figures, superior to humans and inferior to the gods, had been imagined and distributed with a view to
making sense of the evil in the world. Also endowed with superhuman abilities analogous to those of the gods (power, intelligence,
immortality), the evil forces were not on the same ontological level,
even though their divine character was declared by the divine determinative affixed to their names. But they were never inserted into
the lists of the gods. It seems that people did not dwell very much
on their persons, their nature, or their existence, as they have never
been presented very clearly. The same determinative sometimes pre-

cedes the name of an analogous being, the *eṭemmu*, the haunting and dangerous "ghost."

It therefore appears that, for lack of appropriate representations or clear nomenclature, or a decisive and lucid classification within an archaic and perhaps strictly Sumerian vision of things, the terms dingir and *ilu* first denoted, not the unique divine by itself, but everything that, whether good or evil, went beyond the human. The terms were thus applied to beings that were superior to common humans; for example, they could apply to those whom the Greeks called "heroes," a notion unknown in Mesopotamia. Superiority in abilities, functions, prowess, and merits could, without affecting their true *nature*, place stars or mysterious misbehaving agents or, indeed, humans rather close to the edge so that they were induced, more or less consciously, to cross over it, thus becoming "divinized."

The Image of the Gods

The gods' image was thus basically anthropomorphic. In their representations of the gods, the ancient Mesopotamians projected the human model onto a grandiose and fascinating screen.

In the historical era, at least, zoomorphism in the strict sense, or "zoolatry," was never practiced. The use of animal forms in religious imagery came out of a symbolism whose meaning is rarely clear, and which turned certain animals, indeed certain objects, real or imaginary, into suggestions, not representations; animals and objects were less companions than emblems of certain divinities. Although we do not understand why, the dog evoked the warrior goddess Gula; the scorpion, Išḫara, the reflection of Ištar, also destined to be a patron of physical love; the plow, Ninurta, god of agriculture; the lamp, Nusku, responsible for light and fire, etc.; not to mention certain more or less personalized weapons, which were indeed sometimes "divinized" and even introduced into myths, weapons that evoked the acts of the gods who were believed to use them. The system of symbols is quite clearly illustrated on boundary stones, called *kudurru*, on which images of animals or objects symbolized the gods mentioned in the accompanying inscriptions, who were invoked to supernaturally guarantee the official donation of which these monuments were the charter.[25]

If we need proof of the exclusive use of the human figure in representing the gods, let us only think, first, of the vast collection of statues, statuettes, figurines, engravings (on cylinder seals, in particular), and also (more rarely) paintings that archeologists have extracted for a hundred and fifty years from that deep and venerable subterranean "museum." The most ancient objects often appear somewhat naive, indeed truly deformed or "wild," to us; that was perhaps a way of highlighting the otherness, the "different" character of those who belonged to "another world." But the traits are always above all human, and the gods' "sacred" character was easily noted through conventional indicators, sorts of ideograms of divinity, such as the horned headdress of the gods and the *polos* (a tall, cylindrical headdress) of the goddesses, or by accentuating the majestic and hieratic nature of the figure.

The ancient Mesopotamians had a very concrete concept of those images: mysteriously, they *were,* or *contained,* the personality they *represented.* The entire beginning of the poem *How Erra Wrecked the World*[26] details the efforts of that god of sinister designs to convince Marduk to "leave" his cult statue (a core of rare wood, covered with sheets of stamped precious metal), so that, Erra suggested, it might be conveniently "cleaned" and restored to all its former brilliance, tarnished over time. When, in the end, Marduk allowed himself to be convinced, "he arose from his dwelling,"[27] both his statue and the sanctuary that sheltered it, thus opening the way for the misdeeds of the violent Erra, whom his presence would have deterred. Mysteriously, but true, in fact, in the eyes of the faithful, the god's image "enclosed" his person and ensured his "true presence." It was in the name of the same "realism" that, for example, the gods were moved around, in the form of their images, transported by cart or by boat, *intra muros* or beyond, to visit other divinities or even, lying side by side in their closed "bedroom," to spend their honeymoon night together, as in the *hieros gamos* of the first millennium. In the case of military defeat, the gods' images—as well as the kings'— were deported abroad by the conquerors.

Without ever having distinctly seen them, people were thus convinced that the gods, like humans, had real bodies, based on an improved model of our own. Their organs and members are mentioned everywhere: their heads, their eyes, their ears, their mouths, their hands, their feet, and so on. A "theological commentary" from the beginning of the first millennium, in some fifty entries, even details the majestic physical appearance of Marduk in all his bodily components, external and internal, including all bodily fluids, the hair, the lower jaw, the spinal column, the hair of his chest, the blood, tears, earwax, sperm, and so on, to compare them all, following a logic about which we no longer have any idea, to precious elements in nature or in culture:

> 1   His top-knot is tamarisk;
>   His whiskers are a frond;
>   His ankle bones are an apple.
>   His penis is a snake.
>   . . . .
> 11 His heart is a kettle-drum;
>   His skull is silver;
>   His sperm is gold.[28]

The Gods' Behavior

It logically follows that the gods' behavior must also have been a reflection of human behavior. The mythology is greatly edifying in this regard; and even the cult, as we will see below, was based on the gods' needs, which were similar to our own: eating and drinking, clothing and ornamentation, the desire for an opulent and carefree life in big and luxurious "houses" amid celebrations.

In *Atraḫasîs*,[29] Enlil, the king of the gods, dislikes humans because the rising din of their working multitudes prevents him from sleeping. And the gods, like humans, sometimes drank too much beer and then fell into euphoric inebriation, which led them to emphatic and unfortunate generosity. This is what happened to Enki in *Inanna and Enki: The Transfer of the Arts of Civilization from Eridu to Erech*,[30] in which the god, after having drunk a bit, with great careless beneficence abandons to Inanna the complete treasure of the "powers" and secrets that governed civilized life and, once he comes back to himself, attempts in vain to get them back.

The gods were sometimes too human and demonstrated not only our weaknesses but also our sins. *Atraḫasîs* is hardly sympathetic to the king of the gods, Enlil. Not only does it present him as green with fright and completely disconcerted at the news of the strike of the divine workers,[31] but when, in order to sleep, he tries to stop the din of humans,[32] he is completely unreasonable, since instead of simply reducing their numbers, the harsh decision he makes risks eliminating them completely. This is in fact what he ultimately decides upon in ordering the Flood.[33] He thus forgets, or disregards in his exigent impatience, that humans had been created precisely to provide indispensable services to the gods. Even if this is some bitterly lucid vision of monarchical power, indeed perhaps based on specific incidents, the fact that the authors were able to paint such an unflattering portrait of the lord of the gods and of the world says a lot about the anthropomorphism of the faithful!

One of the best examples of this sometimes faulty "humanity" attributed to the representatives of the divine world is provided by the figure of Ištar, who is often modeled after those women who are "enamored of their bodies" and completely dedicated to "free love,"[34] of which she was the patron, and the prerogatives of which she exercised joyfully. One must see her at the beginning of tablet VI of the *Epic of Gilgameš*,[35] seducing Gilgameš and trying shamelessly to attract him into her bed, whereas Gilgameš, forewarned and wary, harshly presents her with her fickleness and betrayals. In a Babylonian hymn from the beginning of the second millennium we learn in a verse in praise of the goddess: "Sixty then sixty satisfy themselves in turn upon her nakedness. Young men have tired, Ishtar will not tire."[36]

Another trait that can also be considered "too human" appears in an old myth written in Sumerian: *Enlil and Ninlil*.[37] Enlil is presented here as driven by a crazy desire to "penetrate" a young and pretty goddess, who is still a virgin and whom he "violates" and makes pregnant, causing a great scandal among the other gods. His subjects immediately exile him as punishment—which does not prevent him from repeating the deed on two occasions with the same goddess, who, moreover, has evidently acquired a taste for him and asks for more!

It is very likely that over time and with the evolution in politics (and even ethics), the memory of the first petty kings, who were still rough, wild, and without grandeur, faded, and a similar image of the gods, one that could well have been that of the ancient Sumerians, disappeared along with it. Similarly, once a human model of a much more grandiose form of royalty was available on which the Semites could model their divinities, these "all-too-human" tableaux, preserved in the mythological tradition, gradually gave way to a truly sovereign and majestic idea of the gods, envisioned as well above the human masses and their weaknesses. Human behavior nevertheless remained the only model for that of the gods.

Everything relating to the gods' "family life" and their family relationships also followed the same logic. The gods were all "brothers," because, as descendants of the same distant ancestors, they all shared the same "nature," the same specific traits. But they were also believed to have had the same strong individual ties among themselves that we have as husbands and wives, as parents and children, as brothers and sisters, over at least three generations, as we can clearly see in the *Epic of Creation:*[38] Anu fathers Éa, and Éa fathers Marduk. These familial relationships, which sometimes appear entangled to us, were one of the keys to the gods' hierarchy and classification.

It was not easy to resolve the problem of the gods' placement within this perspective of the "human model." Although they were never imagined to dwell in the hearts of humans, we have seen that they resided *in* their statues and therefore *in* the sanctuaries where the statues were placed. If the dreamer and prophetess in the letter to the king of Mari cited below cried for a long time after her first dream, it was because she thought she saw in it the temple emptied of its divine inhabitants; and it is even possible that in her second dream she believed she heard the principal one among them desperately calling, "Come back, Dagan!"

But, looking at another ancient and traditional belief, the gods were also, in one way or another, all linked to the portion of the physical universe that they were believed to cause to function. The Moon *was not* the god Sîn, nor was the Sun the god Šamaš, but each of those divinities indeed had to have been in some way in contact with the Moon or the Sun to govern it, since this was his primary raison d'être. It was never, and for a very good reason, specified how these matters were perceived and understood. Nor was the rationale behind the placement of the gods in the universe specified. The *Epic of Creation,* in its global, balanced, and systematized portrayal, places half of the gods (literally, "three hundred," half of six hundred, the great round number in the decimo-sexagesimal system in use at the time) "On High," in the heights of Heaven, and as many "Below," in the antithetical depths of the Earth.[39] And the same epic portrays the gods assembling in the major intermediary sanctuary of Babylon, some "climbing" up from Below, others "descending" from On High.[40]

These are only mythological creations, the products of pure imagination and far from any preoccupation with coherence and logic,
especially since these diverse traditions were born independently of
each other, and no one ever sought to connect them or constitute
them into a single, clear system. The only certainty shared by all was
that all those gods existed, that they came and went, that they acted
and governed things, all in the manner of those superior humans,
the kings.

Loftier Images

We do, however, have a few lists in which names of stars or constellations (which we cannot always identify) are noted in one column, opposite a column with names of divinities, following the old
schema of equivalence, as if they were being set forth as strict equivalents. For example:

> The star of the Plow / (is) the god Aššur
> The star of the Wolf / (is) the god Anu
> The star of the King / (is) . . . Marduk
> The Great Twins / (are) . . . Sîn and Nergal. . . .[41]

These juxtapositions, their listing and interpretation, raise difficult questions with which it would be rash and pointless to deal at
present. In any case, it is not a matter here of listing the various divinities and the associated stars over which they ruled. One can at
least surmise that starting in a certain period—let us say between
the second and the first millennium—for reasons that seem obscure
to us, each god was given a star or a constellation as his symbol and
image. This would seem to be confirmed by the famous passage from
the *Epic of Creation* in which Marduk, creating and arranging the
world, and first of all Heaven, after having installed its divine occupants, had

> made the position(s) for the great gods,
> He established (in) constellations the stars, their likenesses.[42]

Might we not say that the sages of that land, tireless observers of
the celestial population, before they had, in Hellenistic times, transformed their empirical astrology into scholarly astronomy, had
imagined that the starry sky, with its stars and its "figures," which
had been noticed, identified, and named for a long time, unchange-

able in their profile and invariable in their eternal movement, formed a sort of perfect supracosmos, the model and impeccable pattern for our unstable and fluctuating world—something, if we wish, like the "idea," in the Platonic sense, of that changing and perishable universe. If they wanted to emphasize divine "transcendence," how could they not have taken as the most appropriate images of the sovereign gods that luminous population of the sky, brilliant and impassive? The stars, while participating somewhat through "contagion" in divine nature, were not in themselves gods, but they were in the realm of the gods and were also their image, more pure, more "religious," and more striking than that derived from the appearance and behavior of humans. The gods, if you will, constituted a sort of ontological "third order" above the stellar, as the stellar was above the terrestrial.

Another area of the imaginary that has similarly been attached to the mythology of the divine is revealed in a unique and famous document. It is the final piece of a rather lengthy and badly preserved work in which several exegetic texts were assembled in the manner unique to those old scholars, who, from the analysis of *names* easily derived theories on the composition and the value of the *things* named. A final paragraph of this work, isolated and appearing to take into account the successive forms assumed by Sîn, the Moon, from the slender crescent to the full moon, ends, we do not really know why, as if in an appendix, with a sort of table spread out over three columns. On the left a divinity is defined, on the right his personal name is inscribed, and in the middle a number is noted. Thus:

... first of the gods and their father	60	Anu
... king of the universe	50	Enlil
... king of Apsû, lord of the Abyss	40	Éa

and so forth: a dozen great divinities in all. This is the well-known hierarchy of the principal figures of the pantheon; but here, it is in a certain way evaluated numerically: the number 60 is associated with Anu; 50 with Enlil; 40 with Éa; 30 with Sîn; 20 with Šamaš; 15 with Ištar; 6 with Adad.[43] Such a numerical correspondence supposes recondite speculations, of which we no longer have the slightest trace, and which for the most part escape us. It appears at least "normal" that 60, the supreme round number (according to the local decimo-sexagesimal system), was attributed to the supreme chief of the divine dynasty; and that 30 was attributed to Sîn, the moon god (this number was even used as his ideogram), and from that, "Master of the Month," as he was commonly called, a month that, in the lunar calendar (the only one known in the land), regularly included thirty days.

It is of little importance if we are unable to go any farther and determine how each deity ended up with a certain number, or if the dialectic that presided over such a distribution escapes us almost entirely. We can at least accept the idea that Babylonian theologians, in any case beginning in the second millennium, were attempting to suggest the varying ontological superiority of the gods among themselves, in other words, the strength of their specific "divine natures," by figuratively assigning them the most immaterial and abstract concepts, the least "tangible" they had available—numbers— as if they knew that to speak righteously of the gods it was necessary, insofar as was possible, to go beyond the material and carnal reality of humans. This was a lofty, probably isolated vision that nevertheless did not alter the fundamental anthropomorphism of the religious system.

There is no document that clearly states this theory. Moreover, what doctrine has ever been found clearly and formally expressed here? It is even quite plausible that our insistence on isolated propositions somewhat deadens, in fact deforms, the thought of those people, who had neither our need for logic nor our demands for clarity. As we shall later see, the Mesopotamian religion of the Hellenistic Period would perhaps favor such a line of thought, inasmuch as the development of the Mesopotamians' religious vision is not easy to understand if one does not sense, alongside what was preserved unchanged over many long centuries, an internal, practically esoteric, movement by closed circles of scholars toward a certain "purification," an authentic deepening of the representation of the divine. A few traits seem to indicate this; the symbolism, above all astral and numerical, is one such trait. It would not seem admissible, in its existential context, if we did not conceive of this as an attempt to stress both the transcendence and the mystery of the supernatural world, which we will not fail to see as the expression of a meritorious religious depth, at least among certain great minds.

The Origin of the Gods

Where did the gods come from and how did they appear? Where and how did they *mythologically* appear? Like all fundamental questions—and this one necessarily was fundamental, once the gods' existence had been established—it was formulated very early on in the land, no doubt well before writing. The oldest traces of an answer appear among the venerable literary collections discovered at Fâra and Tell Abû Şalābīkh dating from around the twenty-sixth century. Everything in them is basically Sumerian, although already taken and adapted by the Akkadians, as explained above.

Extreme anthropomorphism both necessitated the asking of such a question and suggested the answer to it. On the one hand, it was unthinkable to resort to any kind of absolute by postulating a completely unimaginable "void" or "eternity" (which would have, perhaps, indeed helped to clarify the issue), and on the other, the human model of successive generations provided the answer. That model was therefore very quickly adopted and developed, preferably following a specific presentation: not, as was the case with myths in the strict sense, in the form of a *tale* of a more or less long adventure but, once again giving in to that old passion for lists, by the simple *listing* of ancestors classified in the order of their appearance (which dispensed with a detailed account—in other words, with a formally developed myth), on the model of the lists of the An/Anum type, in which the tale was only implicit. Since the "contemporary" gods had children, it sufficed to go back before their fathers and mothers, going up the chain, through parental and ancestral stages, into an increasingly distant past, following a sequence appropriate to the idea of an immeasurable duration, which the Mesopotamians felt forced to postulate in the presence of such supernatural beings who were immortal and mysterious. But at what point in the past should they stop? For it was indeed necessary to stop at some point!

Several of these lists, more or less detailed, were in use, ending with the "birth" of the principal gods, who were "relatives" of the others, and whose imposing presence made them all the more curious: Enlil, on the one hand, the Lord of the Universe; and Anu, his father, the founder of the divine "ruling" dynasty. Contrary to what we might expect, the listings were not entirely similar, however, except on one or two points. This demonstrates that the authors had reflected and mythologized the issue from diverse angles, "resolving" it according to different perspectives. The systematic and "constructed" nature of such lists is immediately apparent in the number of their elements. They were in multiples of seven: twenty-one for Anu and his ancestors, and twice that for Enlil and his family, who thus go back up the ladder, couple before couple, toward an increasingly distant past, fabulous and ungraspable. Here, for example, is a listing of those who came before Anu, as found in the famous An/Anum list (I: 4–24) (it proceeds from the most recent to the most ancient):

^{d}(u.ra.áš) + ^{d}Nin.uraš	Lord and Lady Earth;
An.šár.gal + ^{d}Ki.šár.gal	universal Heaven and Earth;
An.šár + ^{d}Ki.šár	global Heaven and Earth;
^{d}En.šár + ^{d}Nin.šár	Lord and Lady of the Universe;
^{d}Du.rí + ^{d}Da.rí	Lord and Lady Lasting;
^{d}Làḫ.ma + ^{d}La.ḫa.ma	Lord and Lady Rough-Hewn;
^{d}É.kur + ^{d}Gá.ra	Lord Ekur and Lady Gara;
^{d}A.la.la + ^{d}Be.li.li	Lord Alala and Lady Belili;
$^{d''}$(= A.la.la)ALAM +	Lord Alala-alam (?) and Lady
$^{d''}$(= Be.li.li)ALAM	Belili-alam (?);
^{d}En.uru.ul.la + ^{d}Nin.uru.ul.la	Lord and Lady of the Ancient City;
21 en ama a.a An-na-ke$_4$-ne	(So, in all) 21 Lords, relatives and ancestors of Anu.[44]

To fill in all the divisions or stages of such an implicitly mythological framework they had to call upon various divinities, most of whom, imagined for the circumstances, are not otherwise known to us, and who were paired, along with titles of honor and power, as husband and wife, to give them the status of parents and progenitors of the following couple. Alala and Belili, for example, were believed to be very ancient supernatural beings, about whom we know almost nothing and are unable to translate the enigmatic *alam* attached to their names. Laḫma and Laḫama (perhaps Semitic names) and Duri and Dari are the only non-Sumerian words in the listing. They commonly designated divinities, also very ancient, still "imperfect," rough-hewn, as if true anthropomorphism was only introduced over time within these divine generations, the first couples escaping it, although we are not specifically told, and for good reason, what it replaced. Other Sumerian names leave us completely perplexed, such as Ékur (an opaque homophone of the classic designation of the great temple of Enlil at Nippur) and the incomprehensible Gar(a). Others undoubtedly refer to the universe itself (at that time concentrated in divine couples, since nothing had yet appeared

outside the divinities mentioned), in its various successive and progressive imagined states. The supernatural couples in question were
simultaneously considered divine personalities and the successive
stages of a slowly forming cosmos, which began with the appearance
of a "city," or rather an archaic agglomeration, the mysterious pre-
figuration of all that the universe would later be, and of which no
details have ever been discovered. We are not even told whether the
couples named remained isolated, "alone in the world," or whether,
after giving birth to other divinities, they remained in contact
with them.

The increase in the number of these names, the exact significance
of which is hidden from us, seems moreover to have served, first, to
prolong that fantastic and dark past: one of its stages in some way
calls upon the "pure Duration" (Duri-Dari, certainly a Semitic term;
the Akkadians had therefore added their speculations to those of the
Sumerians in this regard), as if this moment of Anu's ancestry had
no other imaginable purpose than to "continue" and to "last" for an
indeterminate time.

The details of events were far from clear (and even less so for us!).
It is as if, in responding to the fundamental question of the theogony (the origin of the gods, the first to exist), they could only plunge
that great unknown into deeper and deeper darkness, to a starting
place so remote and unimaginable that it could scarcely be discerned, distance and obscurity taking the place of a "beginning."
Each one of these stages marked an advancement in the number
and the condition of the gods who represented them, were responsible for them, or had appeared there, following a progression governed by the notion of the progress and maturation of the cosmos,
which the gods still alone represented, well before the creation of
the world itself. Only at the end (in other words, at the beginning
of the list—reversed!—as mentioned above), did one arrive at the final fruit of that long line: Anu, the father of the most notable "contemporary" god and the founder of the divine dynasty "in power."

A few fragments, apparently to complete these lists, appear to suggest the existence at the very beginning of things, *before* the successive couples, of an isolated divine entity, unique and huge, not
paired up, which, by itself, would have given birth to the first couple
and inaugurated in that way the formidable later evolution set out
in the lists. Simultaneously a supernatural figure, place, and matter, it was believed to be of a watery nature, marine. Perhaps the

ancients were thinking of the huge, flat, uniform, but living fertility of the sea, if the notion was not borrowed from another, more
frankly "maritime" culture. The entity was called "Nammu, the Lady
of the Gods, the Mother who gave birth to the Universe" (*An/Anum*,
I:27–28). She is placed beyond the ancestors of Anu, as if it were
a matter of an individual theogony, even earlier than the oldest
divinities.

This genetic mythology appears to have been taken up again at
the end of the second millennium, both shortened, *told,* as a result,
like a myth and no longer schematized in a list, and evidently, in
this way reworked and clarified by the authors of the famous *Epic of
Creation*.[45] In the beginning, they explain, when Heaven and Earth
did not yet exist, in other words, in the absence of all things in the
universe, including the gods, there existed, not one, but two gigantic divine liquid masses: the salty water of the sea and the freshwater
(they were believed unchangeable and dissimilar). We are still dealing with a "couple": the first member, set forth as the most important, the Mother, was "Sea," or Tiamat (a Semitic name), the distant
doublet of Nammu; playing the masculine role, here understood as
secondary, was Apsû, "freshwater." The two were intertwined, as if in
a formidable and motionless coupling, thus giving birth to the first
divinities, who were considered to be still in formation, incomplete
and more or less "monstrous": specifically the Laḫma and the Laḫama of the list above. It was only after some time that the true gods,
perfected and in their definitive and irreproachable divine state,
emerged from Tiamat and Apsû: Anšar (in Sumerian "universal/total
Heaven") and Kišar ("universal/total Earth")—in other words, "all
there is of Heaven" and "all there is of Earth" (compare An.šár.gal
and Ki.šár.gal above). Finally, the great god Anu was born of that
couple, and Anu engendered Éa, who, with his wife Damgalnunna
("Great Wife of the Prince," in Sumerian), brought Marduk into the
world.[46]

This story of the birth of the gods based on the model of human
generations, following a general schema analogous to that of the lists
but narrated, shortened, and more or less modified and adapted, as
was the rule in the mythological tradition, was reused in other tales,
on a less grandiose scale. We have thus discovered, in a later copy
(late first millennium), fragments of a version (called the *Theogony
of Dunnu*) of the birth and succession of the gods associated with
the Mesopotamian city of Dunnu (unknown to us), where it was evi-

dently conceived and written down.[47] The gods who succeed each other in it, from parents to children, in at least six generations, are obviously the principal members of the pantheon of the city, whose genesis is thus explained; and they live side by side with the cosmic divinities (Sea, Earth, River, etc.), whose presence shows that the local mythographers also maintained a concern with connecting cosmogony to theogony. The succession of these figures, ruling over Dunnu, is almost regularly accomplished through violence: assassinations and incest, of which historical memories must not have been lacking, even if they evoked an ancient, brutal, and "savage" state of existence. Two-thirds of the text is missing, and its importance and complete significance escape us since we know very little about the actors and the unfolding of the story. But it at least provides us with another variation on the theme of the origin of the gods, occurring through the same carnal copulation as that of humans. This theme occurs elsewhere, as in the myth of Enlil and Ninlil, discussed above: Enlil's three couplings were fruitful, and each time a god was born of them, a well-known god whose arrival in the world was thus explained.

Other models, also taken from experience, were used occasionally to answer the same question of why and how the gods appeared. One myth *(Enki/Éa's Part in the Creation of the Universe)* tells how Éa, wishing to fill in the empty frame of the world with everything that might provide for the needs of the gods—sacred buildings, sacred furniture, ornaments, and food—*created* everything by modeling mounds of sacred clay taken from his own dwelling, the subterranean surface of freshwater, Apsû.[48] He *created* not only the raw materials for his plans but first the minor gods "specialized" in the techniques required for such work. The same "creation" of divinities out of modeling clay is found again elsewhere, and it always concerns—this must be stressed—divine figures of the second rank. The idea of their being fashioned (out of clay or other materials, wood, stone, metal) might possibly have been suggested by the conviction that the "real presence" of the god resided in his image.

Undoubtedly inspired by observing plants, which appeared and grew as if by themselves, without the slightest intervention from without, a few authors of myths attributed to the gods the ability to fashion their own appearance: "O Self-Created Fruit!" they said, while invoking Sîn,[49] whose realm and image, the Moon, was born and grew out of itself. The same ability was recognized in Aššur and

Marduk. But the nature of such a feat, which was not easy to accomplish, restricted its use.

Always similar to humans, the gods normally came into the world as humans did, the issue of their parents, or were sometimes produced, in the form of statues and images, by artisans.

The Mythology of the World

Those gods, imagined and arranged in order to clarify the secrets of our universe, a parcel of which each of them ruled over and supervised, how were they and their activities used to make sense of the world's existence and functioning, in a culture that did not believe, as we do, that they possessed almost the last word on things (i.e., via "monotheism" or "science")?

Cosmology

There could not be the slightest doubt that the universe was the work of the gods, since the gods had in fact been imagined with the primary goal of providing an explanation for this cosmos, which was too huge, too complicated, and apparently too well organized for anyone ever to have dreamed for a single moment that it might have been the work of a member of our species or—even less likely—the result of a monstrous series of cumulative and fortuitous chance occurrences (see fig. 1). But before trying to understand that *cosmogony*, we should first ask how, in that time so very long ago, the world as a whole was perceived. Mythological procedure required that one started from the object to be explained in order to construct "calculated imaginations" around it to explain it; *cosmogony* was governed by *cosmology*.

To our knowledge, ancient Mesopotamian scholars never produced, at least not in a preserved written form, a coherent explanation of their "system" of the universe. The allusions that have reached us, from various times, places, and milieux (a circumstance that is already enough in itself to make any conclusions we might draw uncertain), are never very clear-cut, rational, or very systematic: the cosmology itself was mythological. The world around the Mesopotamians was much too huge and secret not to have evoked the most varied visions and reflections from the beginning of time. Therefore, we have only a modest number of snapshot images, taken

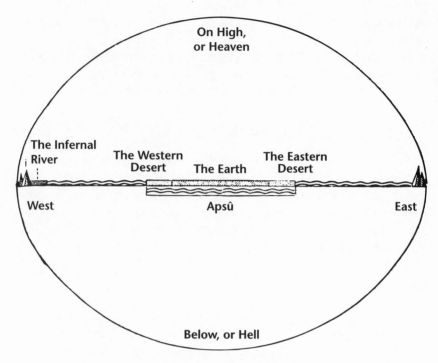

Mesopotamian Cosmography

The ancient Mesopotamians had only an imaginary and mythological representation of the universe as a whole, one difficult for us to understand and seemingly full of inconsistencies and contradictions. They saw it as a huge hollow spheroid whose upper, luminous part formed "On High," or "Heaven," and whose lower, symmetrical, and obscure part formed "Below," or "Hell." It was divided in the center by a sort of central island: "Earth," reflected below by Apsû, a layer of freshwater. Earth and Apsû were surrounded by the salt water of the sea. At the two eastern and western extremities of this system they imagined tall mountains to support the celestial vault, and two depressions that allowed free passage from the space Below to the space On High, and vice versa. The sun emerged from the depression in the east in the morning, for its daily crossing toward Heaven, and sunk into the western depression in the evening, for a reverse nocturnal journey, which brought it back at daybreak to its original point of rising. The western depression adjoined a watery space called the Infernal River.

from various angles, which were always more or less murky or have been made indistinct through age. By putting them all together we can at least create a vague impression of Mesopotamian cosmology: of the world as those ancient thinking minds contemplated, imagined, and above all understood it.

The product of innumerable observations and reflections since the dawn of time, that cosmology was part of the cultural heritage, which was as old as the religion itself; it is impossible to reveal its sources and earlier stages. The cosmology before history might even have existed beyond the borders of Mesopotamia; we do not know very well the role Mesopotamia played: perhaps creating it and disseminating it in all directions, or perhaps receiving it from elsewhere, entirely or in part, and later enriching and adapting it. The fact is that a number of echoes and lineages, even complements, of the cosmology are found in the ancient Middle East, particularly in the Bible.

A few rare texts, each with its own point of view, appear to provide a global image of the world. From around 1200 at the latest, the *Epic of Creation* reveals how Marduk, after having felled Tiamat, the primitive universal mother, built the framework of the universe out of her remains:

> He split her in two, like a fish for drying,
> Half of her he set up and made as a cover, heaven.
> . . . .
> Spreading [half of] her as a cover, he established the earth.
> [After] he had completed his task inside Tiamat,
> [He spre]ad his net, let all (within) escape,
> He formed (?) the . . . [ ] of heaven and netherworld,
> Tightening their bond [ ]. . . .[50]

Perhaps a composite, the entire passage, embellished with a few badly placed gaps, is not extremely clear. In it we can at least discern that the world appeared, when all was said and done, as a gigantic hollow spheroid, made out of Tiamat's own "flesh," in two halves, separated in the middle, and rejoined at the extremities: head and tail. And since their matter was "the sea water" from the body of the primordial mother goddess, that mass, emptied from within, floated in a certain sense in an abyss of infinite water, a cosmic ocean.

The two halves of such a system were designated by two opposing terms, which, along with the antithetical couple, constantly recur in texts: On High, or Heaven (An/*šamû*), and Below, the Earth, with its infernal substructure (Ki/*irṣitu;* we sometimes say "Hell," for economy's sake).

Another difficult document, filled with recondite scholarly and theological commentary, provides a sort of complement to the "doctrine" presented in the *Epic of Creation,* since, focusing on the same Marduk, creator of the world, it notes how that god had arranged the inside of the universal spheroid.[51] It was set up over six levels in all: three for Heaven and as many for Hell. At the very top, there was an "upper Heaven," where Anu reigned; an "intermediary" one, the seat of Marduk, surrounded by the "celestial gods," the Igigi; and an "inferior Heaven," inhabited by the stars and constellations, the images and reflections of the gods. Then, still descending, came an "upper Earth," where humans, whom the text qualifies as "evanescent," to emphasize their natural mortality, "were settled"; the level below, the "intermediate Earth," was the Apsû, the universal freshwater and the residence of Éa; and the sixth, at the very bottom, was the "lower Earth," headquarters of the Anunnaki, the infernal gods, and, according to common belief, the gathering place of human "ghosts" after death.

Earth itself, the domain of humans, superimposed on the Apsû and on "Hell," is not described anywhere as a whole; but if we gather together the few scattered allusions that we have to its mythological geography, a geography quite different from our own and into which it is quite difficult for us to enter on the same level, the best portrait we can create to suggest the idea the Mesopotamians had of it is the following.

On the "fourth level" of the cosmos, below the "inferior Heaven," the diametral plane of the "sphere" was entirely occupied by the huge expanse of the sea, let us say "the earthly sea," although its relationship with either the cosmic ocean (the Abyss, in which floated the enormous hollow sphere of the universe) or the universal freshwater (Apsû) is not very clear. On the external, circular edge of that sea, at the extremities of the world, they perhaps imagined an entire interminable chain of mountains to support the firmament, like the "Columns of Heaven" mentioned in the Book of Job (26:11). Right in the middle of that vast sea was the Earth of humans, our Earth. It resembled an island with varied landscapes but was flat. And the center of Earth, the most noble and most important portion of it, was naturally Mesopotamia.

We have recovered at least one description of this "geography" from around 700 in the form of a map and its commentary.[52] In the middle of the map we see two vast circles that represent "the sea" (literally, in the text, "bitter water," acrid and salty: *marratu*). Inside this Earth-surrounding sea there appears, with parallelepipeds for regions and circles for towns, the entire expanse of Mesopotamia, in all its essential parts, from the Mountain of the North and Armenia to the southern swamps, along the Persian Gulf. And right in the middle of everything, among the few represented localities (we do not know what determined the choice of which localities to put on the map), was Babylon, the center of the world. Beyond the double "marine circle," as if to emphasize that to reach those lands it was necessary to cross the sea or vast expanses of distant lands, five triangles (we can assume there were originally eight, before the tablet was damaged) represent mysterious lands, obviously very much on the fringes and more hinted at than explored. Too little has remained of the text, which explained the origin, the extent, the distance between, or the content of those lands, to provide a satisfying portrait of them. Perhaps one of those lands, in the Far East, evoked the very distant extremity of the world where Gilgameš had encountered the immortal hero of the Flood, far from the rest of humanity.[53] And perhaps another of them adjoined the Far West, where the mysterious "Infernal River" that one had to cross to reach the realm of the dead, in Hell, was located.

Cosmogony

Cosmogony was undoubtedly one of the great mysteries that from well before history most preoccupied at least the religious thinkers in the land, if we judge from the exceptional number of their thoughts on the subject, written down and preserved—not to mention the much more swollen torrent of thoughts that only flowed by word of mouth, and which the current of time has carried away forever.

Concerning the origin of the gods it has been seen that *theogony* was only the first act of *cosmogony*. In other words, the first state of things—let us say, of the universe—was represented (since there was still nothing but the gods) by divinities: distant, mysterious, enormous, unidentifiable, and whose images will never be known. They succeeded each other in consecutive generations, in the manner of human beings, until the birth of the founder of the ruling dynasty, An, from whom other familiar divinities would emerge, and cosmogony itself, the "creation" of *our* world, would begin. That cosmogony was constructed and told a number of times, in many variations.

These cosmogonic tales (still sometimes introduced through theogonic episodes) are surprising first in the variety of the solutions they propose to deal with human perplexity concerning the origin of the cosmos. Protagonists and modi operandi often differed. The demiurges, it went without saying, were always very lofty divine figures but not necessarily the same in each tale, or perhaps they went about their business differently. Here, again, we see the degree to which mythology is not necessarily logical and coherent. Seeking to resolve the same problems in the course of their tales, the authors of the various myths, cosmogonic or otherwise, each in his own time, his own milieu, at his own point of cultural and religious evolution, with his own preoccupations and imagination, aimed primarily to provide a plausible response to the question, in his search for a single *likely* explanation—that could only be multiform and variable— without concerning himself with other answers, or with how they harmonized with his own.

Apart from certain cases, such as the *Epic of Creation*, the product of a known, pretty much datable historical situation—the "elevation" of Marduk around the end of the second millennium—it is almost impossible to pinpoint accurately the dates of those multiform tales, any more than we can so many other literary pieces. If we manage, most often without great difficulty or audacity, to date the *copies* that have reached us, how can we know, for lack of other information, just how far back their *originals* go, themselves rooted in a long and ungraspable oral tradition? The fact that Mesopotamians preferred accumulation over substitution is part of the problem. Rather than attempting here to arrange the texts in an illusive chronological order, it is preferable to stress their variety and rich imagery by presenting them as representatives of their explanatory systems: the imaginary middle term they each proposed to cast light on the origin of things. A certain number of these myths, in some sense carrying on the tradition of the genealogical lists of the gods, start with the great binomial Heaven/Earth (An/Ki) and culminate with the birth of An. It remained to fill in that general framework of the world, to explain where all that we see around us originally came from.

To my knowledge, there is no Mesopotamian cosmogonic myth that deals with the origin of the whole cosmos, as is found in the biblical Book of Genesis. Most of the tales are content to fill in only pieces of the puzzle.

Furthermore, unlike the theogonic lists, realities normally appear in them, not as the issue of a couple of "parents," but as the product of a deliberate operation, most often not carnal, that is attributed to one of the highest and most powerful gods (never a goddess, whose role was not to create but to give birth), either isolated or associated with others: An, the ruler of Heaven; more rarely Enlil; most often Enki/Éa, the "producer and shaper" par excellence (Nudimmud); and finally, Marduk.

Their mode of intervention, their "creative act," if you will, is never analyzed or described as it unfolds. The verbs used to refer to it, very often recurrent, are all of a stock meaning, vague and ambiguous: taken from the vocabulary of industry and of the activity of people, they do not refer to a single and precise operation, but they above all note the result of it: "to make something appear" *(šupû)*; "to draw" a figure *(eṣēru)*; "to establish on its foundations" *(šuršudu)* or "to erect" *(ramû)* a building; "to give shape" to a construction *(bašāmu)*; "to establish it solidly" *(kunnu)*; "to manufacture" or "to make" something *(epêšu)*. The most frequent verb, just as imprecise, is *banû,* which could be interpreted as the "manufacturing" of an object, the "building" of a structure, even the "procreation" of a child, and above all—the context made it specific—as the "modeling" of a statue or an object out of clay, or as its "manufacture" from a certain material. All of which already promises a great variety of cosmogonic myths! The only constant element that was assured in every myth, whatever its expression might be, was the relationship of causality between the demiurge and his work. The Mesopotamians did not want to be, and, it must be said, they could scarcely have been, more specific; but they held fast to what was essential: the world was the work of some supernatural being.

Here is a selection of these creation myths: some are in Sumerian and are possibly older; others are in Akkadian. Most often they were not composed in isolation as independent "explanations" but were included in other works: notably collections of exorcisms, to justify a ritual; of prayers, to reinforce a request; or of what we call "tensons," types of poetic contests between two personalized entities written with an economy of words, whose purpose was, in the course of the "confrontation," to establish their value and superiority through (tacit) reference to their prototypes at the time of their creation.

Around the beginning of the second millennium (I know nothing for certain of what came earlier), the exordium of a tale in Sumerian concerning Gilgameš presents the first formation of the world, be-

ginning with the original spheroid, Heaven/Earth, which was still
blended together and made up one mass, as a gigantic *wrenching
apart,* an initial *separation,* inaugurating the ordering of that enormous primitive chaos:

> 1   In those days, those ancient days,
>   In those nights, those ancient nights,
>   In those years, those ancient years
>   . . . .
>
> 8   After On-High had been moved away from Below,
>   After Below had been separated from On-High
>   . . . .
>
> 11   After An had carried off On-High,
>   After Enlil had carried off Below.[54]

This recalls, from somewhat afar, the first verses of *Atraḫasîs* (from
around 1700, in Akkadian), in which the three greatest gods "draw
lots" for their respective domains, which are at first all blended together, as if it were a matter of a formidable compact mass to be divided up.[55]

The theme of *procreation* is also employed. At the beginning of the
Sumerian tenson *Tree against Reed* (turn of the third millennium),
Heaven/An and Earth/Ki, already separated, are a married couple,
and the former, impregnating the other with the spermatic liquid of
the rain, impregnates her with vegetation, beginning with the trees
and the reeds,[56] just as the ground becomes covered with vegetation after a rain. Another tenson, in the same language and from the
same time, portrays a god, in this case Enlil, who "inserts his penis
into the mountainous region, thus impregnating it with Summer
and Winter, the fortune of the land,"[57] the two essential local sea-
sons. The framework and condition for all agricultural and stock-
raising activity are personalized here.

And here is another creation scenario which comes very close to
resembling a *generation.* Written in Akkadian and dating fairly early
in the second millennium, it involves oral exorcism rituals meant to
cure toothache. It prescribes the extraction of the dental nerve that
is hidden in the gums, under the tooth, and which was considered
to be a "worm." One first explained to the "worm" that it deserved
its extraction, because its prototype, just barely created, refusing to
follow the advice of Éa, who wanted it to live in a "fruit to suck,"
had unfortunately preferred a jaw. Here is how the worm's creation
is recounted:

After Anu had created heaven,
Heaven had created earth,
Earth had created rivers,
Rivers had created canals,
Canals had created marsh,
Marsh had created worm—[58]

This was a "cascading" creation, somewhat along the lines of genealogical lists. The verb *banû* is used everywhere, and therefore the
exact "how" of the operation is not specified. But it took place in
steps. And it is clear that although the narrator went straight to the
only creature that interested him—the worm—he meant to imply
a similar process for all others.

The modeling of clay is the key process in another tale in Akkadian, dating perhaps from the middle of the second millennium,
and which was recited before a ceremony intended for the renewal,
or re-renewal, of a sanctuary. Here, again, everything is centered on
this one-time goal—the restoration of the sacred edifice—and the
tale refers only to the temple, namely its construction and everything that was required for its building, its decoration, its opulence,
and finally "the service of the gods" that took place in it, in the form
of lavish ceremonies and food offerings.

When Anu had created heaven,
And Éa had created Apsû, his dwelling,
Éa took a wad of clay from that Apsû,
Out of which He created the god Kulla (patron of brick-making),
To preside over the renewal of the Temples![59]

After which, Éa created "cane fields and copses," the sources of other
construction materials; then the gods, keepers, and patrons of the
various wood-, metal-, and stoneworking techniques; then the great
centers of food production, of harvesting and of cultivation; then
the gods who presided over the preparation of food for liturgical
meals; then the king, responsible for putting everything for the service of the gods in the sanctuaries; and finally human beings, the
only true executors and achievers of all that work. We will note an
oddity in passing, one more testimony to the "illogic" of mythology:
here a number of divinities are created from modeled clay, whereas
elsewhere their birth is explained as the result of pure and simple
procreation by parents.

A very short myth, recited only in some exorcism prayers in Akkadian, from the first half of the second millennium, might suggest that Earth had been created *(banû)* by River,[60] which the ancient Mesopotamians considered to be supernatural and divine (the "god of the flow of water," Íd/Nâru, was a well-known object of devotion). It seems that this "holy River," in a land that was rather prone to drought and whose rare river water not only ensured and maintained vegetation and life but divided and gave shape and limits to the region, was a creative force. The tale is not developed or explained well enough for us to consider it otherwise than as a possible cosmogonic suggestion.

Several of the greatest gods, the members of the illustrious triad, were associated, if not with the very act of creation, at least with its planning. The authors obviously borrowed the model from the "industrial manufacturing" of a known implement, which the experts first had to design and manufacture before passing it to the "assembly line." In these cases as well, the tales kept to a certain order of things and left it to others to develop their explanatory merits.

Thus, in the prologue to a tenson between two members of the animal kingdom:

1   The greatest gods, gathered in a Council,
     To create Heaven and Earth,
     To form the Azur, consolidate the Land (?),
     Brought the animals to life:
5   Great Wild beasts, Wild beasts, Wild insects . . .[61]

In the introduction to a great astrological treatise, it was imagined that the same members of the august triad gathered to "firmly establish" *(kunnu)* the world of the stars, not only with the goal of regulating time—days and months—but, through their movements and respective positions, to provide humans with the "presages" that would announce their futures to them, following the basic belief in "deductive" divination.

When Anu, Enlil, and Éa, the greatest of gods,
Had, in their council, drawn the plans of the Heaven and the
    Earth,
And they had assigned the major astral gods
To produce the Day and to assure the regular procession of
    Months,
For the astrological observations of men,
One then saw the Sun rise,
And the Moon shine forever right in the Heaven![62]

The most detailed, impressive, and famous cosmogonic portrait (dating to the final quarter of the second millennium) no doubt had the greatest impact, without for all that being imposed categorically everywhere, which would have been against the very spirit of "prehistoric religions." It is the *Epic of Creation*. We call it that rather improperly, for its primary goal was not at all theo-, cosmo-, or anthropogonic, even if it indeed touched on those three areas. Its ancient users cited it, following their customs, by its *incipit: Enûma eliš,* "When On High. . . ." In some eleven hundred verses evenly divided over seven tablets, it is a long poem, in Akkadian, in a lofty and austere style, more didactic and stiff than truly lyrical, and by chance, we have recovered it almost in its entirety.[63]

According to its authors, it was not primarily a pedagogical work but an *apology:* it meant to *demonstrate* that Marduk, a latecomer in the pantheon (the son of Éa, he was only of the "third generation" of gods) and scarcely known before the first half of the second millennium, indeed deserved to become the primary god, their ruler, and the master of the world and of humans, thereby succeeding Enlil, who until then had occupied that supreme place alone and uncontested. Their demonstration in four arguments is both rigorous and complete.

First of all, Marduk deserved the highest place among the gods because of all of them he was the most perfect, in a certain sense, "the most god." The epic begins with a *theogony,* summed up above, to establish that assertion. Its guiding principle is the conviction that the gods, over time, through an endless evolution as unfolded in the theogonic lists, like all living beings, had developed toward increasingly more accomplished achievement—did not the intelligent author of the *Theodicy* advance that "a first child is born a weakling, / But the second is called an heroic warrior"?[64] The theogony of the poem is therefore constructed on this motif: it begins with gigantic, prodigious, but rough and primitive forces (Sea and Freshwater), which first produce rough-hewn and incomplete divinities (e.g., Laḫma) and only afterward the supernatural beings in full possession of their nature and their advantages: Anu and his son Éa. In the logic of this rising lineage, Marduk, the son of Éa, the last-born of the gods, proves at his birth to be "ten times, fifty times," more of a god than the others: by his very perfection, he is therefore the most worthy of being placed above them.

This is all the more true since they owe him their lives: Tiamat,

the mother of them all, was incited by the "former" gods to annihilate them, and it was Marduk who heroically proposed to defend
them, and who beat and felled the enormous, deadly goddess.

He similarly deserved to be placed at the head of the world because he was the inventor and the author of it, having arranged and
created it, as we saw above, from the formidable remains of Tiamat.
At this point the authors of the poem provide more detail than is
useful for me to repeat here to better specify (without always being clear!) how Marduk, in order to create the cosmos, indeed used
everything from the gigantic cadaver, in addition to its formidable
hide: from its head he made the mountainous mass of the north
of the land (the Caucasus), and from its two eyes, the two rivers,
the Euphrates and the Tigris[65] (in Semitic the same word designates
"eye" and "source"), and "he heaped up high-peaked mo[unt]ains
from (?) her dugs."[66]

Finally, Marduk was to be the ruler of humans because it was he
alone who had the idea for them and who "created" them, as we
will see.

This ample synthesis is obviously tightly connected to an entire
long tradition of myths (oral, above all, but also written): theogonic
lists and tales, whose constructs the authors reworked, reordered,
and, to us, somewhat clarified in a definite direction. With the elevation of Marduk, which the tale must have been instrumental in
establishing, the work was diffused throughout the land, and even
beyond (its philosophical influence on the Greeks could still be detected in the fifth century A.D.[67]). Copies have been recovered, most
often damaged, from the south to the north of the country, and its
text, which we know was occasionally recited in its entirety, at least
in Babylon, during liturgical ceremonies, was remarkably stable.

In the eyes of its authors and users, the epic never represented a
"holy book," a "religious authority," or a true "doctrine" to be imposed as the only authentic and credible one; all such notions are
diametrically opposed to a "popular" religion such as the one in that
land. It is enough to note that after its promulgation, even if the
clergy of Babylon managed to praise Marduk to the skies, that god
never truly replaced once and for all, much less ousted, Enlil. He was
never introduced into a new version of the ancient triad, which was
still found, after as before the epic, in its traditional form: Anu, Enlil,
and Éa. Mesopotamia, I must repeat, preferred accumulation (even
if it was illogical!) to substitution.

Another indication that the cosmogony presented in the epic was at best only one "imagination" among others is that once it was promulgated, new myths, addressing the same questions, were still developed and were apparently no less well received. Let us look here at one of them, which was similarly recited during a ceremony to inaugurate a sanctuary that was either new or had been restored. We only have some forty verses of it, known through two or three independent fragments from the beginning of the first millennium, in other words, *after* the diffusion of the *Epic of Creation*. Here, too, Marduk was the unique demiurge, but his portrait was presented quite differently. To begin with, the authors insisted on the "negative" state of things before creation, on their "not yet being," if I may say so, and the authors wrote only of sacred constructions—sanctuaries and the cities of which those edifices were the center—since they were in fact the subject of the composition:

1   No holy dwelling, no temple in its holy place,
    Had yet been built . . .
    No reed had yet emerged from the ground,
    No tree had appeared,
    No brick had been laid,
    No brick-mold had been made,
    No dwelling had been built,
    No city constructed. . . .[68]

The myth, borrowing a description from the *Epic of Creation*, but from a completely different angle, and even rediscovering, from long ago, the old solitary Nammu, imagined original nonbeing as an immense expanse of marine water:

10   All the (future) territories were (still) but sea!

It was then that Marduk created that indispensable seat of all constructions, cities, and buildings—the Earth, which cosmology represented as a sort of immense flat island in the middle of the marine expanse, an enclosure filled with earth:

17   Marduk then constructed a raft on the water's surface,
     Produced dust and heaped it on the raft.

And since the terrestrial base henceforth enabled buildings to be constructed on it, Marduk, with that goal in mind and in order to serve the gods, created workers for these undertakings—human beings:

19   To leave the gods idle, in this place for happiness,
      Marduk created mankind.

And so that humans would have what they required to provide for the needs of the gods, Marduk then created everything they might need for their work, beginning with sources of food: animals and plants.

From this rapid and varied look at the cosmogonic horizon, there emerges a double axiom to attribute to Mesopotamian thought and religion. First, completely absent from that culture was the idea that something had come from nothingness. There was never any notion of an ex nihilo creation. At the beginning of the world, at the beginning of everything, there was an enormous chaos, something huge and compact, in which everything was included and mixed together, and from which everything had gradually been extracted, made explicit, and put into place, through the intervention of an actor: a demiurge.

Second, that demiurge had always been a god: whatever means it employed—and, of course, quite a few had been imagined!—its action had always and everywhere been decisive. In other words, in the cosmogonic domain, as everywhere, mythology left an open field for fantasy as to the *process* but remained firm and unshakable on the *causes*. Is this not logical and expected, since from the dawn of time, if the existence and the presence of supernatural beings had been postulated it was precisely in order to resolve the unsolvable enigmas posed by the presence and the workings of the world?

The Government of the World

Without ever being clearly stated, everything seems to indicate that the ancient Mesopotamians viewed the functioning of the universe —its never-ending routines as well as its more or less abrupt turning points, the functioning of nature as well as that of the society of human beings and of each individual—as only the continuation of creation. Once the world appeared and began to exist, everything that occurred in it, like its origin itself, was wholly due to the gods' intervention alone, and it was the only determining cause. On this level, the gods' actions—unlike their cosmogonic interventions, which were always clearly specified (we will see a bit later how such an action and universal intervention burst forth in the divinatory system)—were ordinarily more diffuse, especially for the rabble, and only in certain cases was it judged necessary to designate the authors of an intervention by their names. Divine action vis-à-vis the functioning of things in the world and the life of individuals was rather anonymous: it was "the gods" who ruled everything, and usually no one was concerned with specifying and designating which gods were functioning in specific cases. As in the cosmogony, what was important was knowing that everything was governed by them, and that people were aware of that fact. There was no use in going any farther than that universal, and sufficient, conviction.

In this realm the fundamental metaphor was always taken from earthly royal power and the government of the land. In the lofty supernatural hierarchy as well as down below, all authority remained concentrated in the hands of the sovereign but was, in fact, delegated by him, in a sort of "pyramid of powers," to his many representatives, who, from top to bottom, worked only in his name; authority usually appeared only as "coming from On High," without any further specification.

Of course there remained, at least vaguely, the old conviction that each of the gods was fundamentally connected to one of the elements in the world, controlled the functioning of it, and had his domain there: storms, wind, rain, and snow were attributed to the activity of Adad; the movement of the sun to Šamaš; that of the moon to Sîn; the raising of grain depended on Ašnan; and the raising of sheep and goats on Laḫar; while the powers and effects of fire were connected to Gibil; and so on.

Furthermore, insofar as individual people were concerned, popular devotion had developed the notion that each individual had his own "personal god" and "personal goddess" to take care of him and assist him, gods whose functions have never been made very clear, but to whom a person was connected by a specific bond of dependency, and who more or less played the role for that individual that the great gods played with regard to the various elements in the world. No doubt, in his religious life, in the other aspects of his life, and in his vision and perception of things, each individual had more or less to make allowances for his god, tell him what was occurring in his life, and watch him direct his existence—through means that were apparently too personal and intimate for us to be told very much about them.

Thus the gods constantly intervened everywhere and participated in everything, like kings in the affairs of their kingdom. And like kings as well, the gods expressed their will through their "words" *(amatu)* and their "commandments" *(qibîtu)*, which were not necessarily spoken but were believed to be inscribed, in a certain sense, in the unfolding and the routine of events and things. Even if, at least in cosmogony, it does not appear that people knowingly placed value on the self-efficacy of those words and orders, they were recognized as having a strength and qualities proportional to those of their august emitters: thus what came out of the mouths of the gods was "sublime" *(şîru)*, "powerful" *(gašru)*, and "imposing" *(kabtu)*, like the authors themselves, and above all, still like them, "unchangeable," "impossible to modify and even less to suppress" *(ša lâ innennû, lâ uttakkaru)*; only their authors were capable of revoking or altering their commands.

These words and wishes of the gods could be written down: the entire doctrine of so-called deductive divination, specific, as we shall see, to the Mesopotamians, was based on the notion that the gods were free to communicate their will concerning the future, both good and bad, to humans as they saw fit by "inscribing" it in things of nature, as they were creating them. But they could also announce the future "face to face," by spelling it out or revealing it, perhaps in a dream. This was at the foundation of everything that, in personal or social life, compelled a person to act or prohibited him from doing so.

Beyond the writing or the words of the gods to express their will and their actions on things, people were interested in going back as far as the "thought" that precedes and forms discourse: as far as "intent" *(uşurtu)*, as far as mental "decision" *(purussû)*, going back in this way to the "inner" zone of the gods' minds, where their wills ripened and were formed, where their decisions were made. In this regard, the strongest and, no doubt, to the ancient Mesopotamians, the richest and most significant term, as well as the one most characteristic of their way of viewing things, was *šimtu* (in Sumerian nam or nam.tar): "Destiny," "Fate," the "Future," foreseen and desired, of the world, of a land, or of a person, such as the gods had "fixed," "imposed," and "decided" it *(šâmu)*. Just as here on Earth the great political decisions concerning the future of the land and of its subjects were made and decreed by the sovereign, after having been, if necessary, planned and discussed in the "assembly" (the one or several various political councils that the ruler convoked and heard), so too was an "Assembly" (ukkin/*puḫru*) of the gods imagined, in whose sessions, presided over by the king of the gods, they debated and decided the destinies of the universe, of the gods, and of human beings.[69] The result of these constricting and irrevocable deliberations was inscribed by the "secretary" of the council on a tablet: the "Tablet of Destinies" *(ṭuppi šimâti)*. The act of writing them down thus recorded, reinforced, and memorialized forever the "governmental" wishes of the gods. This tablet assured its possessor of supreme power over the entire universe of the gods and of humanity, all of whom found themselves ostensibly mentioned in it, each with the particular fate that was to befall him. It is that tablet, in the *Epic of Creation*, that Marduk, after Tiamat's death, ripped from the hands of the god Qingu, the impostor, and "sealed it with a seal and affixed it to his chest,"[70] for it would henceforth be he who would be the universal master of things. And in the *Myth of Anzû*, the entire working of the universe is disorganized and blocked and the gods rendered incapable of intervening efficiently from the moment when Anzû the traitor hid the Tablet of Destinies, along with other talismans of power, from Enlil.[71]

All of these "destinies" seem to have been more or less tacitly viewed as composing a huge "plan," conceived and to be carried out by the gods, one that bore on the entire future of the world and all its components: objects, plants, animals, and humans. The *destiny* of each person corresponded to his *name*. The name *was* the thing named, sounded out through pronunciation and materialized by being put down in writing. Through the *destiny* that the gods had assigned to each being, the gods conferred what we call its "nature" upon it, in the ancient and philosophical sense of the word: everything it needed to accomplish the role that the gods had assigned to it in the vast mechanics of the universe. Even the gods had their own destinies. However, since we lack explicit documents to support the notion, we should not for all that be led to think that in the name of "Destiny" the ancient Mesopotamians ever truly went so far as to adopt the Hellenistic concept of *heimarmene*, Divine Fate, a universal Necessity, impersonal, implacably ruling the entire universe and each of its components, from the gods to the smallest things. Nevertheless, in the first millennium at least, the word "destiny" was sometimes preceded, preferably in the plural, by the determinative for god, which conferred upon it the nature of those who were masters of it and turned it into something like a personalized and supernatural being. "May there be peace," one reads in an exorcism prayer, "in the heart of your god and your destiny, with the hand of your god and your goddess!"[72]

It is not easy to find a place, in the mechanism of the gods' government of the world, for the mysterious term "m e," which seems moreover to have had a role primarily in a traditional Sumerian and archaic vision of things. It certainly refers to a power, a privileged power, reserved for certain gods, normally the most highly placed: An and Enki, above all; Inanna, it seems, having obtained it only tangentially from Enki, as is explained in a famous myth *(Inanna and Enki)*.[73] A long list of those "m e" was drawn up, with more than a hundred columns. The list concerns only elements relating to high urban culture, which at first only Enki had possessed in the beginning in Eridu, but which, in a moment of drunkenness, he had generously given as a gift to "his daughter," Inanna, who quickly transferred everything to her city of Uruk, thus giving it access to high civilization, which until then had been limited to Eridu. The "m e" were, foremost, cultural facts, the effects of the ingenious creative abilities of the gods—Enki above all—mythologically imagined, in these circumstances, as so many pieces of a treasure.

The word by itself is impossible to translate exactly (it was already difficult to translate into Akkadian, which had more than one equivalent for it); sometimes a lengthy paraphrase fits best, because it simultaneously evoked several semantic fields that seem dissimilar to us. There was something ontological about it, as it obviously referred, in one way or another, to the "nature" of the things in question; but the "m e" seem to entail an aspect of that nature that was simultaneously precious, rich, and above all secret, known only by the divinities who had mastery over the things. At the same time, possessing those "m e" conferred upon the gods an indisputable prestige and power, which they took advantage of and which they even kept for themselves. Inanna, descending to Hell, the place filled with dangers, had brought all the "m e" she had available with her (seven), to protect her body like so many clothes and jewels.[74]

It is possible that "m e" comes from an archaic mythological vision—hence its obscurity—which above all stressed the intervention and authority of certain gods over the cultural life of humans. But it is not clear that we must go any farther and recognize in them and in their possession and wielding a universal and basic element in the government of the world in its entirety; we need only to recognize through them the ability of certain great gods to intervene efficiently in a given sector of nature, of culture, and of life.

The End of the World

As for the end of the world, the documents we possess do not tell us much about whether the old sages of Mesopotamia ever thought much about it. Berossus[75] attributed a doctrine to them according to which the total duration of the world was to be "twelve times twelve *sars*," a *sar* equaling 3,600 years, which equals 518,400 years, of which in his time, 432,000 years of ancient reigns from the Sumerian King List had already passed;[76] plus 34,080 or, according to another chronology, 33,091 years, from the end of the Flood to the First Babylonian Dynasty; plus 1,564 years from that dynasty to Alexander the Great, the contemporary of Berossus. Therefore, only twelve *sars*, or 43,200 years, of existence were left.

It is probable, since Berossus was a witness and not only well aware of the traditions of his land but in general quite reliable, that he echoes authentic speculations—of which the vertiginous qualities are in no way surprising to anyone familiar with the fantastic numbers that the Sumerian King List attributes to the old kings, especially those before the Flood. But for lack of documents, we can be certain of nothing, nor speculate further. And in any case there is the greatest possibility that if such speculations were made, they were in no way official or representative of the religious system. Finally, in what remains of his book, Berossus says nothing of the true problem: did the sages whose lucubrations he was reporting think of the end of *a* world (to be replaced by what?) or of the absolute end of *the* world, which would then disappear forever?

The Mythology of Man

Considering the gods' constant and universal intervention in the universe, the ancient Mesopotamians sought and imagined answers to the fundamental questions raised by the existence of human beings.

Universalism

It must first be noted that although the ancient Mesopotamians considered their land and its inhabitants as the center and pinnacle of the world, they were nonetheless conscious that the action of the gods extended well beyond that: they had a universalist vision of their gods.

In that land there was never any notion of what we call "racism." The idea of "foreigners" (*aḫû;* in Sumerian, bar) mattered only on the linguistic, economic, and political level; and those "foreigners" were the objects of opposition, aversion, or rejection only insofar as, in the random and more or less ephemeral conflicts of interest, they were considered to be "enemies" (*nakru;* in Sumerian, kúr) and fought as such.

The traits, both natural and cultural, that distinguished "others" —the color of their skin, physical peculiarities, clothing and customs, incomprehensible languages—to our knowledge never seem to have inspired barriers or hatred or even true alterity in Mesopotamia. All people were foremost, indisputably, people.

When the names of gods that belonged to foreigners (such as Šušinak, Laḫuratil, and Ḫumban of the Elamites; Melqartu, Baal-ṣapûnu, and Aštartu of the Phoenicians; Atarsamaim, Rusa'u, and Nuḫa'a of the Arabs; Ḫaldia and Bagbartu of the Urartians) were written, they were uniformly adorned with the determinative of the "star," which identified them as gods. Thus, they were considered not as "idols" but as ontologically on the same footing as the members of the Mesopotamian pantheon. There are no cases where in one way or another those foreign gods' divine character was ever at issue.

Accustomed since the time of the Sumero-Akkadian symbiosis not only to the multiplicity and the variety of divinities but to their mutual syncretism, the Mesopotamians similarly easily added foreign divinities to their own: in addition to the West Semitic Dagan, who was equated with Enlil, indeed, adopted as such, we possess, for example, a list of Kassite divinities in which each is associated with a corresponding Mesopotamian divinity: Maratta was Ninurta; Šiḫu was Sîn; and Kamulla was Éa; and so forth. The foreign pantheons were tacitly considered as what they were: the product of different cultures, with their members playing a role analogous to that played by the indigenous gods of Mesopotamia. It was as if, on the supernatural level, they had recognized the existence of a certain number of *divine functions,* of which the titularies bore, depending on the lands and the cultures, different names and personalities—a bit like political offices, which were pretty much the same everywhere; only their names were different, as were those of the individuals who held the offices. Just as one did not feel obligated to serve the rulers of other lands, one felt no obligation to serve foreign divinities. One was not interested in them as such or in the way they exercised their power; people did not construct myths concerning them. Such things applied only to the gods of one's own land. But it went without saying that whatever it might specifically have been, the role of the indigenous gods was *universal.* Just as their cosmogonic interventions were not limited to Mesopotamia, however preeminent it may have been, but extended to the entire universe, the gods' role vis-à-vis humans was similarly extended to all people and was universal.

As we saw above, Enlil was "the great and powerful ruler who dominates Heaven and Earth / Who knows all and understands all"; Enki was "the Sovereign of all men together"; and it was said of Šamaš:

10   With the brightness of your light their path is seen.
11   Your dazzle ever seeks out [. . .]
15   Šamaš, at your arising mankind bows down
16   . . . every land.
21   You climb to the mountains surveying the earth,
22   You suspend from the heavens the circle of the lands.
23   You care for all the peoples of the lands,
24   And everything that Éa, king of the counsellors, had created
        is entrusted to you.
25   Whatever has breath you shepherd without exception. . . .[77]

Ištar was celebrated as the "queen of the inhabited world, who governs the peoples."

Everything in the following sections, all of which comes under the auspices of the gods of Mesopotamia, should consequently be understood to apply to all humans.

Anthropogony and Humanity's Reason for Being

An interesting fact, even if it is of lesser significance, is that unlike the various cosmogonies that have come down to us, we have practically only a single mythological presentation of the origin of human beings. From a few Sumerian phrases, regularly used elsewhere to note the growth of plants and their emerging from the earth, we have come to believe in the existence of an anthropogonic theme that presented the first appearance of human beings on the model of that of plants: by "emerging from the ground," by "emersion." But because we do not have any explicit tale based on this motif, it is therefore likely that it was not a true *explanation* but a purely literary *metaphor,* as is perhaps the case with the "creating River."

The only "calculated imagination" that responded, to our knowledge, to the eternal question, "Why do human beings exist?" appears in a few mythological writings. The clearest expression of this theme is also the most ancient: the great poem *Atraḫasîs*. This work, in Akkadian, was apparently composed shortly before the oldest fragments we have recovered of it: they are signed and dated to the reign of the king Ammiṣaduqa (1646–1626), the fourth successor of the great Ḫammurabi of Babylon. We call this work by the name of its hero, who plays the role of the king of the land: Atraḫasîs, the "Supersage." [78] It is a poem of some 1,200 verses, spread over three tablets. Only about two-thirds of it remains, which is more than enough for us to determine its structure and meaning. We will summarize it here, not only as an essential testimony to the religious thought and "mentality" of those ancient ancestors regarding anthropogony, but also because, expressed in language that is noble, dignified, and clear, it is one of the great and pure masterpieces of the thought and literature of Mesopotamia in the glorious Old Babylonian Period. In addition, it is easy to see in it the prototype of the first chapter of the Bible, in Genesis, although Genesis treats the theme in a spirit completely different from that of the Mesopotamian prototype. [79] By repeating and adjusting, while strongly rethinking, a few traditional mythological motifs, the anonymous author of *Atraḫasîs* produced a powerful synthesis, coherent and persuasive, of the entire "history" of humanity, from humans' first appearance, through the entire "mythical era" of the formation of things, up to the dawn of the "historical era," which henceforth unfolded without any further fundamental innovations.

There is no mention of theogony in it: the gods existed, that was all! And the only allusion to cosmogony, as we saw above, is the initial dividing up of the mass of the world among the three principal gods—like heirs who would have drawn lots for their shares of an inheritance. The tale begins at the time when only the gods existed; human beings had not yet been created. The gods had to organize themselves in order to obtain through their own work all the goods and services they needed. As later among the humans, the upper class, the leaders (the Anunnaki), forced the lower class (the Igigi) to perform works of drudgery. And those lesser gods toiled endlessly to manage and work the earth, like a huge cultivated field.

At the end of interminable years of such work, they were exhausted and dejected to find themselves exploited in such a way, and they went on strike, refusing to continue their drudgery and even destroying their tools, thereby burning their bridges behind them. They demanded, in sum, not only to be relieved of their heavy labor but to be dealt with on the same level as their leaders, whose nature, after all, they shared. There was much panic in the divine society, which was henceforth threatened with poverty and famine. The gods then met in a council, and the most intelligent and ingenious among them, Enki/Éa, proposed the salutary plan he had come up with.

It involved the creation of a substitute for the worker gods, which was to be the Human. His body would be shaped out of clay, not only because in that land it was the ultimate omnipresent raw and plastic material, but because it implied the inevitability of death: recalling the earthly powder into which old bones fell, "to die" was "to return to one's clay." That Human, constructed in that way, could therefore never, as could the Igigi, interrupt his work to attempt to obtain a superior condition, one equal to the gods. But it was necessary to "animate" that clay, so the substitute built with it would be in a good condition to fulfill his laborious mission as best he could, just like his divine predecessors: the clay was therefore molded along with the blood of a second-level god who was immolated for the purpose.

In fact, Enki/Éa's plan, thus summed up, was much more intelligent and clever and merits a more precise and detailed description, as does the reasoning of the ancient theologians. It was based on one of those assonances which were not always, as we might think, purely phonetic and random but reflected a truly ontological and thus meaningful order, insofar as the ancient Mesopotamians were persuaded—we have already seen a few examples of this—that the *name* of a thing was indeed the *thing* itself. Thus the god that Enki/ Éa chose to make up the Human, a certain Wê, was otherwise unknown in the pantheon (and, indeed, perhaps created for the circumstances). As the author of the plan strongly stressed to explain his choice, Wê was picked, on the one hand, for his quality as a "god" *(ilu)* and, on the other, because he was endowed with a "spirit" *(ṭêmu).* By adding to Wê the mention of his divine nature, *ilu,* one obtained the Akkadian word for "human being": *(a)wêlu,* or *awîlu.* And if one also joined to the name Wê the reminder of his "spirit," the combination gave *(w)eṭem(m)u,* which designated everything that remained of a person after death: "ghost." [80] In this way Enki/Éa constructed a substitute for the gods in its composite reality, both semantic (from the "Wê" and the "god," on the one hand, and from the "Wê" and "spirit," on the other) and in its ontological reality *(awîlu,* on the one hand, and *(w)eṭemmu,* on the other: the "man" that it would be during its life and its time for work, and the ghost that would remain afterward, as a distant and pale shadow of divine immortality, so that he would never seek immortality further and thereby reject his basic mission). The mission of human beings, even if it is not explicitly stated in the text of *Atraḥasîs,* was nevertheless clear: human beings would be (like the earlier Igigi) workers for the gods, providers for the gods, servants of the gods, laboring on their behalf throughout their mortal lives as men *(awîlu)* before necessarily stopping work at their deaths, when they became ghosts *((w)eṭemmu).*

Submitted to the general assembly of the gods, and immediately unanimously applauded, the ingenious plan was undertaken right away. First of all, it went without saying, in that culture, which had experience in such fine points of a craft, they needed a simple yardstick—a prototype—called *lullû.* For this initial step the Great Lady and universal mother of the gods, she who had once belonged to the great tetrad, Bêlit-ilî, intervened, rather mysteriously, it seems, since nowhere is there mention of any sexual conjunction—was it passed over in silence as being too precise, or "vulgar"? To create a being as important and "close" to the gods, in which, as the text emphasizes, there would be "a blend of god and man," how could they do without the assistance of the supreme Mother? [81]

It was only once the human prototype was achieved, and once again approved by the gods, that it went, as in industry, into "assembly-line production," through the process of reproduction that henceforth became commonplace. Conception is presented here simply as a "deposit" into mysterious "matrices" of the clay of the "prototype" (no doubt mixed with the blood of Wê—the text does not elaborate on this) by apparently fourteen goddesses chosen for the purpose. This was followed by a gestation period of ten lunar months (the initial month counted as a whole month), then by the birth of the *seven* anticipated couples, the ancestors of all people: *seven* "matrices" for men and *seven* for women. It appears (the gaps in the text make this unclear) that those fourteen first "mothers" (goddesses then took their place) indeed inaugurated and henceforth forever ruled over the ritual of childbirth, a notion that then became traditional (but we know almost nothing about this, however).

Such is, in a sketchy form, the only well-known myth of Mesopotamian anthropogony, which emphasized the "theocentric" existence of humans: they were servants of the gods by natural vocation. The tale does not stop there, however. It still had to "explain" many facts that were inseparable from our lives and that were not necessarily included in that initial creation: the existence of illness and great scourges in nature; the means to avoid them; as well as, ultimately, a few specifics, such as the normal duration of human life. That life, it was believed, although from the outset destined to be extinguished by death, had first been extraordinarily long: a sort of more or less fantastic summary of the ancient history of the land, the Sumerian King List, mentions ancient figures who lived for 64,800 years!

The afflictions that plague humanity are explained in the *Atra-ḫasîs* in the following way. The first humans, beyond the reach of what might inhibit their reproduction and endowed with almost endless life, immediately multiplied to such an extent that, all the while enthusiastically tending to their tasks to the satisfaction of the gods, they became so noisy that Enlil, the king of the gods, being unable to sleep and having become increasingly irritated, decided to destroy them.

He therefore sent them Epidemic, Illness, and, next, Drought and resulting Famine. But each time the humans escaped, because Atra-ḫasîs, their king, called upon the help of his supernatural protector, Enki/Éa, their "inventor" and creator, who had every reason not to see them disappear. This god taught them how to dispel and rid themselves of misfortune: through the ritual interventions of exorcism.

Thus, since the inhabitants of Earth were becoming increasingly numerous, boisterous, and noisy, and since their din continued unabated, Enlil, who still could not sleep and who was impatient, eventually made the harsh—and, it must indeed be said, stupid—decision to destroy them by resorting to the incomparable and absolute weapon of the Flood (a literary and mythological theme that was unknown up until then): a formidable general flood that was caused by enormously rising rivers and torrential rain. Faced with this new and deadly threat, Enki/Éa, anxious not to see the gods return to the catastrophic situation from which he had saved them by creating the very humans Enlil wanted to destroy, very creatively arranged to preserve at least one man (Atraḫasîs) and his family by placing them in an unsinkable boat along with what they needed to restore the fauna of the world. Once the Flood was over and his plan of salvation had succeeded, in order henceforth to prevent the overpopulation that would once again deprive the irascible Enlil of his rest and calm, which would again lead him to make new fatal decisions, Enki/Éa took a number of conservative measures. He reduced the life span of each person to the one we know today, and he introduced sterility among a certain number of women and infant mortality. Thus ended the long and clear tale of *Atraḫasîs*.

In perfect accord with the general vision of things, the tale seems to have responded rather well to the mythological curiosity of its readers and listeners so that, at least to our knowledge, they never had to imagine any other. They even disseminated it, since, without citing the other ancient sources in which it ended up, we find it powerfully adapted to "monotheism" in the first chapters of Genesis. In Mesopotamia it was altered slightly at times but did not change in broad outline at all. For example, the authors of the *Epic of Creation* [82] naturally attributed the plan to Marduk, leaving it to Enki/Éa, his father, simply to execute the idea. And, no longer being interested in the astute reasoning behind the choice of the god Wê to explain the nature and destiny of humans, they replaced him with Qingu, the leader of the revolt quelled by Marduk; Qingu was immolated as punishment for his "sin." Another myth, possibly originally written in Sumerian, which clearly accepts and is based on the same explanations offered in *Atraḫasîs,* emphasizes above all the ingeniousness of Enki, who went even farther than simply creating human beings and went on to astutely find an explanation and a useful occupation for even the "rejects" of humanity: the paralyzed, the blind, the sterile, bisexuals.[83]

A third tale, also Sumerian, which has reached us in rather poor condition, revolves, especially at its end, around the Flood and its hero (who was called Ziusudra, "prolonged life" in Sumerian, because in the end he is granted immortality); it stresses the repopulating of the Earth after the extreme elimination of the first wave of humanity.[84] We also have a rather short myth, in two parallel versions, Akkadian and Sumerian, to explain how the gods, after having created Earth as a vast cultivable field, brought humans into the world, who would work it and exploit it for the gods' benefit.[85]

All these tales are quite evidently inspired by *Atraḥasîs* and retain its essential vision. We have not found anything in that land from an earlier time that suggests the development of other, similar anthropogonic imaginings. And in everything that came later, the same framework, the same thread, and the same presentation of that noble, intelligent, and elevated myth have been preserved, manifestly transposed, as well, from the political hierarchy on Earth: just as subjects had no other purpose in life than to obey their king and his representatives, and to provide those rulers, through their constant labor, with what they needed to lead an opulent and leisurely life, free of all worries and thus free to govern their people with a view to their prosperity, so, too, was humanity "invented" and placed in the world only to serve the gods. It is a vision whose intelligence, religiosity, and wisdom we cannot help but appreciate.

The Gods' Government of Humanity

The government of humanity followed the logic of that primary metaphor: as owners and masters of the universe, which the gods had created and arranged, they were similarly the masters and lords responsible for their servants, the human beings—humans in general but also each person in particular. As we read in the hymns to Enki and Šamaš above, they were "the Sovereign of all men together" and they "care for all the peoples of the lands."

Nothing shows better the degree to which the ancient Mesopotamians were convinced of the universal and constant intervention and meddling of the gods in the life of each person, as well as in the workings of the world, than the generalized practice of divination. We will explain its workings later and will limit ourselves here to a rough sketch. The ancient Mesopotamians readily accepted "revelations" by the gods concerning the danger that might befall the king at any given moment:

> If on the 29th of the month of Ayyar [April/May] there is a solar eclipse: the king will die.[86]

The entire life of each person, public or private, as well as the working of the world, was entirely within the hands of the gods:

> If a lizard crawls on the bed of a sick person: his illness will leave him.[87]

The gods alone were responsible not only for the dangers incurred by the king in a given circumstance but also for everything from eclipses of the sun to a lizard's deciding to crawl on the bed of a sick person; the gods were also responsible for the consequences of all events, from the death of a king to the healing of a sick person.

How did the gods intervene in a person's existence? The ancient Mesopotamians did not seek a precise answer to such a question any more than they did to that concerning the government of the world. How might they have answered it? Might not the question have appeared pointless? From the moment they were persuaded that the gods acted and intervened in everything and everywhere to lead human affairs as they saw fit, that the gods were the absolute masters of all of human existence, was it truly important—indeed imaginable—to follow step by step the mechanism of their activities, since they were confident of its reality? Just like their attitude regarding the government of the world, a certain number of general terms could be invoked pertaining to the intervention of the gods. The strongest and most eloquent was "destiny": *šimtu*, the effect of a decision made and carried out by them. But unless one wanted to stress the intervention of a certain specific god, one invoked divine action only generally, without ever being tempted to follow the unfolding of the process from beginning to end, from the formulation of the express will of the god (and, moreover, of which god?) to its inevitable execution through the effect of that same all-powerful will. It was enough to be convinced—and they were!—that the gods were the true agents of everything that occurred or was sustained on Earth, in the life of each person as in the workings of the world.

The gods could, in fact, proceed exactly in the manner of chiefs of state: by expressing their wills, to which their subjects had only to conform. Everything in the cultural tradition that had been received by all and sundry beginning in childhood and reinforced through education, and which governed, positively or negatively, each person's behavior, all that was normative, in every realm of human behavior—religious but also legal, social, or simply routine —was seen as the express will "of the gods" (collectively) and therefore constituted nothing other than their intervention in our conduct and our lives. We will later see the religious repercussions of such a way of viewing things, which could put all those who went against the gods' will in a condition of "sin" and of "revolt" against them. At least it was clear and undeniable that the gods inevitably directed and governed all people, during their entire lives. But what about afterward?

Death and the Beyond

In the very model and prototype of the human, as it had been conceived and fine-tuned by its inventor and creator, Enki/Éa, death was included, fated, unavoidable, and no less cruel. The *Epic of Gilgameš* was there to recall that the greatest efforts the hero undertook to avoid death had been in vain. And when, having reached the end of his long and terrible voyage, he finds himself face to face with the survivor of the Flood, Utanapištim, from whom he hoped to learn the secret of his privileged immortality, Utanapištim at first simply says to him:

286 Mankind, whose offshoot is snapped off like a reed in a cane
        brake,
      the fine youth and lovely girl
      · · · · · · · · · · · · · ·
290 No one can see death,
      no one can see the face of death,
      no one can hear the voice of death,
      yet there is savage death that snaps off mankind.
      · · · · · · · · · · · · · ·
298 For how long has the river risen and brought the overflowing
        waters,
      so that dragonflies drift down the river?
      The face that could gaze upon the face of the Sun
      has never existed ever.

> How alike are the sleeping (?) and the dead.
> The image of Death cannot be depicted.
> (Yes, you are a) human being, a man (?)!
> 305 After Enlil had pronounced the blessing,
> The Anunnaki, the Great Gods, assembled.
> Mammetum, she who fashions destiny, determined destiny
>   with them.
> They established Death and Life,
> 309 but they did not make known "the days of death."[88]

In fact, at the end of his long and exhausting pursuit, Gilgameš had obtained nothing. Even that pitiful substitute for indefinite life, the "plant of rejuvenation," ultimately escaped him. Even if someone was of the stature and importance of that great man who did not want to die, no one was made to last forever: this is the primary fact that the Mesopotamians quickly integrated into their religious system, even if, very, very long ago, they admitted, considering their polytheism and their anthropomorphism, the extremely rare exception of a few eminent men of the past who had passed into the ranks of the immortals, of "gods."

How did they view death itself? Not having, as we do, that vague phantasm of an incorporeal element to "animate" our bodies and to keep them alive through its presence, then to cause their death through its disappearance, they considered humans fated, through their own destiny, to a successive double condition. As long as they had blood in their veins and breath in their nostrils, alternatively inhaled and exhaled, they were alive, by themselves: as was taught in *Atraḫasîs*, they were truly "men," *awîlu*. At the moment when, emptied of their blood or after having exhaled one last time, breath ceased to return into them *(napištu)*, their condition changed into that of a "phantom," *eṭemmu;* they were dead!

However, death was not nothingness, a notion that was far too unimaginable, as we have already seen, for the ancient Mesopotamians ever to have considered it. They found themselves simply before a cadaver, a body-and-nothing-else *(pagru)*, fixed and appearing deeply asleep ("How alike are the sleeping and the dead!" as Utanapištim said), which, according to the land's immemorial tradition, was to be committed to the earth, in an individual grave.

But foremost, the deceased had not completely disappeared from the existence of the survivors: in their memories, in their dreams, or in their obsessions and fears the dead person came to them, not only so they would think of him, but so they could see him again, vaguely, and even believe they heard him speak, cry, wail. And since in those times they did not, as we do, truly separate the things of their oneiric lives from those of real life, they were convinced that that vague profile, aerial, foggy, evanescent, and untouchable, truly *was* all that remained of the deceased himself, in his new condition as "shadow," as "specter," as "phantom": *eṭemmu,* as Enki/Éa had decreed at the moment when he planned humans and their entire destiny, in life and afterward. They most likely thought (we have never been told this) that this *eṭemmu* existed in the living *awîlu,* only in a latent existence. But at the time of death, while the body, buried in the ground, "was returning to clay," *the phantom,* thus introduced under the ground, was by that fact conveniently placed to go to the huge, black cave of Below: the symmetrical and antithetical opposite of On High, where it joined the countless multitude of other specters, assembled there since the beginning of time and forever to lead a gloomy and mournful existence, lethargic and sluggish forever after, an existence that was suggested by the rigid and pensive cadaver, as well as the fabulous image of a Below of black night, of heavy silence, and of endless, weighty sleep.

This ultimate and definitive resting place for humans was anticipated from their beginnings through their nature and destiny by their creator himself. Each person upon dying automatically went there, without undergoing any real form of "judgment" in order to be granted a more or less bearable or "fortunate" condition: the last sleep was the same for everyone! At best those jurists and formalists seem sometimes to have imagined the dead person "summoned" Below and to its perpetual sleep by a divine "decision," along the lines of those taken by the sovereign to assign one of his subjects to a certain post.

But the imagination cannot be stopped, especially when it grapples with a problem as crucial as that fatal future we all share: the new and definitive existence into which we are thrown by death. Building upon these simple, clear, and so well-defined facts that came out of the very charter for the invention and creation of human beings, over time people's imaginations devised multiple mythological products and phantasms, which were easily contradictory, like everything that comes out of the imagination alone.

First of all, these notions organized the afterlife and Below along the lines—the only ones known—of Earth and Heaven, based upon the system of the pantheon. They projected the image of the city on it, the residential center of populations living closely together, and as if the deceased were locked away in it and were held there by force, they turned it into a formidable citadel, surrounded by fortifications of powerful, unattackable, sevenfold ramparts. In *Ishtar's Descent into the Netherworld*,[89] in order for her to enter into it, she was made to pass through, one after the other, the seven gates of that wall, thereby stripping her, gradually, of everything that had made her a living being equipped for life. This City of the Dead was sensed to be lugubrious, crushing, and haunted only by sluggish, melancholy, and floating inhabitants, far from any light or happiness. It was, as the poem begins,

1   To the netherworld, land of n[o return]
     . . . .
5   To the house which none leaves who enters,
     . . . .
7   To the house whose entrants are bereft of light,
     Where dust is their sustenance and clay their food.
     They see no light but dwell in darkness,
10   They are clothed like birds in wings for garments,
     And dust has gathered on the door and bolt.[90]

This dark and multitudinous community was also called *Arallû* or *Ganzer*—terms whose meanings are unknown—or the "Great Below" or *Irkallu*, from the Sumerian iri.gal, the "Great City." It was naturally organized along the lines of the cities of our world and was under the control of the gods as well. We know that out of a concern for symmetry the pantheon was divided into two equal groups: "three hundred On High" and "as many Below." Those On High were obviously superior, as was fitting, since there figured among them the most notable, the most powerful, the great creators and rulers of the world. The divinities relegated to Below, magnificently lodged and treated in spite of the dreariness of the location, were, like those On High, ranked in a hierarchical order, with a supreme chief at their head. It seems that a long time ago (perhaps under the influence of the Sumerians, who were much less "macho"), they had preferred a woman for that role, Ereškigal, the well-named "Lady of the Great Place" in Sumerian. She was later replaced by a male warrior god, assigned to the great hecatombs to increase the number of his subjects: Nergal (from the Sumerian nè.iri.gal, "Chief of the Great City"). An Akkadian myth, in two versions, the shorter of which must be, at the latest, from the middle of the second millennium, resolved the conflict between the two traditions by explaining how Ereškigal, at first an "old maid" and alone at the head of her dark kingdom, had married Nergal, in one version after being brutally conquered by that ruffian soldier, and in the other, following a romantic episode.[91]

The rulers of Below, like those of On High, were regularly assisted in their councils and decisions by an elite corps of divinities, who were ultimately called Anunnaki. It was they, in fact, who decided (it was commonly said "to judge") the cases of each *eṭemmu*, certainly not to grant it a more or less satisfactory infernal existence depending upon its merits, since the "merits" in question, no less than "morality" or "good conduct" on Earth, played not the slightest role in one's orientation after death, which was identical for everyone and definitively set by death itself; but in order to confirm, following the rules, the dead person's entrance into his new existence and his new residence, a bit like a clerk scrupulously maintains the register of those who are imprisoned.

But because it was impossible not to imagine that the existence of the dead was made up, as is ours, of an infinite accumulation of inequalities, and because it was, in particular, unbelievable that the kings and the highest-ranking figures could ultimately fall to the ranks of the miserable populace, the ancient Mesopotamians very early on no doubt (the royal tombs of Ur, true and exceptional testimony to the macabre pomp reserved postmortem for the royal figures and their sacrificed court, are from around the twenty-sixth century; the custom was undoubtedly abandoned later on), in spite of their basic conviction that death and the afterlife were the great equalizers of human destinies, maintained the idea that the level of existence of the *eṭemmu* was no more equal than the destiny of the former *awîlu*, their fate in the Beyond depending more or less, not on their behavior, but on their conditions of life on Earth, even if death had introduced them into a routine of despondency and torpor. In truth, the mythology was not logical.

As in many lands, and throughout time, the dead were also feared, and many depressing misdeeds were attributed to them (in Mesopotamia, mental illness was often ascribed to their intervention). Against them, as against all evil creatures ("demons" and other worrisome or fearsome phantasms, whose status, this must be emphasized, had nothing to do with Below, to which they do not appear

ever to have been truly linked), people traditionally armed themselves by ritually asking the gods, through appropriate "exorcisms,"
to keep them, as well as the other "evil forces" who were believed to
inflict punishment for "sins," far away. In spite of the thick and
impenetrable walls of the terrible infernal fortress, which were supposed to prevent the *eṭemmu* from going the wrong way on the "path
without return" that they initially took, that same path (whether
it passed through the grave itself or was via an earthly detour toward the Distant West, undertaken by crossing a "river" [or a "border river"?], one side of which mysteriously bordered Below, in a
boat, under the eye of an implacable boatman) seems to have been
traveled daily in both directions by processions of "specters" who
came to terrify and mistreat the living, then were sent back where
they came from by exorcisms.

The most fearsome, it was said, the most relentless, those whom
it was necessary to neutralize at all costs, were those whom the vicissitudes of their existence had left without a grave. They had not
been introduced into their definitive space and were incapable,
given their condition, of penetrating into it themselves. They therefore wandered, vagabonds and heinous, like thieves, in deserted and
dark places, easily throwing themselves, like wild beasts, onto whoever had the misfortune to pass within their reach.

There were other just as vindictive and fearsome phantoms, those
who did not receive or no longer received the meager subsidies of
drink and food necessary to maintain their pitiful existence from
their descendants, who had disappeared or were simply forgetful.
For the duty of the family remained in force. What might be called
the cult of the dead was the responsibility of the head of the family:
a little water, poured from time to time onto the grave, with a few
scraps of food, and at the end of each month, when the Moon disappeared and, in a certain sense, died, a family meal, which was
called *kispu* (in Akkadian, this name alluded to the "sharing of the
flesh"), to which the dead relatives were ritually invited.

One kept the memory of the deceased alive, but ordinarily without going back further than three generations: those that came before, with the exception of the most illustrious, were henceforth
only the objects of a collective and vague memory. In their gloomy,
sleepy existence they had been absorbed by the great universal forgetting—the true death of a person.

Hedonism

Onto a tablet from the middle of the first millennium, an unknown copyist or scholar, taking the text from who knows where, recorded this panorama of human life, which had been reduced by Enki/Éa, after the Flood, to a suitable duration:

> At forty, it is (still) pleasant;
> At fifty, the days become shorter;
> At sixty, one is respectable;
> At seventy, a reprieve from existence;
> At eighty, old age;
> And at ninety, decrepitude![92]

After which, one had only to await death: to close one's eyes forever to light, movement, joy, to lose oneself, forever after, in the subterranean night, in a state of shadow, drab and sluggish. Wasn't this enough to inspire a certain pessimism concerning human life? During those too rapid years, without the slightest "moral" or altruistic ideal, one knew oneself to be above all assigned, through one's own nature and destiny, to work in the "service of the gods," a rather unexciting prospect, after all.

To be sure, those sovereign masters had only rather good-natured dispositions with regard to humans, provided that everyone did his duty as a good "servant"; and people even believed they could count on the gods' help if they had not been good servants and were expecting to be punished. But any true communication with the gods was inconceivable, so powerful and beyond reach were they believed to be: the only imaginable relationships were those of humble domestics vis-à-vis lofty and distant masters, without any other pleasure than that of accomplished duty, which has never truly delighted anyone. The human condition, however one looked at it, thus did not have, in itself, anything exalting or what might lead to what all people have never ceased to look for: happiness—not the small delights of which life is never too stingy, but the happiness of fulfillment. And the religious system did not make things easier. Each person was thus reduced to attempting, as best he could, to find his own happiness in the great or small immediate joys that his own life could provide. This is what we call *hedonism*. And it is indeed hedonism that the mysterious Tavern Keeper preached to Gil-

gameš after reminding him how chimerical his relentless pursuit of
an inaccessible endless life truly was:

> Gilgamesh, where are you wandering?
> The life that you are seeking all around you will not find.
> When the gods created mankind
> they fixed Death for mankind,
> and held back Life in their own hands.
> Now you, Gilgamesh, let your belly be full!
> Be happy day and night,
> of each day make a party,
> dance in circles day and night.
> Let your clothes be sparkling clean,
> let your head be clean, wash yourself with water!
> Attend to the little one who holds onto your hand,
> let a wife delight in your embrace.
> This is the (true) task of mankind (?).[93]

And the epic pretty much suggests that its hero had, in the end,
derived that lesson from his failure: returning to his capital, he can
speak only of that lesson—in other words, he no longer thinks about
anything but his duty as a king, which he had carried out so badly
before, and which he now envisions with a true enthusiasm, in spite
of (or because of?) his failure.

In ancient Mesopotamia, insofar as we are able to understand it,
humanity's only ambition, given their condition and the idea that
their religious representations gave them of it, was not to change
their lives but to succeed in them. It is striking how the notion of
success is at the foundation of all the efforts that we note or assume
among these people when they are pondering their behavior.

A complete, highly significant literary genre whose very ancient
testimonies already figure among the most venerable literary collections known to us, those found at Fâra and Tell Abû Ṣalābīkh, dating to around 2600, brings this to light through the many fragments that have remained, first and foremost in Sumerian and later
in Akkadian. I refer to the *Advice of a Father to His Son,* in which we
see a father addressing his son, "to teach about life," by conferring
his own experience and wisdom upon him:

> 19 Do not guarantee (for someone), that man will have a hold
>   on you.
> 22 Do not roam about where people quarrel, . . . [You will be]
>   made a witness in the quarrel!

35 My son, do not commit murder, do not cut yourself with
    an axe!
54 Do not have sexual intercourse with your slave girl, she will
    call you: Traitor!(?)
38 Do not speak (?) with a girl if you are married (?), the slan-
    der is strong.
158 Do not beat a farmer's son, he will beat your irrigation canal.
IV:4 Love alone maintains the family: hatred destroys it.[94]
72 Do not marry a prostitute, whose husbands are legion,
    A temple harlot who is dedicated to a god,
    A courtesan whose favours are many.
    In your trouble she will not support you,
    In your dispute she will be a mocker;
    There is no reverence or submissiveness with her.
135 Every day worship your god.
    Sacrifice and benediction are the proper accompaniment of
        incense.
    Present your free-will offering to your god,
    For this is proper toward the gods.
    Prayer, supplication, and prostration
    Offer him daily, and *you will get* your reward.[95]

All this advice makes up a sort of "code of good conduct," the observation of which (this is repeated and stressed) was to ensure the
success of each undertaking and, consequently, success in all of life
—with a little luck, of course (in Akkadian, "to have luck" was "to
have a god"—*for oneself*). Even religion and its obligations, as we
see, were exploitable in the same sense: they demanded of people
only to provide, through their work, the "service" of the gods, and
from this one concluded that such service would be, if not remunerated, then possibly compensated with divine favor.

All of this was, we might say, at least from our own point of view,
a common, rather down-to-earth, "pragmatist" notion: it ignored
not only heroism but apparently any attempt to live slightly above
oneself. We can nevertheless well understand that it was able to fill
the horizon of the ancient Mesopotamians and communicate a certain wisdom to them, perhaps above all a certain prudence and circumspection, indispensable to hedonism and to "success."

CHAPTER SIX

Religious Behavior

The Theocentric Cult

Quite logically, the fundamental metaphor that inspired every representation of the gods also governed every aspect of the religious
behavior of the faithful: since the faithful viewed the gods as sovereigns, they had to be treated accordingly. The faithful were convinced that humans had been created and put on Earth for the sole
purpose of ensuring, through human industry and solicitude, that
the gods led an opulent and worry-free life, free to concentrate on
the government of the world and its inhabitants.

In Mesopotamia, the cult, the "active" function of religion, therefore revolved around the "service to the gods," their "maintenance."
This involved providing the gods—just like subjects provided their
king—with "room and board," that is, all the goods and services, in
quantity and quality, of necessity or luxury, and in the style, pomp,
and magnificence worthy of their majesty, to fulfill all the needs and
desires that anthropomorphism endowed upon them.

But the king was also all-powerful in the land, and his subjects depended entirely on him, as master, not only for their lives but also
for their tranquility and happiness. He was capable, on a whim, of
reducing them to nothing or of heaping good things upon them,
provided he was moved enough through offerings, ostentation, and
requests. Similarly, the ancient Mesopotamians prepared an entire
series of rituals for the gods, both oral and those involving the performance of some activity, a good number inherited from ancient
"magic," in the hope of obtaining from the gods, at the very least,
the suppression of human misfortunes and pain. Here we have an
entirely different aspect of the cult: it was anthropocentric, and what
I call "sacramental," by reason of the specific presentation of its activities. It is necessary, therefore, in order to be clear and sufficiently
complete, to deal separately with the two aspects of religious behav-

ior: the theocentric cult and the anthropocentric, or sacramental, cult. I will begin with the theocentric cult, the objective of which, following humankind's fundamental purpose and "vocation," was to provide the gods with all the goods and honors they desired.

The Temples

First, we will discuss the gods' "shelter"—their houses. These were not only to shelter them but to isolate them in peace and allow them to lead, separately and among themselves, a peaceful and refined existence in a magnificent solemn place where their subjects knew they could be found and could admire them, take care of them, and request their benevolent aid—again like the sovereigns in their palaces. The Sumerian word for "palace" was "Great House" (e.gal, Akkadianized into *ekallu*), and a sanctuary was called "house" (e; in Akkadian, *bîtu*)—we translate simply as "temple." A temple was further defined by the name of the god to whom it was dedicated: "temple of such and such a god."

Each temple was dedicated to a divinity, of whom it was, like the palace for the king, the true dwelling place *(šubtu)*, through the ages constructed along the somewhat constant general lines of a simple private home. In the center was a courtyard, around which individual "apartments" were placed, reserved for the god who resided there and for the personal, familial, and official lives of his entourage. Some rooms were used for meetings of the assembly and the council, and other rooms were used for the various ceremonial activities that were required by etiquette and ritual. There was also, of course, the necessary space allotted for the needs of the personnel.

I am speaking here of the "major temples," those dedicated to the greatest of gods, to the patrons of major cities, especially political and religious capitals, such as the famous sanctuaries of Enlil in Nippur; of Enki/Éa in Eridu; of Anu and Inanna in Uruk; of Aššur in the city of the same name, in Nimrud, and in Nineveh; and of Marduk in Babylon. At a distance from the rest of the city, like a sacred neighborhood (they called it the "city of the gods"), surrounded by tall and massive walls, each temple contained a number of buildings of all sizes and configurations. But there were also temples throughout the entire land: in every city, town, and tiny village. They were distinguished by specific names: *parakku, papâḫu, a/eširtu, kiṣṣu, kummu,* and still others, whose exact significance we can only rarely grasp, a significance which must have changed over time and depending on the location. The simplest of these places of worship could have consisted of one or two rooms.

Of all these "dwellings of the gods," the most spectacular, present in every important city, sometimes in more than one version, and adjoining the sanctuary itself, was the *ziqqurratu* (which we simplify to *ziggurat*), literally (in Akkadian) "the preeminent," given its shape: a multifloored tower, which could include from three to seven stories, increasingly narrow the higher the story and connected by a staircase or ramp. It was usually about thirty meters high; but the most imposing, that of the temple of Marduk in Babylon (immortalized in the Bible in Genesis 11 as the Tower of Babel), was as high as ninety meters—we have its specifications and description in an intact tablet from the first millennium. The origins of and the reasons for this characteristic building, indeed its purpose and use, remain a mystery to us: did it respond to a specific religious model? Which one? Did it reflect—and how?—the sanctuary itself, located perhaps at its base? This is unlikely. Did they want to be closer to Heaven, or to bring Heaven closer to Earth? And what occurred in the chapel at its summit, in any event usable by astrologers and astronomers for their observations (but that was obviously not its primary function), and of which archeologists have still never found the slightest vestige, as they have been eroded for a very long time. It is only at the end of the third millennium that we note the development of ziggurats in their traditional form, and we are uncertain where that fashion might have come from.[1] Before then, we find only slightly raised sanctuaries on terraces.

Regarding the sanctuary itself, at the foot of the ziggurat when there was one, the center of interest was what we call the cella, let us say, in biblical language, the "holy of holies." This was the true sacred residence of the divinity. Its "true presence" was ensured there by its image or, better, its precious cult statue. Apparently sitting alone in the middle of the room or by one of the walls, and sometimes hidden behind a curtain, the statue may have been accompanied by images and statues of members of its family or its supernatural companions placed on separate pedestals or on banquettes along the walls. A long exorcistic liturgy entitled *Šurpu*, apparently involving Marduk in his temple in Babylon, suggests a good hundred such statues, in twelve groups, set up and distributed in a manner that is not clear to us.[2] Images, statues, or statuettes most likely ensured the gods' "real presence." We will read a document below in which a woman dreamed that the temple cella was completely empty of its principal statue as well as all the others, which must have meant that the gods had deserted the cella—a bad omen. In a second dream she heard the gods being called to go back to their places.

Perhaps above all in the most ancient times, the temples, along with their personnel, played an essential economic and political role in the land. It was as if their occupants, through their very "presence," communicated something of their own "numinosity," that "supernatural brilliance" *(melammu)* that indicated the divinity. We have recovered a collection of glorifying hymns (in Sumerian) dating at the earliest from before the middle of the third millennium in which the temples themselves are celebrated, as are—obliquely— the specific divinities who inhabited them. Here are a few lines addressed to the great sanctuary of Inanna in Uruk:

> 199 Well grown fresh fruit, marvelous, filled with ripeness,
> Descending from the midst of heaven, shrine, built for (?)
>   the steer,
> Eanna, house with seven corners, lifting the "seven fires" at
>   night,
> Surveying the seven . . .
> .   .   .   .
> 207 The great queen of heaven and earth, Inanna,
> Has, O Eanna, placed the house upon your . . . , has taken
>   her place on your dais.[3]

This status of the temples, and their importance in the life of the land, caused them to be given—as if to personify them—"names" that were significant and just as sacred, by which they were known and commonly cited. All are in Sumerian—the custom was therefore ancient—and begin with the generic term é, "temple": É.anna, "Temple of Heaven" (and of An, the god of Heaven) in Uruk; É.kur, "Temple-Mountain," dedicated to Enlil in Nippur; É.sag.íl, "Temple of the Eminent Pinnacle," which described the greatest and most famous of all, that of Marduk in Babylon. The multifloored towers, just as sacred, also received such names: for example, the ziggurat of É.sag.íl was called É.temen.an.ki, "Temple Support of the Universe." We have counted some thousand such titles in all, which tells us a lot about the increase, through time, in the number of sacred buildings in the land, as well as about their role and their place in its religious vision of the gods and the world.

One of the monarch's most eminent and most constraining ex officio obligations was to make sure the temples were in good condition: to erect them, to restore them, to improve them as required, to equip them luxuriously. What the king thus piously did went straight to the divine sovereigns of the world, while the humans, their king at the helm, in this way realized their innate vocation as "providers" for the gods. The kings willingly glorified themselves, notably in their dedicatory and commemorative inscriptions, for their zeal in religious behavior, frequently taking the titles of "curators" and "servants" of the sanctuaries. Thus Išme-Dagan, ruler of Isin, between 1953 and 1935, wrote:

1   (It is I,) Išme-Dagan,
      the curator (of the temple) of Nippur,
      the supporter (of the temple) of Ur,
5   the perpetual servant (of the temple) of Eridu,
      the pontiff (of the temple) of Uruk,
      the powerful king, the king of Isin.[4]

There is an Akkadian myth dating from the beginning of the first millennium, mentioned in the previous chapter, that conveys perfectly the lofty idea people had of the temple. It was considered to be the essential and primary part of the universe, the highest and most indispensable reality for the good functioning of the universe, and whose construction had been, it was thought, foreseen and desired by the Creators themselves, at the very origin of time. Therefore, we can understand perfectly why the temples attracted all the activity in the land: works of construction, of decoration, all carried out in the "service to the gods." And through the countless number of them that have been discovered during the past hundred and fifty years of excavations, archeologists have been able to sufficiently prove the interminable and powerful efforts of that ancient land to provide its lords and masters with magnificent residences throughout its long history.

At least one question remains: to what degree were those sacred buildings accessible, and to whom? There is a chance that as a rule—at least for practical reasons of keeping order—the public was no more easily allowed into them than they were into the palaces of the kings. Yet at the end of the famous poem called *Ludlul,* the subject, liberated from his misfortunes by Marduk and restored to a happy state, wanders around in a pious pilgrimage of gratitude, going through one portal after another (there are thirteen in all) in the great Ésagil of his liberator, while carrying out various devout and obviously ritual acts as he goes along, during which he receives appropriate favors from his god:

> 79 [In the] "Gate of Prosperity" prosperity was [given me,]
> [In the] "Gate of the . . . Guardian Spirit" a guardian spirit
>   drew [nigh to me,]
> [In the] "Gate of Well-being" I found well-being,
> In the "Gate of Life" I was granted life, . . .[5]

The temples, at least some of them, were therefore more or less accessible to the common "faithful," who were free to carry out their devotions there.

For lack of an indigenous equivalent as forthright as the above, we will cite here a few words from a biblical apocryphal work known as the Epistle of Jeremiah. Of a moralizing and devout nature, it aimed to ridicule the gods of Babylon in favor of "the only true god" of the Bible, but beyond its biting mockery, it betrays the emotions of the eyewitness who, even while deprecatory, reveals something of the spectacle and the amazement that a visit to a temple in Babylon could arouse:

> [Their idols] are overlaid with gold and with silver; yet are they but false, and cannot speak . . . and [the priests] deck [the idols] as men with garments, *even* the gods of silver, and gods of gold, and of wood. Yet cannot these gods save themselves from rust and moths, though they be covered with purple raiment. They wipe their faces because of the dust of the temple, which is thick upon them. . . . Whereby they are known not to be gods: therefore fear them not . . . their eyes be full of dust through the feet of them that came in. . . . They light them candles, yea, more than for themselves, whereof they cannot see one . . . and men say their hearts [their "soul" of wood] are eaten out, when things creeping out of the earth devour both them and their raiment: they feel it not when their faces are blacked through the smoke that cometh out of the temple: upon their bodies and heads alight bats, swallows, and birds; and in like manner the cats also.[6]

The Ministers of the Cult

More immediately responsible on everyone's behalf for "serving" the gods in their temples, the ministers of the cult, like the personnel of the king in his palace, formed a distinct social category, all the less clearly imaginable for us in that we are so far from it, especially in the religious realm, in which our concept of "clergy" can distort our understanding.

First, even if at least the high-ranking priests were officially inducted into their profession (the position was often inherited from their fathers and, perhaps, at times was divinely assigned) through some rite of passage or ceremony dedicated to the supernatural figures they were to serve (presentation to their images, anointing, purification of the initiate), those were only introductory formalities that had no obligatory impact on the priest's person or life, on his spirit or heart, or on anyone else's. This differs from our somewhat ontological vision of priests, who are interiorly transformed, so we think, by their priesthood. Not only, as we shall see, was the priesthood also conferred upon women, who could even occupy major positions in the cult hierarchy, but members of the clergy regularly married and led the same lives as everyone else (even if childbearing was prohibited to certain high-ranking priestesses, who were reserved, in a certain sense, for the gods alone). Their position therefore hardly consumed their entire existence: like all professionals, they were exercising a profession, no more, no less. Beyond their ceremonial functions nothing truly distinguished them from the average mortal, except, in a few cases at least, for a certain way of wearing their hair, a certain style of headdress, or a certain robe. Moreover, these characteristics were not reserved only for them and only indicated their obligations.

Although the documentation we currently possess is quite voluminous, it does not answer all our questions about the clergy, especially since some members of the clergy, in addition to their strictly ceremonial and "sacred" duties, also had administrative responsibilities in their temples that were easily overwhelming. Granted, the religious conservatism of that land—which we will see demonstrated more than once, in particular in the liturgy—authorizes us, *positis ponendis,* more or less to transpose what we learn about an individual, a sanctuary, or a ceremony to other places and times, naturally taking into account the obligatory evolution and variation of things. But although (we somewhat expected this!) the scribes of the land left us scholarly nomenclatures listing the placements of professionals of the clergy, the duties and specific obligations that corresponded to those names (which are often obscure) are not explained anywhere, or only within the detail of a few rituals, which therefore leaves us with a vague, incoherent idea of them. No doubt the ancient

Mesopotamians had a better idea, even if they did not have a generic term, in Sumerian or Akkadian, to designate the "clergy" as such. However, rituals scrupulously describe the role of a certain officiant during a ceremony, which clarifies his activities more than his function:

> [12] . . . The *kalû* priest, standing, will then sing the chosen hymn. . . . [21] Then, another *kalû* will sing the *eršemma* lament, accompanied by kettle drums. . . . After which a *šangû* priest, in front of (the statue of) the goddess Ištar, will pour from his *šâhu* cup a libation of water; and a *pašîšu* priest will do the same before the inscription (marked on the statue); another, to his right, and another, on his left.[7]

But those were scattered and common gestures, noted in their order of occurrence, and it would be quite a stretch to claim to be able to derive from them an overview of the roles assigned to the *kalû,* the *šangû,* the *pašišu,* and the others. Therefore, it is wiser, for lack of enlightening documentation, simply to leave each one with their original denomination without claiming to go any further. At the cost of a more scholarly approach, let us look at a few descriptions gleaned from many varied contexts, to further our understanding, to some degree, of a few clerical specialties. It is important to note that as in the case of the names of divinities, most of the oldest designations of priests were Sumerian, sometimes transposed into Akkadian or translated: there is therefore a chance that most of the clerical and thus liturgical tradition originated with the Sumerians, even if their Akkadian successors made some modifications later on.

The king was also the sovereign pontiff, a position that he had undoubtedly exercised fully in the most distant periods, perhaps also as an heir to the Sumerians. But in time he rid himself of the title, keeping only its most prestigious functions.

The same archaic influence of the Sumerians might explain the importance of women in the liturgical service and the clergy. The Mesopotamians were proud of this and readily noted the absence of priestesses as marking the primitivism of certain foreigners: "whose god knows no consecrated *nugig* or *lukur* priestess."[8]

At the top of the clerical hierarchy, all of whose members were regularly attached to *one* divinity, in *its* temple, the officiants were designated by a single word, a masculine or feminine e n, "Lord/Lady." Let us use the terms "archpriest" in the temple of a goddess (e.g., Inanna in the Éanna of Uruk) and "archpriestess" of a god (e.g., Enlil in the Ékur of Nippur). This complementarity suggests, at least in the present case, a strict connection between the priest and the divinity; and the splendor of the cultic decorations of these "superior priests" suggests that each one was more or less considered to be the alter ego of his or her complementary divinity, even on the conjugal, and therefore sexual, level. The Sumerian term that designated a female cleric who had almost as high a position as the archpriests was nin.dingir, "Lady Goddess" (in Akkadian, *entu*, from the Sumerian en feminized). It, too, suggested the same complementarity, including a ban on becoming pregnant, as these priestesses were "saved" for the gods.

In the rest of the clerical cohort, which, like other sectors of society, seems to have been rather well organized, each with its "head" or "chief" (gal/*rabû* and ugula/*waklu*), women appear always to have maintained their feminine role: devoted, as women, not only to the gods, as we have just seen, but also to men. In that land where the primary goddess, Inanna/Ištar, was the patron of "free love," prostitution was not far removed from religion, even if, in time and with Semitization (?), it is not clear how the practice evolved. A number of priestesses seem to have practiced such prostitution; we do not know whether they practiced it in their professional or personal lives. We are aware of a few "specialists": the nu.gig (Sumerian, meaning unknown), called *qadištu,* "the consecrated," in Akkadian; the nu.bar, in Akkadian *kulmašîtu,* both untranslatable; *ištarîtu,* "consecrated to Ishtar," who were not considered mere prostitutes (terms for prostitutes were *ḫarimtu*/sal.kar.kid, "the separate," and *šamḫatu,* "the joyous," both terms without religious connotation). A woman who had an opposite role, but no doubt in the name of the same religious views, was called lukur (Sumerian, "servant of the temple," "hierodule") or, in Akkadian, *nadîtu* ("left fallow" due to the prohibition against pregnancy). Not only was she forbidden, under penalty of death, from frequenting "bad places," notably the "cabarets," but she might have been forced to live more or less cloistered and "in a community," in the *gagû,* a sort of nunnery, outside the temple. They were the daughters of local faithful (like most priestesses, especially of high rank, they were refined and exceptionally cultivated, could read and write, and some of them composed beautiful poems) and at a young age were promised to a god by their families and spent their time either doing "needlework" or, more willingly, conducting business, simultaneously demonstrating, at least in their copious correspondence, an astonishing piety. One of their group played the principal role during the ancient *hieros gamos,* or holy marriage ceremony (see below).

Unlike their female counterparts, the priests were apparently devoted only to the divinities and to the ceremonial implied by their cult. The highest ranking in their normal hierarchy would have been the *šangû* (from the Sumerian sanga, perhaps related to the name of authority *iššakku,* itself derived from the Sumerian ensi?). We have seen him cited above, during a ritual, and officiating with two other representatives of the clergy: *kalû* (from the Sumerian gala), for whom was notably reserved the execution of laments and sad songs; and *pašîšu* (the past participle of the verb *pašâšu:* "to anoint," possibly stressing a votive "anointing" that he received). There were many others, which it would be tedious to present and even to list. Some bore the Akkadian title of *erib bîti,* "admitted to the temple," to highlight their frequent participation in services and the fact that they moved around freely in the temples, which was most certainly not the case with the general populace. The *ramku* (in Akkadian, "sprinklers"), for example, were primarily responsible for the many purifications with lustral water. And a whole division specialized in music and song: besides the *kalû,* there were the *nâru* (nar), the *zammeru,* and so on. Some appear only rarely, such as the *šešgallu* (Akkadianized from the Sumerian šeš.gal, literally, "big brother," "older brother"), who had almost no function (or hardly ever bore that title) except on certain liturgical occasions such as the feast of the New Year. We will later look at the essential functions of the members of the specialized clergy in the section on the sacramental cult.

Since homosexual love was perfectly tolerated in the land, provided that it did not harm anyone, it should not be surprising to see professional homosexuals here, as if to balance the "religious" prostitutes mentioned above: the *assinnu,* the *kurgarru,* the *kulu'u,* and even, on occasion, the *kalû,* who had rather a bad reputation in this regard, although we do not really know why. Nor do we know under what conditions they exercised their profession or their duties. But we occasionally see them dressed as women, holding strictly feminine accessories (such as a spindle) in their hands in addition to manly weapons, as if to point out their sexual ambiguity, and taking part, at least in honor of Ištar, in ritual, ambiguous, or lascivious dances. They were not, however, formally integrated into the clerical corps, and their specific designation referred above all to their condition and to their way of making love. They did not perhaps in fact belong to the clergy and the temple and were summoned there only occasionally to play their role in a few specific ceremonies.

This was the case for many professional people, in themselves foreign to the sanctuary and its occupations, but whose services were called upon when needed. Certain rituals required the celebrant to appeal to such professionals: a carpenter, a metalworker, a butcher . . . to create a certain wooden object, a certain precious piece of jewelry, as required by the ceremonial, or to "behead a sheep" that was to be sacrificed. Cooks must be considered separately, however: in that capacity they were indeed members of the clergy and played an active role in the "service to the gods." They no doubt had their homes within the confines of the temple, where they were needed every day. Did the other independent workers live in town, or were they settled within the holy perimeter along with their tools and their workshops? The latter case is certain only for those who took care of everyday needs: aside from cooks, those who did laundry, maintenance, cleaning, and so on. It is possible that at least the greatest sanctuaries thus assembled *intra* (or *extra?*) *muros* a group of "specialists" and technicians, who, without being strictly speaking members of the college of priests, were habitués of and collaborators in the temples, and lived there as priests did.

Some high-ranking priests, of both sexes (such as the two e n noted above), had their official dwellings in the temple, in what one called, in Sumerian, the mi.pàr (of obscure meaning), Akkadianized into *giparu*. In addition, the priests of apparently all categories were expected to learn how to perform their duties, which could be more or less complicated; and, except for those who had second-level positions and duties, the priests were required to read and write and to learn Sumerian, which necessitated many years of education in a school that was no doubt within the confines of the temple or connected to it, with teachers, workshops for preparing tablets, and libraries. The temple, no doubt, even more than the palace, was an intellectual center, and more than one religious, literary, or scholarly work must have been created there.

The "houses of the gods" therefore, with their sanctuaries—their "hearts"—with their rooms and buildings devoted to the cult, and with the necessary personnel, were true "cities," sorts of sacred neighborhoods ("the city of the gods"), where many men and women, foremost, naturally, the priests, lived together near their divinities, whom they served according to their special roles.

The priests lived *within* the temple and made their living *from* it, according to the rule: "the priest lives off the altar." However, because we lack relevant documents, we are unable to unravel the details of their daily lives: economic, social, and even personal. Apart from a few sparsely noted details, we do not even know how they looked during the ceremonies in which they officiated. Ancient images sometimes show them entirely nude; but that practice, inherited perhaps from the ancient Sumerians, must have rapidly died out. Others present them "disguised" for the event, notably as fish: no doubt to represent the "holy carps," a reference to the Seven Sages, civilizers of the land, in the famous myth related by Berossus.

The resources of the clergy are described no more clearly. We know only that, thanks to the intelligent exploitation of its lands, its herds, and its other goods, not to mention the opulent donations of the king, their "curator," and of other faithful, sometimes from throughout the land, the temple formed a true economic power, so rich that it occasionally played the role of moneylender and banker. There was also, as we will soon have occasion to note, the vast accumulation of food offered each day to the gods. In truth, the priests normally wanted for nothing, which did not, however—it is human nature—put a stop to corruption.

The Maintenance of the Gods

Our religious vocabulary is strongly influenced by biblical ideology, and one of its central terms is "sacrifice," which we take only in its *negative* sense: we believe we "sacrifice," religiously speaking, in order to lose something, to renounce it, to suppress it, to destroy it, thinking that by doing so we are paying homage to God or expiating our sins. In Mesopotamia, the corresponding term (siskur in Sumerian and *niqû* in Akkadian) was understood, immediately and everywhere, as something *positive*. Every "sacrifice" was exclusively a gift, an offering, presented to a divinity for its benefit or pleasure, something that was necessary, useful, or agreeable to that divinity: an immolated animal ("sacrificed" in the usual sense of "destined to death"); a beverage poured as a libation and thus transmitted to its recipient; a precious or rare object, which the recipient was imagined to need, or want, to derive benefit or pleasure from it.

The cult, and this was only logical, was therefore necessarily anthropomorphic, as well: if the gods had created human beings, as
was taught in *Atraḫasîs,* it was, from the gods' point of view, out of
necessity, out of the need for material goods that humans alone were
able to produce and present to them. Through their industry, their
technology, and their work, humans not only met their own needs
but, above all, out of natural vocation and by virtue of the will of
their creators and masters, functioned as servants and providers for
the gods. From such a perspective, religious behavior focused on that
fundamental duty of "maintaining" the gods: of providing them
with all the goods and services, and luxury, that were indispensable
to them; not, of course, to keep them alive—were they not by nature immortal?—but to guarantee them, like the subjects their king,
an existence that was not only bearable but opulent and pleasant,
as befitted the masters of the universe.

It goes without saying that on religious occasions the beneficiaries of such maintenance were represented by their statues, their images, which ensured their actual presence in the temple.

The area in which we can perhaps best grasp this religious notion,
which is so far from our own, is that of the *feeding of the gods,* a primary necessity, daily and perpetual, concerning which we are for-
tunately rather well informed, as much as concerns the specific food
as its preparation and consumption. A good number of "technical"
terms evoking acts of the daily cult imply a reference to food and to
its provision: *kurummatu* (pad in Sumerian), *nindabû* (from the Sumerian ninda.ba, "to offer bread"), *sattukku* (sá.dug), whose precise
liturgical meanings are not always clear.

Dating from the second half of the third millennium, and continuing practically up to the end of Mesopotamian civilization around
the beginning of our era, a great number of tablets we have found
illustrate perfectly, each in its own way, many aspects of that daily
"sacrificial feeding," which made up the essential part of the cult.
Some of the tablets appear to be lists of divinities, of a city or a
temple, and mention the various rations of food that were respec-
tively apportioned to them, proportional to their dignity or their
importance—in other words, they note the devotion that the faithful demonstrated toward them.

But we above all have a true torrent of information relating to the
provisioning of the sanctuaries: the recording of quantities, sometimes quite impressive, of food of all sorts, conveyed to the temples

and placed in their storerooms. We have learned the most fascinating information from the thousands of tablets excavated at the ancient site of Puzuriš-Dagan (present-day Drehem), a short distance to the southeast of Nippur, the old religious capital of the land. These tablets concern the famous Ékur, the major temple of Enlil, at Nippur. The huge amount of documentation that has been dug up, dating from the end of the third millennium, allows us to envision a sort of enormous warehouse in this small locality and an immense livestock yard, augmented and provided by "shipments" (mu.du in Sumerian and *šurubtu* in Akkadian) from the governors of all the cities and towns of the land, who made their donations in a sort of duly calculated "rotation" (in Sumerian, bala), whose system recalls that of the Greek amphictyonies. Provisions of all sorts are mentioned: grain, fruits and vegetables, dairy products, all types of large and small livestock and fertilizer, game, and so on. To give an idea, here is just a snippet from one of those texts in which livestock is recorded—curiously counted in multiples of 6:

> For the ceremony (?) of the first of the month there was sent:
>
> —from the city of Umma: 6 steer three years old; 24 cows two years old; 360 liters of butter, and as much cheese.
>
> —from the locality of Maškan-dudu: 240 sheep; 240 goats; 180 lambs; 120 ewe-lambs; 60 pigs.
>
> —from the locality of Bàd-an: 180 sheep; 420 goats; 120 lambs; 120 ewe-lambs; 160 fowl; 60 pigs.
>
> —from the city of Maškan-šapir: 120 sheep; 120 lambs; 120 ewe-lambs; 120 fowl.
>
> . . . .
>
> —from the locality of Urusagrig: 40 sheep and 20 goats.
>
> —from the city of Isin: 30 sheep and 20 goats. Rotation of the governor of the city of Sippar.[9]

We do not know the ultimate destination of this mass of animals for slaughter. It is possible that the capital at that time, Ur, kept its tithe from it and that some animals were sold to enrich the coffers of the Ékur and its clergy. But since, after all, the primary purpose was to "feed" the divinities of the Ékur, that must necessarily have been how most of these offerings were ultimately used.

Since we are unable to respond to specific questions on those points for that period of time, perhaps, taking a giant leap across the centuries, it will be enlightening to insert here the text of a famous tablet found in Uruk from the third century B.C., which explains rather distinctly the cultic use that was made of so much food.[10] The well-known conservatism of the liturgy in Mesopotamia, as everywhere, enables us, since we are not seeking a meticulously recorded history in chronological order here (which would be, as we have already said, impractical for our purpose), basically to disregard such gaps in place and time.

The arena for the document in question was one of the great temples of Uruk, whose titular gods were Anu, his wife Antu, and his "hierodule" Ištar (another hierodule appeared under the name and personality of Nanaya), with their "court" of minor divinities. Our tablet transcribes a ritual program employed to oversee, over the entire year, the quantities and quality of food necessary for the daily maintenance of the gods. The continuous ceremonial of the daily cult included the four meals that were to be provided every day to the divinities of the temple: a large and a small meal in the morning and the same in the afternoon. Such was apparently the common routine in the land, at least among the rather well off inhabitants. Our list has ninety-nine long lines. Without citing it from beginning to end, we will at least give an idea of it, for it says a great deal that is of interest to us here.

The text successively deals, in as many paragraphs, with the four elements that seem to have made up, at least at a certain level of Mesopotamian society, a meal worthy of that name: (1) beverages (primarily beers, of various qualities; also wine and milk); (2) grain products (barley and spelt, in flour form, to make "round loaves," "biscuits," and cakes [?]); (3) fruit (dates, of various quality; figs, grapes, raisins, as well as "sweets" and treats, not specified otherwise, and whose precise meaning, as well as composition, escapes us); and (4) meat (cows, sheep, some previously fattened on milk or barley; geese, ducks, and other fowl, as well as their eggs). They had evidently chosen here only the products most worthy of the presumably refined palates of the recipients, since other, much more common food—such as pork and fish—is not listed, apparently being viewed as not fitting for the gods' table, as well as vegetables and various condiments, the choice of which referred to the preparation of the dishes (we have learned this from our "culinary texts"). Here, then, is only the section dealing with grain products:

Every day of the whole year, for the principal regular offerings [we would say: "to assure the daily office, fixed once and for all—the gods, like humans, eating every day!—and constant, which made up the ordinary liturgy"], there will be needed 648 liters of barley and spelt, which the millers (after turning it into flour) will provide daily to the temple cooks, in order to prepare the four meals for Anu, Antu, Ištar, and Nanaya, as well as for the other minor gods around them. From the above they will take 486 liters of barley flour and 162 liters of spelt flour, from the mixture of which the cooks [the bakery was thus part of the kitchen] will prepare and bake 243 "round loaves." Out of that total the same cooks will prepare and deliver 30 round loaves for the table of Anu: that is, each time 8 loaves for the large and the small morning meals, and 7 for the large and small afternoon meals. 30 loaves will also be needed for the meals of Antu; 30 for those of Ištar; 30 for Nanaya; and 15 for the four meals of the divinities in their company. Also to prepare: 1,200 "biscuits" (fried?) in oil, to accompany the "cakes" of fine dates. . . .

Of note: the miller, when he mills the above-mentioned grain, must in doing so recite the formula: "O celestial Plow! In the field we harnessed the seeder plow! . . ."; and, while kneading the dough, and putting it in the oven to make loaves, the cook will recite this formula: "O Nisaba, holy Abundance, rich Allowance! . . . (We have not found the texts of these two prayers.)[11]

Here, also to enlighten us, is the end of the paragraph devoted to meat. Their daily total is rather astounding in itself, when one realizes that it was meant to feed a dozen "people" at the most!

That which makes, in all, every day, for the four meals of the above-mentioned gods: 21 top-grade sheep, fattened and without flaw, fed on barley for two years; 4 specially raised sheep, fed on milk; 25 second-grade sheep, not fed on milk; 2 large steers; 1 milk-fed calf; 8 lambs; 30 marratu birds (wild bird, not identified); 20 turtle-doves; 3 mash-fed geese; 5 ducks fed on flour mash; 2 second-grade ducks; 4 dormice (?); 3 ostrich eggs and 3 duck eggs.[12]

If one adds up this meat-based food over the entire year, one obtains truly overwhelming figures, given the small number of those eating: 18,000 sheep; 720 steers; 360 calves; 2580 lambs, etc. Actually, the old stockyards of Puzriš-Dagan were not overly big!

At least in the presence of such a Pantagruelian feast we can imagine something of the richness, the magnificence, and excess of the gods' table and of the trouble that the ancient Mesopotamians took to feed their gods, or in other words, to ensure their daily liturgical cult—their "maintenance."

The above list concerns only the raw materials. All those provisions, before being served, had to be made edible and tasty by culinary work. It is plausible that cooks occasionally resorted to the ancient method—still in use—of direct cooking over fire, by grilling or rotisserie. But the thirty-five refined and scholarly recipes that have been discovered on three tablets from around the sixteenth century deal especially with "cooking with water." One can assume that this more versatile, more highly refined, and more subtle technique must have been used along with many others to prepare the food offerings with even more refinement and sumptuousness.[13] All of this further enhances our view of the regular liturgy in Mesopotamia of long ago.

Regarding the actual ceremonial of the meals that constituted the heart of the liturgy, we have almost no accounts. No doubt, in serving the gods, the food was presented to the images of the recipient gods on platters placed within their reach, in the temple cella, on those rich portable platters that at that time took the place of our dining tables (the Mesopotamian concept of sacrifice/offering hardly admitted an "altar" strictly speaking, on which one would have only "immolated" the victims; we know, with some certainty, of almost no such immolations) and in the richest and most precious serving dishes that could be found. The ritual cited above makes a few references to them: vases, goblets, cups, plates, and bowls of silver and gold, sometimes inlaid with rare jewels. One might conjecture that the statues of the gods, in their "holy of holies," were usually veiled with curtains and that only the priests dedicated to their personal maintenance were able to pull back the curtains to "contemplate their faces" and to serve them.

We may as well respond here to the question that immediately arises: how should we imagine the consumption of the food thus offered to the gods with the obvious intent of seeing them eat it, which was, however, impossible for their hieratic images to do? The direct response, which our archives do not appear to provide, is most likely found in a sort of supplement to the biblical Book of Daniel: "Bêl and the Dragon." "Following the ceremony of the laying out of the dishes, the priests carried them away"[14] to eat the food themselves, possibly sharing it with the other temple personnel (but according to what rules?) and possibly selling what remained. In any case, we can see how those outrageous meals must have played a role in the economy of the sanctuary.

The "four meals of the gods," which, from one year to the next, gave rhythm to the liturgical day in Mesopotamia, somewhat like our "canonical hours," were naturally not the only "feasts of the mouth" that were offered to the gods. There were others: official ones, sometimes banquets offered to a certain divinity or to all of them on festive or special occasions; and private feasts, which each individual, depending on his devotion, his opportunities, or his means, could offer, or rather perhaps have officially offered to the gods by an appropriate person, let us say, to thank the gods or implore them for some good fortune or favor. Thus, after a lion hunt King Aššurbanipal (668–627), who had killed four beasts, had himself represented pouring a libation onto the cadaver of one lion—in other words, something to drink in "offering" *(muḫḫuru)*—for Ištar, whose victorious "Bow" he mentions, to thank her for his triumph.[15] Everyone was thus free to make such offerings to the gods, primarily of food, appropriate to his devotion and to his means. In a ritual against bad dreams we find, addressed to the patron god of dreams: "The *bārû*-priest brings you (an offering of) cedar (perfume), the widow (only) madga-(and *kukkušu*)-flour, the poor woman (some) oil, the rich from his wealth brings you a lamb."[16]

That offering recalls that in Mesopotamia festive meals among mortals, and consequently the liturgical ceremonies for the gods, were often accompanied by the burning of incense *(nignaqqu,* "incense burners," borrowed from the Sumerian níg.na) made from myrrh, herbs, kindling, and aromatic shavings of juniper, cedar, and cypress, to enhance the magnificence and pleasure of the feast with their odor.

Music and song were similarly required at those feasts. Thus, it is quite likely that the official and ceremonial meals of the gods, especially the most festive ones, were accompanied by music from all sorts of instruments: stringed (e.g., lyres and harps), wind (e.g., flutes, horns, and trumpets), and percussion (e.g., large and small drums, tambourines, bells, and rattles), which are rather well documented in our archives, even if it is not always possible to find their modern equivalents or relatives in our own instrumentation, nor to know the true nature of their melodies, or whether the music was accompanied by recited or sung lyrics—but we will return to this later.

The Maintenance of the Gods in Their Daily Lives

Several allusions suggest that the gods were "washed" periodically and ritually, that baths were given to (the statues and images of) the gods, and that this gesture, through a concern for purification, cleanliness, and good health, which was shared among the great as well as the less great of the world, was in a realm different from that of the feeding in the "service to the gods."

We are much better informed about the gods' clothing, above all about their collections of outfits (túg.ḫi.a/*lubuštu*). Similar to lists of food, we have lists of clothing, such as the fifteen or so festive out-fits that King Nabû-apla-iddina of Babylon, in around 900, gave to the god Šamaš and to his partner goddess and wife.[17] We also have inventories of cash and of "trunks" or "armoires" (pisan/*pisannu*) in which treasures were placed and kept. Clothing and jewelry, could be locked up, preserved, and inventoried together. For example, here is a list from the Old Babylonian Period (around 1700–1600) concerning the goddess Ištar installed in the temple of the little town of Lagaba (site unknown), in the north of Babylonia. Here is its beginning and end:

1   2 finger-rings of gold,
     1 *vulva* of gold,
     19 fruit (-shaped beads) of gold,
     2 rods of gold,
5   2 breast-ornaments of gold,
     2 ear-rings of silver,
     1 pea (?) of carnelian,
     4 (beads of) lapis lazuli,
     6 cylinder seals,
10   2 stamp-seals (?),
     1 cord of yellow metal-alloy,
     6 breast-ornaments of ivory,
     1 great ring of carnelian,
     2 kaunakes,
15   3 [large] coats of linen,
     6 woolen ribbons,
     4 ribbons of flax (linen),
     5 beautiful gowns (?),
     1 tilt (?)
     . . . .
34   new addition in the case,
     2 beautiful gowns (?),
     2 loincloths,

37 dress of Inanna is this, which is
    ·   ·   ·   ·   ·   ·   ·   ·
    besides that in the case,
    under superintendence of Awel-Ishtar,
    Ahum-waqar,
    and Šamaš-gamil,
45 Dumuzi 27th
    of the year Samsuiluna, the king, made the throne for the
        shrine of Nin-gal.
    —it was the twenty-first of the reign of that king, which
        would bring us to 1728.[18]

Another famous inventory, from around 1400, was found in Syria, in the city of Qatna. It lists the treasures in a *šukuttu* (jewelry case) of the local goddess Nin-égal. Through the years the inventory was recopied four times, each time with the addition of new pieces that the faithful had contributed as offerings to the treasure. The inventory lists sixty-eight carefully described items, fifty-two of which are necklaces *(kišâdu)*, whose beads and pendants are counted and described (shape and color).[19]

The "maintenance of the gods" as concerned festive clothing and precious jewelry was thus in no way inferior to the pomp and ceremony surrounding their food offerings.

The "Social" Life of the Gods

The gods were not confined to the august dullness of their cellae. Like the kings in their palaces, the gods had in their temples and at their disposition palanquins *(tallu)*, carts *(narkabtu,* etc.), and transport boats *(eleppu,* etc.), in which they could, using their three-dimensional images, be taken in processions or travel elsewhere—always in the manner of sovereigns.

The theme of the "voyages of the gods" is found more than once in the religious and mythological literature. *The Visit of Nanna-Sîn to Nippur* is a typical example.[20] It is a rather long myth, in Sumerian, from the end of the third millennium, in the time when the kings of Ur governed the land. It relates in detail how, from his temple in Ur, the capital, the god Nanna-Sîn went one fine day by boat to Nippur (some hundred and fifty kilometers upstream) to visit "his father and mother," Enlil, the king of the gods, and Ninlil, his wife, in their great and famous sanctuary of Ékur. Nanna-Sîn first decides to go there (verses 1–16), and he praises the city, the goal of his

travels (17–36). In order to prepare a boat worthy of this solemn ex-
cursion, as a great one of this world might do, Nanna-Sîn sends em-
issaries charged with bringing back the best materials from everywhere in the land and beyond, precious and rare materials needed
to build all the pieces of a perfect vessel (37–82). Then there is a
break in the tablet covering the time of the building of the boat. He
then loads it with riches of all kinds which he plans to distribute os-
tentatiously along the way, and above all to bring as offerings to the
temple of Enlil (156–96). And then he leaves (197). The convoy is
stopped five times along the way, as if to sidetrack it, especially the
treasures it is carrying, to the sanctuaries of the cities on its route:
Enegir, Larsa, Uruk, Šuruppak, and Tummal. But it continues right
along to Nippur (198–252), where it finally docks (253–58). Then,
following proper etiquette, Nanna-Sîn asks to be introduced into
the dwelling of his father, the Ékur, while showing the sumptuous
offerings that he has brought (259–308). Once in the presence of
Enlil he displays his gifts before him; and Enlil, very happy, offers a
great welcoming banquet for him (317–25). Nanna-Sîn then thanks
him for his magnificent welcome, and—this is his opportunity!—
presents him with a list of requests for the fortune and prosperity of
his own capital, Ur (327–39). Enlil grants him everything (340–48).
And the tale ends with an address to the king of Ur, to remind him
that he derives his power from Enlil, and to pray to that god to grant
him a long life (349–52).

Under the guise of a mythological tale, this is obviously a "pilgrimage" ritual through which the fruitful encounter of the two divinities, carried out by transporting the image of the son, Nanna-
Sîn, to that of his father, Enlil, was organized both as a testimony of
Ur's allegiance to Nippur and to its sovereign god, and as a request
for benediction and favor. The question remains as to whether in the
course of his pious journey Nanna-Sîn was represented by the king
of Ur in person or was represented through his cult statue alone.

All of this ritual movement of the gods' images, in both positive
and negative circumstances (just like the king and his court, the
gods' statues and effigies were sometimes held hostage by the conquerors in a war), again suggests that the images being moved were
truly believed to be the "gods" in person, and that their mobility
and "freedom" were an important part of the luxurious and blessed
life that was provided to them.

Prayer

Prayer, just like the maintenance of the gods, was a central activity of the cult, although it is viewed from a completely different angle. From the moment a person imagines the existence of invisible, imperceptible, supernatural figures above him whom the unsolvable enigmas of the world and of his own being force him to implore, supernatural masters to whom he attributes all-powerfulness as well as the ability to intervene everywhere in the affairs of the universe, above all in his own, it is inevitable that in times of need that person will turn toward those beings. And, however distant, sublime, and crushing he considers them, seeing them as his interlocutors, he tells them everything he has in his heart: his feelings, his desires, his fears, his anguish, his needs, his regrets, his repentance, and his dreams—everything that we sometimes feel forced to exteriorize, primarily in the vague hope that a positive response will be given to those requests. Prayer is above all individual and spontaneous: it is normally a primary and virtually instinctive religious gesture.

Given the dearth of personal testimonies, we are fortunate that a few examples of personal prayers to the gods have survived. On a tablet where he commemorates his restoration of the temple of Ištar in Arbela, as well as his scrupulous execution of the wishes of his father, Esarhaddon (680–669), with regard to his two sons, the great Aššurbanipal (668–627) continues:

> Thus I've done good for the gods and for men, for the living and for the dead. But then, why do illness and sadness, difficulties and prejudice continue to plague me? Discord in the land, complaining in my Palace, troubles and failures of all sorts, are constantly against me! Illness of the body and the heart have completely shriveled me up. I spend my time sighing and complaining. Even the day of the Great Feast I remain in despair. . . . O my god, reserve such a fate for the impious, and allow me to find happiness once again! How long are you going to abuse me so, and to treat me as one who respects neither gods or goddesses?[21]

In another tone, the king of Babylon, Nebuchadnezzar II (604–562), prayed to Marduk:

> What is there besides you, my lord? You have promoted the reputation and vouchsafed an honorable career to the king you love, whose name you pronounce, who is pleasing to you. I am the prince

whom you preferred, your handiwork. It was you who created me and vouchsafed me kingship over all peoples. According to your favor, O lord, which you are always ready to bestow upon all of them, make your sublime lordship merciful upon me, instill in my heart reverence for your divinity, grant me what you please that you sustain my life.[22]

We naturally do not have as many such expressions of profound emotions from commoners, even educated ones. But we can, here and there, either stumble upon them or infer them. In particular, the personal names given by parents to their children conveyed such sentiments, and almost all can be taken as "ejaculatory prayers": Dan-Nergal, "All-powerful is Nergal!" Rabi-melammu-šu, "Great-is-his(= the patron god)-supernatural-brilliance!" Šamaš-rêmanni, "O-Šamaš-take-pity-on-me!" Mannu-kî-Aššur, "Who-can-equal-Aššur?" Ištar-ummi, "Ištar-is-like-a-mother-to-me!" Everywhere we find the same positive attitudes toward the gods: a person admitted to being stunned by their luminosity, their transcendence, their majesty; one was aware of their good deeds and trusted in their benevolence; they were revered, feared, respected; and the expression of these feelings indeed constituted a form of prayer.

This manifestation of the heartfelt emotion evoked by the basic feelings toward the supernatural world, which were spontaneously addressed to its representatives, was introduced into the official cult and organized to accompany the various activities involving the maintenance of the gods. It was most likely the effect of the same logical transposition of royal etiquette, which always served as a model for that cult. People were not content simply to provide the sovereign and his entourage with the material consumer goods and services, the most indispensable, the most useful, the most exquisite. People were aware that, like us, they needed not only bread but also praise, celebrations, exaltation, confidence, flattery, glory, endless reminders of their prerogatives and their superiority, as well as the humble dependency of their subjects. What was said and repeated to kings had necessarily, a fortiori, to be said and repeated to the gods whose service one was seeing to. Such was the official, public, liturgical prayer: an essential component of the cult.

We do not have what is necessary to delve into the "origins" and follow the first developments of this verbal and literary aspect of religious behavior. It is, however, rather clear that, regarding the pantheon and a few other phenomena in their religion, the first dis-

cernible contribution in this area can be attributed to the Sumerians. It is obviously not that we assume the Semites lacked such a
way of addressing their gods. But it is a fact that the oldest known
official prayers in the land, the oldest addresses to the gods, the oldest appeals to their help, the oldest hymns to their glory and to that
of their residences, inseparable from them, were composed in Sumerian. When and how were these pieces recited and what place did
they have in the archaic liturgy? Since we know just about nothing
about that liturgy, we cannot answer these questions precisely. We
are at least assured that these venerable couplets must have been,
from the beginning, accompanied by music: solemnly chanted or
sung in the temple by qualified singers, solo or in a chorus, with the
accompaniment of various instruments.

In the third millennium several instruments gave their names to
compositions (tigi and adab, e.g., which were sorts of cymbals; balag
and zami, which were types of lyres), obliquely evoking in this way
their regular sonorous accompaniment, but also a certain number of
constants in style, imagery, as well as "metric" and "strophic" structure—as so many distinct literary genres. There were also other categories of prayers: "dialogues" (balbale), which were sung or modu-
lated by two people or two choruses, and "eršemma," whose name
evoked the "plaintive" tonality (er in Sumerian was "tears," "lamen-
tation"), regularly performed by female officiants, priestesses, their
very text written in that so-called feminine dialect (eme.sal) that
was reserved for them in literature.

After the disappearance of the Sumerian scholars and poets, their
Akkadian successors were at first content to imitate them, to translate and to adapt Sumerian hymns and prayers, like so many of the
other literary works. Still influenced by them, the Akkadians quickly
gave free rein to their own inspiration and genius, no doubt perpet-
uating ancient pieces—such as the eršemma, henceforth, however,
reserved for specialized priests, the kalû (which, given the ambiguous
reputation of those priests, no doubt justified the "feminine" eme.sal
in which they were always written)—while perfecting new ones, following the development and the requirements of their religion.

Other models and structures of official prayers thus saw the light
of day in the Akkadian language—even if they were still readily given
a name in Sumerian, since that remained the literary language of the
land. There were not only hymns and solemn prayers (ikribu) but
"prayers with raised hand" (a common gesture of both reverence

and communication: šu.íl.lá), "addresses" to Šamaš (ki.Utu.kam),
"prayers of repentance" *(šigû;* this word is not of Sumerian origin), "laments to appease the heart (of the gods)" (ér.šà.hunga), and others.

We do not have to lose ourselves here in the detail of this eu-
chology, of its presentation, its vocabulary and style, much less its
history, which is, moreover, not often discernible to us. It is a fact
that from the time of the Sumerians official prayer in Mesopotamia
had become literature. That is—*assueta vilescunt!*—it was quickly
"formalized," easily fixed into clichés, the reiteration of which muted
the earlier vivacity and fervor, invading the text to the detriment of
emotion and lyricism—a general defect, moreover, of the literature
of the land.

Instead of detailing its formularies, its themes, its images, its turns
of phrase and motifs, it will perhaps be better—as we have already
done with regard to "religious sentiment"—to cite *in extenso* a selection of a few "songs of glory" *(zamar tanitti):* hymns or speeches
that should give an even more "emotional" idea of the Mesopotamians' stance regarding prayer. Their religious sentiment, already sufficiently analyzed and defined, is expressed here quite clearly in a
profound attitude of fear and respect, of basic and "centrifugal" dependency, to which was readily added at times a strong conviction
of guilt and a pressing desire to free oneself from the misfortunes provoked by one's sins. The latter two motifs permeate specific types of
prayers and addresses to the gods, which are more immediately connected to the personal and "sacramental" cult; we will discuss this
at greater length below.

Here is an ancient hymn (end of the third millennium) in Sumerian, sung, perhaps, as a dialogue (balbale) to the god Ninurta. His
glory and good deeds are celebrated—an oblique way of counting
on him and of reconciling oneself with him, so that he will continue his benevolence, thus ensuring the prosperity of the land and
its sovereign:

    1   O Wellborn! O Wellborn!
        O king whom Enlil has named!
        O Wellborn! O Wellborn!
        Ninurta whom Enlil has named!
        I wish to celebrate your name, O my king!
        Ninurta, I, your man, your man,
        I wish to celebrate your name!
    5   O my king, the sheep has given birth to the lamb—

The sheep has given birth to the lamb—
The sheep has given birth to . . . the lamb,
And I, I wish to celebrate your name!
O my king, the goat has given birth to the kid—
The goat has given birth to the kid—
The goat has given birth to . . . the kid,
10   And I, I wish to celebrate your name!
O my king . . . !
My king, son of Enlil, I wish to celebrate your name!
You fill the canal with perpetual water,

. . . .

R.5   You make the speckled barley grow in the fields,
You fill the pool with carp and perch (?),
You make the reeds and rush grow in the cane-fields,
You fill the "forest" with wild grazers,
You make tamarisks grow in the steppes,
10   You garnish gardens and vineyards, with honey and wine!
And you will grant the palace a longer life! [23]

Again in Sumerian and dating, on the whole, from the beginning of the second millennium, here is a rather long "song," accompanied by percussion instruments: a hymn of a type called tigi, to the glory of the great Enki. He is covered here with praise, stressing how he was closely connected to the highest of gods: An and Enlil, to whom he was associated through his responsibilities and above all his power. The insistent reminder of his creative activity and his absolute power over the destinies of everything and everyone was obviously—a convenient, discreet, and well-known procedure in prayers of requests—a flattering invitation for him to once again deserve such admiration, by continuing to make the most favorable decisions for the land and for the people. The piece was composed in three equal parts, separated by what we call, very analogously, "response" and "antiphon," but whose Sumerian expression, sagidda and sagarra, referred to musical notation and thus completely escapes us. The tigi was composed on the orders of, and primarily on behalf of, the sixth sovereign of the ancient dynasty of Isin, Ur-Ninurta (1923–1896), and it was above all toward him that the author wanted to channel the benevolence and the efficacy of Enki (the public prayer did not render the common interest abstractly):

1   Master of the commanding eye, the one who is seated on the
      earth,
          whose heart, far-reaching, knows all things,

Enki, who spreads wisdom wide,
    noble leader of the Anunna,

expert who instituted incantations, word-rich,
    the one who keeps his eye on decisions,
guide who gives advice from sunrise to sunset,

5   Enki, master of all the right commands:
    I want to praise you the way you should be praised.

An, your father,
    king,
    the master who brought all seeds forth,
    who settled all the people on the earth,

made you ward of the *me* in heaven and earth,
    raised you up their prince—

    to open the holy mouth of Tigris and Euphrates Rivers,
        to fill them full with joy,

    to make thick clouds give out the waters of *hegel,*
        to make them pour down *heavy* rain on all the fields,

10   to raise high the head of Ašnan over the furrows,
        to cover the steppe with grass and herbs,

    to plant orchards and gardens of honey and wine,
        to make them reach far like forests—

An, king of the gods, has made you author.

Enlil, his noble *sag-kù-gál* name,
    clothed in great awe,

presented you:
    you are the breeding master of all things,
    a junior Enlil.

15   Of him who alone is god of heaven and earth,
    you are his younger brother.

In your hand he has set all fate-decreeing below and
    above,
        just like him.

The right decision that comes out of your mouth
    is supreme [?].

With the god who makes the judgment clear,
    for the people who live out even to the very edge of *kur,*

    you tend their food and drink,
    you are their very father.

20 O Master, they praise your noble name as their god,
    the way they should.
           It is a *sagidda*

O Nudimmud, have your holy worded word lavish
Ur-Ninurta
    with glory,
    let him have no rival.
            It is its *gišgigal*.

Great master, you were first to walk on heaven and earth,
        you made your name shine forth.

O Enki, you gathered all the *me* that are,
        you fixed them at the Abzu.

    Of the holy dwelling place you chose,
        the Abzu,
        noble shrine . . . ,

25   you made its *me* foremost of the *me*,
        you brought its *giš-ḫur* acclaim.

        you made its shadow cover all the lands from sunrise to
            sunset,

        you made its awe and *melam* reach up to holy heaven,
            like a heavy cloud,

        you filled the Ekur with terror,
            that holy dwelling place of An and Enlil.

Given a scepter in its midst
        in keeping with
        the *me* dealt out to all the great gods,

30   you create myriad . . . seed [?],
        you planned and brought to life humankind.

O Father Enki, when you take your seat
    in your fate-decreeing dais
            It is a *sagarra*.

May king Ur-Ninurta who has been endowed with glory by
    Enlil,

he for whom the house of wisdom
            where you have gathered [?] expertise supremely

            you will have opened:
                become the leader of the Black Heads.

35 Terror fit for godship make the lion of kingship

shine out upon whatever he touches,
        as long as humans live.

Once presented the heavy tribute of the lower and upper sea,
Ur-Ninurta will carry it all to the Ekur of lapis lazuli.

May Enlil,
        having cast upon him his jubilant eye,

40 multiply good days and blissful years of life
        during his reign.

    O Father Enki, clothed in great awe,
        at your occult utterance

    let the Anunna, your divine brothers, rejoice with you.

    O son of An, noble one,
                who has accepted the glory they have given:
                your praise is good.

                It is a *tigi* of Enki.[24]

The "song" we will read next is a bit unusual, but its style, its lyricism (for once!), and its strength are both too surprising and too typical of great Sumerian poetry for us not to include it in this small eucological collection. In fact, it is part of a myth in which Enki (once again!) is supposed, like Sîn, to go visit Enlil in Nippur, ostensibly to ask him to approve of the new temple that he had had built in Eridu. It is thus more or less a liturgical song of dedication, and it is possible that it was composed on the occasion of the restoration of the sanctuary, which archeologists have attributed to King Amar-Sîn (2046–2038), a ruler of the Third Dynasty of Ur. Following a short reminder of the circumstances of the renovation of the sanctuary, Enki's "page," Isimud, sings a vibrant and rather admirable praise of it: it is clear that through the building in which the god was believed to reside, it is indeed Enki himself, closely connected to his residence, that the poet wants to celebrate:

1   In those days,
            once the fates had been decreed,
        after the year *ḫegal,* heaven-born,
        had broken through the earth,
            spreading through the land like plants and herbs,
        King Enki,
            lord of the Abzu,
5   Enki,
            lord who decrees the fates,
        built, of silver and lapis lazuli blended as one,
            his house:
        its silver and lapis lazuli, luminous as the day,
        the shrine sent joy through the Abzu.

    The *mùš-kù,* with cunning hand turned out,
            breaking free of the Abzu,
10 press up to Nudimmud, the lord.

The silver house he built there,
    decked it out with lapis lazuli,
    adorned it overall with gold.

In Eridu by the bank he built the house,
its bricks discoursing, and its echoes ring.
15 Reed hedges roaring like a bull,
the house of Enki, resounding,
nighttimes the house carries praise to its king,
        sings it sweetly.

Sukkal Isimud to king Enki
    with affection speaks,
stands at the house,
    pours forth the voice,
20 stands at the brickwork,
    gives voice:

"House built up of silver and lapis lazuli,
whose base is planted in the Abzu,
treasured by the prince out of the Abzu,
feared by the high Tigris and Euphrates:

25 "you send joy through the Abzu of Enki—

"your lock, unrivaled,
your bolt, a fearsome 'noble beast,'
your roof-beam, the 'Bull of Heaven,'
    a *mùš-kù* cunningly turned out,
your mat, lapis lazuli,
        adornment for the roof-beam,
30 your vault, a bull with horns raised high,
your gate, a 'noble beast' gripping a man,
your doorsill, a lion rising up against a man—
Abzu, pure place, decorous,
Sea House:[25] your king has set his foot towards you.

35 "Enki, king of the Abzu,
adorned your foundation with carnelian,
honored you with sacred incantations.

"House of Enki that fires the *lalgar*,[26]
    bull that presses closely to its king,
40   that roars with lust,
        that reechoes in harmony,
Sea House with reed hedges tied together by Enki,
    you from whose midst the lofty dais is raised up,
    whose threshold is the arm of the heavenly *mùš-kù*,
Abzu, pure place, where the fates have been decreed,
45 The cunning lord, king Enki,
Nudimmud, lord of Eridu,

in the 'wild ram's' midst—on which no man has ever
   gazed—
has had your *abgal* loose his hair down over his back."

"Eridu, beloved of Enki,
50   Sea House, brimming over with *ḫegal*,
          Abzu, life of the land,
              beloved of Enki,
          House built on the edge,
              fit for the *me* of crafts,
Eridu, whose shade stretches over the midst of the sea,
          the billowing sea, unrivaled,
55   the high river, awesome,
              that strikes terror in the land,
Sea House, powerful,
          noble,
          firm-standing,
House by the seaside,
          a lion in the midst of the Abzu,
Noble House of Enki that pours wisdom over the land:

"your din, like the rising high river,
60   makes music for king Enki,
          sweetly at his holy house it plays it,
              the lyre,
              the *algar*,
              the harp,
              the *algarsurra*,
              the *ḫarḫar*,
              the *sabitum*,
              the *miritum*,
              that fill the house,
the sweet sound, the lip-freeing harp,[27]
65   there resound, according each its own feeling,
          eagerly the holy *algar* of Enki plays for him,
          the seven *tigi* resounded there.

"unbending the command of Enki,
[his] word thus firmly grounded."

70 [Thus] at the brickwork did Isimud give voice,
     at the Sea House sweetly he sang.[28]

After this, the tale of Enki's voyage to Nippur continues, along with
his fortunate encounter with Enlil.

Next is a liturgical "song" in Akkadian (divided into quatrains) of
completely different tone, sung to the glory of Ištar, that supernatural figure who was, nevertheless, so "human." It, too, ends with a

prayer for the king, Ammiditana (1683–1647), the fourth successor of Ḫammurabi, around the end of the Old Babylonian Period. The king therefore remained at the center of the liturgical cult: he presided over it as "curator" of the temples and as chief purveyor of the gods, and he was supposed also to be the primary beneficiary of that cult.

i

Sing of the goddess, most awe-inspiring goddess,
Let her be praised, mistress of people,
    greatest of the Igigi-gods.
Sing of Ishtar, most awe-inspiring goddess, let her be praised,
Mistress of women, greatest of the Igigi-gods.

ii

She is the joyous one, clad in loveliness,
She is adorned with allure, appeal, charm.
Ishtar is the joyous one, clad in loveliness,
She is adorned with allure, appeal, charm.

iii

In her lips she is sweetness, vitality her mouth,
While on her features laughter bursts to bloom.
She is proud of the love charms set on her head,
Fair her hues, full-ranging, and lustrous her eyes.

iv

This goddess, right counsel is hers,
She grasps in her hand the destinies of all that exists.
At her regard, well-being is born,
Vigor, dignity, good fortune, divine protection.

v

Whispers, surrender, sweet shared captivation,
Harmony too she reigns over as mistress.
The girl who invokes (?) finds (in her?) a mother,
Among women (?) one mentions her, invokes her name.

vi

Who is it that could rival her grandeur?
Her attributes are mighty, splendid, superb.
Ishtar this is, who could rival her grandeur?
Her attributes are mighty, splendid, superb.

vii

She it is who stands foremost among the gods,
Her word is the weightiest and prevails over theirs.
Ishtar stands foremost among the gods,
Her word is the weightiest and prevails over theirs.

viii

She is their queen, they relay her commands,
All of them bow down before her:
They go to her (in) her radiance,
Women and men fear her too.

ix

In their assembly her utterance is noble, surpassing,
She is seated among them as an equal to Anu their king,
She is wise in understanding and perception.
Together they make their decisions, she and her lord.

x

There they sit together on the dais
In the temple chamber, abode of delights.
The gods stand in attendance before them,
Their ears awaiting what those mouths will command.

xi

Their favorite king, whom their hearts love most,
Ever offers in splendor his pure offerings.
Ammiditana offers before them
His personal, pure libation of cattle and fatted lambs.

xii

She has asked of Anu her spouse long life hereafter for him,
Many years of life for Ammiditana
Has Ishtar rendered to him as her gift.

xiii

By her command she gave him in submission
The four world regions at his feet,
She harnessed the whole of the inhabited world to his yoke.

xiv

What she desires, this song for her pleasure
Is indeed well suited to his mouth,
        he performed for her Éa's own word(s).
When he heard this song of her praise, he was well-pleased
    with him,
Saying, "Let him live long, may his (own) king always love
    him."

O Ishtar, grant long life enduring to Ammiditana,
        the king who loves you, (long) may he live![29]

The next prayer, addressed to Marduk, also in Akkadian, adds a
certain nuance (which is the foundation of many others) not only
by insisting on the greatness and the glory of the god it is celebrating but also by advancing a feeling of guilt, of "sin" and of fault, as

well as an awareness of the punishment to be expected for those misdeeds, and a request for absolution and for pardon. These feelings are expressed in many public and, especially, private prayers.

1 O warrior Marduk, whose anger is the deluge,
   Whose relenting is that of a merciful father,
   I am left anxious by speech unheeded,
   My hopes are deceived by outcry unanswered,
5 Such as has sapped my courage,
   And hunched me over like an aged man.
   O great lord Marduk, merciful lord!
   Men, by whatever name,
   What can they understand of their own sin?
10 Who has not been negligent,
        which one has committed no sin?
   Who can understand a god's behavior?
   I would fain be obedient and incur no sin,
   Yes, I would frequent the haunts of health!
   Men are commanded by the gods to act under curse,
15 Divine affliction is for mankind to bear.
   I am surely responsible for some neglect of you,
   I have surely trespassed the limits set by the god.
   Forget what I did in my youth, whatever it was,
   Let your heart not well up against me!
20 Absolve my guilt, remit my punishment,
   Clear me of confusion, free me of uncertainty,
   Let no guilt of my father, my grandfather, my mother,
        my grandmother, my brother, my sister,
        my family, kith, or kin
   Approach my own self, but let it be gone!
   If my god has commanded (it) for me,
        purify me as with medicaments.
25 Commend me into the hands of my (personal) god
        and my (personal) goddess for well-being and life,
   Let me stand before you always in prayer, supplication, and
        entreaty,
   Let the fruitful peoples of a well-ordered land praise you.
   Absolve my guilt, remit my guilt!
   O warrior Marduk, absolve my guilt, remit my guilt!
30 O great lady Erua-Sarpanitu, absolve my guilt,
   O Nabu of the good name, absolve my guilt,
   O great lady, Tashmetu, absolve my guilt,
   O warrior Nergal, absolve my guilt,
   O gods who dwell <in> Anu's <heaven>,
        absolve my guilt!
35 The monstrous guilt that I have built up from my youth,
   Scatter it hence, absolve it sevenfold.

Like my real father and my real mother,
Let your heart be reconciled to me.
O warrior Marduk, let me sound your praises![30]

From the dozens of prayers that have been found, we could cite even more varied examples, both public and private, from all times, throughout the endless history of the land. To suggest, at least, the wealth of themes and eucological schemas, let us in concluding at least point out a local procedure—original and completely unique—of addressing the gods: by correspondence! Based on the model and in the style of missives, private or official, of which we have thousands of examples from just about all times, a certain number of requests were composed, in Sumerian, first, and later in Akkadian, and were addressed (this is the word!) personally to the divinities from whom one hoped to obtain some advantage or favor. This type of "written request" was not reserved for personal needs, and the author, either clearly presented or more or less hidden, could just as well have been the king, or a representative of power, speaking in the name of all his subjects.

The piece we have here, from the Old Babylonian Period (around 1700), is rather on the private side. We know nothing about the circumstances of its composition or about its sender, whose name was very common and could thus have been borrowed or fictitious. It is interesting that it is addressed directly, not to the great divinity whom he wished to reach, but to his own personal god, whom he calls "his father," who was assigned the role of playing the honest courier. Discovered in several identical copies, the present letter was perhaps meant to be used in a scholarly tradition, given to students or apprentice scribes to copy as an exercise, or to be disseminated, as a model, so that it might be used just about everywhere.

1   To the god, my father,
    You will say (this):[31]
    Here is what Apil-Adad, your servant, says to you:
    "Why have you become indifferent to me?
    Who then could give you
5   someone like me?
    Send a message
    to Marduk, who loves you,
    to ask him to make my sin
    disappear.
    Then I will go (to the temple) to contemplate

10   your face
       and kiss your feet!
       Further, concern yourself (also)
15   with my family, big and small,
       and, for them,
       take pity on me!
       May your support reach me! [32]

The Liturgy

The cult itself, that is, the collection of religious practices performed
in the name of the gods, rendering them homage worthy of their
greatness, was normally celebrated in the temple by the clergy. It
blended rituals that involved the performance of some activity,
more or less complicated manipulations and mimicry that primarily related to the maintenance of the gods, with oral rituals, that is,
recited and sung prayers. The active rituals materially represented
the oral rituals, and the oral rituals gave a clear and intelligible voice
to the others.

The rituals were scrupulously put down in writing to transmit
them word for word and gesture for gesture down through the ages,
reflecting and contributing to the conservatism of the religious system. We have a sizable collection of such ritual tablets, which are of
varied content. Some, such as the one cited above, were simple accounts of provisions or articles to be used; others provide the script
for only one of the participants (thus we have a portion of the duties of the *kalû*); finally, others detail either a specific ceremony or a
more or less lengthy entire liturgy. To us the most important and the
most eloquent are the latter texts, because they enable us to consider and often to better understand a ceremony in the liturgy. Here
is a short excerpt, which is better than a lengthy commentary. It
comes from a tablet of the Seleucid Period and is thus relatively recent, but there is the greatest likelihood that, from copy to copy, its
text goes much farther back. It concerns a nocturnal celebration in
the temple of Anu in Uruk:

> . . . Once the priestesses of Anu in Uruk are seated at the door of
> the sanctuary, the officiant will mix wine and perfumed oil to make
> a libation to Anu, Antu, and all the gods of their entourage; and
> he will rub the mixture into the frame and panels of the afore-
> mentioned door. After which (for a fumigation) he will garnish

the golden incense burners and will offer the same gods a bull
and a sheep. The evening meal will then be served to them. . . . At
the first arrival of night, on the roof of the high chamber of the
ziggurat, at the moment when the stars of "Anu-the-greatest-
in-Heaven" appear and, in Ursa Major, of "Antu-the-greatest-in-
Heaven," hymns will be sung: "The King Anu Resembles the Marvelous Brilliance of the Stars" and "The Beautiful Star Is Rising." At
that moment a golden platter of offering will be prepared for the
two Stars.[33]

We have not discovered the complete texts of the two hymns
(alas, not unusual), but their titles allow us to guess the excessive richness of the eucological and liturgical literature, which has in large
part been lost. It sometimes happens, however, that chance stingily
smiles upon us. We should note here that the largest number of rituals—ordinarily the shortest but very detailed—relate to the exorcistic ceremonial, of which we will look at a few edifying examples.
For the time being, however, we will consider only the strictly "divine" cult, performed and intended only for the benefit of the gods.

The cult concerned "ordinary" and daily rituals, such as seeing to
the meals of the gods, and also those performed less frequently and
on more solemn occasions, such as "feasts" (ezen/*isinnu*). Some cultic activities were motivated by unforeseen, unusual circumstances.
We might cite here the ritual preparation of the hide of a cow intended to be stretched to form a sort of liturgical kettle drum called
a *lilissu*. We have almost complete details of this.[34] The animal, duly
chosen and "without defect," was led in great pomp into a defined location in the temple. There, during purifications and offerings to the
gods through exorcisms and prayers—some of which were whis-
pered into the animal's ear, as if to confide them secretly to it, thereby
conferring upon the animal responsibility for being a go-between
with the gods—it was sacrificed and skinned, following all rules. The
skin was then tanned, no less ceremoniously, and stretched over the
lilissu. Most celebrations, however, were cyclical, repeated regularly
to commemorate natural or supernatural events, dating from times
past, even lost in prehistory, or memorializing more or less recent
events, but they are all, in any case, almost always beyond our reach.
The succession of all these ceremonies, which were more or less solemn, depending upon where they took place and upon the specific
tradition, constituted what we might call the Mesopotamian "liturgical year."

The year (mu/*šattu*) itself, the major unit of the division of time, was composed of twelve lunar months (itu/*warḫu*), each with twenty-nine or thirty days (u/*ûmu*), depending on the moment when one noted the disappearance of the moon. If twelve months, give or take a few days, was not enough to cover the annual revolution of the sun, when the difference became troublesome the authorities proclaimed the addition of a "supplementary month," to be inserted after the sixth or, more commonly, the twelfth month. An intermediate sub-division, between the month and the day, resembled something like our week.

The list of twelve months, each with its own name, had a long history behind it, richly informative but too complex and moreover too little known for us to delve into it here. In the time of independent city-states, each city-state not only had its own routines and worldview, including, not least, its own pantheon, but each also had its own names for the twelve months. Month names were based on agricultural matters (the months of farming, of harvesting, etc.) and on local celebrations (the month when a certain feast was held). At the turn of the third millennium the calendar of the religious capital, Nippur, overshadowed all the rest and replaced the others almost everywhere, with a few exceptions (in the north of the land, notably in Assyria, as well as the "peripheral" kingdoms, such as Ebla and Mari). The Sumerian names were replaced by new terms, sometimes taken from Sumerian (such as Nisan, from nisag: "first fruit") or from Akkadian (Tešrît, "beginning"; Waraḫsamna [also spelled Arakhsamna], "eighth month"); some names are etymologically obscure. Some month names referred to traditional religious celebrations: Dumuzi, for example, the name of the fourth month, recalled the myth of the god of that name who was sent by Inanna/Ištar to the Netherworld, from which he climbed back six months later—an ancient image of vegetation, which disappears during the hot season only to reappear in the cold season.[35] The name Elul may refer to rituals of "purification" *(elêlu)* that were practiced during that month. Nisan marked the beginning of the year, although the month name Tešrît, "beginning," tells us that there had been a time when the new year was calculated as beginning six months earlier.

Here is the classic Mesopotamian calendar, which reached as far as Palestine and into the Bible and from there into Judaism. The months did not correspond exactly to ours, but overlapped them:

Hot Season
1. Nisan   (March–April)
2. Ayar   (April–May)
3. Siman   (May–June)
4. Dumuzi   (June–July)
5. Ab   (July–August)
6. Elul/Ulul   (August–September)

Cold Season
7. Tešrît   (September–October)
8. Arakhsamna   (October–November)
9. Kislim   (November–December)
10. Tebet   (December–January)
11. Šabat   (January–February)
12. Adar   (February–March)

We have enough information to attempt to reconstruct, at least in part—and at the cost of prodigious labor—the Mesopotamian liturgical year. Notably in "occasional literature," that written with a specific, ephemeral purpose and concerned with day-to-day occurrences, such as administrative and economic texts, as well as letters, we find a great number of assertions about and allusions to festivities and celebrations of divinities, of rituals and observations performed in their honor. One example out of a thousand is this delivery statement from the enormous archives of Puzriš-Dagan, dating from around 2040:

> 1 fattened cow for Enlil; 2 cows for Ninlil (his wife) . . .
> 1 fattened cow for Nintinugga (old warrior goddess) and
> 1 fattened cow for the Feast of the Sowing.
> Everything received by the functionary Lusaggata. Seal of control
> . . . Month of Kisig-Ninazu [the fourth month of the ancient calendar of Ur, whose Sumerian name referred to the "wool merchants" of Ninazu, who was also a warrior god and was linked to the infernal pantheon], the evening of the 15th. The year (of the king Amar-Sîn—2046–2038) after Lady Enmaḫgalanna was raised to the dignity of great priestess (e n) of Nanna.[36]

We learn here that at least in Ur, in 2040, around the 15th of the fourth month, a "Feast of Sowing" (noted elsewhere) was celebrated for Enlil and his divine entourage, accompanied by various offerings of meat-based food.

A few centuries later, around 1780 in Mari, a different feast is mentioned:

There was delivered: 1 liter of cypress ointment; 1 liter of an ointment compound (?), and 1 liter of cedar ointment, for the god Nergal on the occasion of the Feast of the Chariot of Nergal. In the
month of Liliatum (in Akkadian, "Evening"; it was the ninth month
in the calendar of Mari), the 7th (day), in the year after the year
when Ṭâb-ṣilli-Aššur was eponym.[37]

This festival centered on a chariot destined for the god of the Netherworld, Nergal, and was to be celebrated on the seventh day of the
ninth month.

More than a thousand years later (around 670), Marduk-šakin-
šûmi, one of the representatives of the king of Nineveh, Esarhaddon
(680–669), wrote a letter to his sovereign, no doubt not long before
the seventh day of the sixth month:

1   [To the king, my lord: your servant Marduk-šakin-šûmi . . .]
R.2   [The king, my lo]rd, knows that Bêl is dressed (for the festival)
        [on the 7]th of Tishri (VII); on the 8th day the gate (of the
        temple) is kept open, and the procession of Bêl sets out as in
        the month Nisa[n (I)].
        [The cerem]onies of the city of Der are conducted in the same
        way. [In fa]ct, [the king], my lord, should (now) decide what t[o
        d]o (with these ceremonies) [and send word] (about it).[38]

It is a matter here of a festival in honor of Marduk (Bêl, an Akkadian
word for Marduk), which was to take place, at least in Babylon (and
also in another city, Der, 100 kilometers to the east), after the sixth
day of the seventh month. A statue of the god was to be clothed in
advance in his ritual raiment, then led in procession. Another document, speaking of the same festival, fixes the opening of the doors
of the temple and the beginning of the procession on the eighth of
Tešrît. The ordering of the festival and the procession must have been
incumbent on the king. The one who reminded the king of this was
an "exorcist," no doubt connected to the temple where the ceremony
was to take place, and he must have had some authority there, at
the very least in liturgical matters, as delegated by the king.

We can easily imagine all the details that this literature might provide concerning the many official religious activities: their dates,
their cyclic recurrence, their dedicatees, their officiants, the order of
activities, and the rituals involved. To mute our enthusiasm we must
add that, with some exceptions, many details and important facts
are unintelligible to us. Those people spoke of things that they were

perfectly familiar with, and thus they could speak cryptically about certain elements or ignore them completely. For example, do the dates in them refer to the *writing* of the text, the *preliminaries* of the festival, or the *carrying out* of the festival? The ceremony might have included a vigil, a preparation of one or several days—whence possible differences in the dates given in different documents. And the duration of the celebrations was not necessarily indicated; that is the case above. A cloud of uncertainty thus diminishes our satisfaction in the information about the liturgical year available to us, whose complete contents will always escape us.

What emerges at the very least from an attempt to make use, even imperfectly, of such a vast amount of material is that the activity of the temples throughout the land must have been intense and constant. Very few days went by without here and there people celebrating some more or less grandiose and solemn ceremony, festivity, or unfolding of the "service to the gods." In fact—and this goes hand in hand with our interest in penetrating and understanding the religion of this ancient land—the king, the great one responsible for and governing the cult and the activity of the sanctuaries, and the clergy, the professional executors of the rituals, as well as the ones who lived off the cult, were not the only ones active in it. All Mesopotamians believed in their original and fundamental mission as servants and providers of the gods, and the divine cult was one of the cardinal points and the primary driving force of their political lives.

To obtain a better idea of the luxury and the splendor of that environment, without getting lost in a labyrinth of details, we will set our gaze on two revealing moments of the liturgical year: a great festive ceremony and an important festival that concerned everyone.

HIEROS GAMOS

The *hieros gamos,* or "sacred marriage," of a pair of gods, the celebration of which no doubt dates from a long time ago—to the time of the Sumerians, who appear to have had a more "realistic," if not perhaps "too human," view of their divinities—is attested in documentation only from the end of the third millennium and the beginning of the second, in southern Mesopotamia, where we have recovered a huge amount of information about it. This risks being deceptive, however, as we might be tempted to extend the importance of the specific accounts to the entire history of the land, or even to other towns and other temples, about which we know nothing.

Here, at least, in a few words, is how things occurred, in Ur and in Isin, at the turn of the third millennium. The two "divine spouses" were Inanna and Dumuzi, probably an ancient "divinized" sovereign, whom the people traditionally greeted as the "first lover" of Inanna, who was well known as patron and model of physical love, all of which conferred upon the festivities an emotional and amorous, indeed, a frankly erotic tone. Preparations for and the celebration of the marriage gave rise to a series of love songs, a few of which have been found, that are sometimes sensitive and lyrical, always captivating, in which were recounted the first loving contact between the two "intended," in a tone that was tender and timid, yet passionate. Here are a few lines from one of the songs:

12   Inanna, at her mother's command,
     Bathed herself, anointed herself with goodly oil,
     Covered her body with the noble *pala*-garment,
     Took along the . . . , her dowry,
16   Arranged the lapis lazuli about her neck,
     Grasped the seal in her hand.
     The Lordly Queen waited expectantly,
     Dumuzi pressed open the door,
20   Came forth into the house like the moonlight,
     Gazed at her joyously,
     Embraced her, kissed her.[39]

The marriage itself was celebrated either in the temple or in the palace—our sources are not very explicit. Yet they stress a detail which is the most surprising and should be noted: the wedding night was actually consummated by the king in person, playing the role of Dumuzi, and by a lukur priestess playing that of Inanna. The carnal union of the two was believed both to concretely represent and to mystically "achieve" that of Inanna and Dumuzi. Here is an exalted and fiery song of one of those female officiants addressed to her royal lover, Shu-Sîn (2037–2029), the fourth ruler of the Third Dynasty of Ur, believed to describe, or to suggest, the wedding night:

1   "Bridegroom, dear to my heart,
     Goodly is your pleasure, honey-sweet;
     Lion, dear to my heart,
     Goodly is your pleasure, honey-sweet.

5   "You have captivated me, I stand trembling before you.
     Bridegroom, I would be carried off by you to the bedchamber;

     You have captivated me, I stand trembling before you,
     Lion, I would be carried off by you to the bedchamber.
     "Bridegroom, let me give you of my caresses,
10   My precious sweet, I would be laved [?] by honey,
     In the bedchamber, honey-filled,
     Let us enjoy your goodly beauty;
     Lion, let me give you of my caresses,
     My precious sweet, I would be laved [?] by honey.

15   "Bridegroom, you have taken your pleasure of me,
     Tell my mother, she will give you delicacies [?]
     Tell my father, he will give you gifts.

     "Your spirit—I know where to cheer your spirit,
     Bridegroom, sleep in our house till dawn,
20   Your heart—I know where to gladden your heart,
     Lion, sleep in our house till dawn.

     "You, because you love me,
     Lion, give me pray of your caresses,
     The lord my god, the lord my good genie,
25   My Shu-Sin who gladdens the heart of Enlil,
     Give me pray of your caresses.

     "Your place sweet as honey, pray lay a hand on it,
     Like a *gishban*-garment, bring your hand over it,
     Like a *gishban-sikin*-garment, cup your hand over it." [40]

The day after the wedding a great banquet (this was usual for all marriages) was offered to the divine spouses and to the people, there as witnesses to the ceremony, to prolong everyone's jubilation and to give the festival its joyous and liberating tone.

Our texts insist on the goal and the anticipated results of such a festival: it was to provide the land with abundance and prosperity, even more than "fertility" as such. For even if "mythology is not logical," we must remember that neither Inanna nor Ištar after her were ever wives, in the strict sense of the word, or mothers, which rendered them unsuitable to represent anything connected to maternity. It is undoubtedly preferable to view the celebration of the so-called marriage, on both the divine and the royal levels, as an affirmation that just like the god above, the king on Earth also in a certain sense received, along with the ability to ensure an heir through marriage, the fullness of his prolongable powers as an authentic and lasting ruler of the land, henceforth capable of fully exercising those powers for the good of his people. In any event, this was the festival of love, and what we read about it still conveys a bit of its emotional resonance to us.

For lack of documents, we know almost nothing about the way in which that annual celebration, which must have been held near the beginning of the year, possibly in the second month, was organized elsewhere and in other centuries, with other protagonists and, most likely, other rituals.

In the Neo-Assyrian Period, some thirteen or fourteen centuries later, at the very least in the north of the land, in Assyria, in Kalḫu/ Nimrud, the festival had lost its "realism," a possible effect of an already ancient change that has been readily attributed to the Semites. The king and the priestess no longer appeared in it, and things henceforth occurred only between the god and the goddess concerned—in Nimrud, it was Nabû and his "wife," Tašmêtu, whose cult had been imported from Borsippa, in Babylonia. Here is what an "official" wrote to King Esarhaddon around 670:

> On the 3rd of Iyyar in the city of Calah the bed of Nabu will be prepared; Nabu will enter the bed-chamber. On the 4th the return of Nabu (will take place). The crown prince knows (that) I am the overseer of the temple of Nabu, your god; I intend to go to Calah. The god will come out from the dark shrine of the palace; when he goes from the shrine of the palace into the park, a sacrifice will be offered there. The charioteer of the deity will go into the sacred stable; he will bring forth the god and carry (him) in the procession; (then) he will bring him in (again). He, proceeding with solemn pace, will go his way. The merchants who have their sacrifices ready shall perform them. Whoever offers 1 qa of his food may eat in the temple of Nabu. Let (the officiating priests) complete carefully the prescribed rites of their deity for the preservation of the life of the crown prince my lord; let them do whatever the crown prince my lord shall write. May Bel and Nabu, who in the month Shebat grant protection, guard the life of the crown prince my lord. May they prolong your reign to the end of time.[41]

Another officer of the king specifies and sums up the same ritual in these terms in a letter that he writes to him, perhaps at the same time:

> Tomorrow, (that is) on the 4th (of Iyyar) toward evening, Nabu and Tashmetum will enter the bedchamber. On the 5th, they shall be given of the king's food to eat.[42]

Apart from the "representation" of the wedding by the king and a priestess in person, the essential ritual was thus indeed the same as that of fifteen centuries earlier and in the south of the land. The festival took place at the beginning of the second month of the year, Ayar, and it happened in Kalḫu as in Babylon (since the author of the first letter above places Marduk [Bêl] on the same footing as Nabû). And the culmination of the celebration was, after a few preparations, the encounter of the two divinities in the marriage bedroom and in their marriage bed, where they were obviously each represented by their own statues. The next morning the "newlyweds" were offered the great traditional feast, in which the faithful could take part, at least those who were associated with the offerings. And the anticipated result of the festival was always to provide a long and happy life to the king and, consequently, prosperity to the people.

The *hieros gamos,* in sum, all the while honoring and "serving" the gods in an anthropomorphic perspective, was thus also a ceremony to reinforce the power of the king.

THE CELEBRATION OF THE NEW YEAR

Since we do not know as much about the innumerable other festivals that occurred throughout the land and that, century after century, marked the liturgical year, we cannot spend as much time on them. But it is a fact that the celebration of the New Year (in Sumerian, zag.muk, "threshold of the year"; in Akkadian, *rêš šatti,* "beginning of the year") was also very politically, as well as religiously and emotionally, charged. Its primary and essential significance was above all "cosmic." During the festival the gods were exalted in order to renew not only time, with the entrance into a new annual cycle, but the universe itself, as if the gods were re-creating the universe in order to launch it once again into continuing duration. Rituals and details of the ceremonies necessarily varied among specific towns and temples and more or less throughout time. We have uncovered fragments regarding the festival as it was celebrated here and there, in Uruk (involving Anu), for example, but above all in Babylon (fragments dating from around the end of the first millennium), where the festival, as was fitting, was centered on Marduk in the glorious Ésagil and its outbuildings. The festivities filled a dozen days, and although we have retained information concerning only the first half, we do have various scattered allusions that enable us to make a few reasonable conjectures concerning the rest of the schedule. Complex and quite varied, this ritual should give a true idea of the major fes-

tivals in the land. We shall provide a summary of the ritual by citing a few excerpts from it in order to make contact, as it were, with
that old Mesopotamian crowd, simultaneously and joyously celebrating its gods and the eternal rebeginning of everything organized
and ruled by those gods.

The succession of ceremonies was rationally divided into days, of
which the ordered schedule has been minutely noted. The first day
of Nisan, or the first day of the New Year, does not as such appear to
have had the importance that we traditionally confer upon it: it was
only the beginning of the festival. The temple was simply opened
and prepared, through purifications, for the imminent celebration.

> On the second day of the month Nisannu, two hours of the night
> (remaining?), the [šešgallu] priest shall arise and wash with river
> water. He shall enter into the presence of the god Bel, and he shall
> . . . a linen *gadalū* in front of Bel. He shall recite the following
> prayer.[43]
>
> O Bel, who has no equal when angry,
> O Bel, excellent king, lord of the countries,
> Who makes the great gods friendly,
> O Bel, who fells the mighty with his glance,
> Lord of the kings, light of mankind, who divides the portions—
> O Bel, your dwelling is the city of Babylon, your tiara is the
>   (neighboring) city of Borsippa,
> Broad heaven is the "totality of your liver."
> O Bel, with your eyes you see all things,
> [With] your oracles you *verify* the oracles,
> [With] your glance you hand down the law.
> [With] your . . . you . . . the mighty;
> When you look (at them), you grant them mercy;
> You show them the light, (and) they speak of your valor.
> Lord of the countries, light of the Igigi deities (who) bless—
> Who (does not speak) of you, does not speak of your valor?
> Who does not speak of your glory, does not glorify your
>   sovereignty?
> Lord of the countries, who dwells in the temple Eudul, who
>   grasps the hand of the fallen,
> Grant mercy to your city, Babylon!
> Turn your face to the temple Esagil, your house!
> Establish the "liberty" of the people of Babylon, your
>   subordinates.[44]

The text adds here that there are "twenty-one lines (of writing)" referring to a specific, secret prayer in the liturgy of the Ésagil: no one
was supposed to know it, except the officiant. After which:

[After] [the *šešgallu*] speaks the recitation, he shall [open the gate].
The *ēribbīti*-priests [shall arise] and perform their rites, in the traditional manner, [before] the deities Bel and Beltiya. (40) [The *kalū*-
priests and the] singers (shall do) likewise.[45]

What follows is in part lost: it appears that the *šešgallu,* after having fixed his (?) seal on the crown of Marduk, recited a new address
to that god about the "enemies of Babylon," cursed by Bêl for having
ravaged Babylon and other ancient religious cities (Uruk and Nippur,
in particular). A lacuna follows, which covered the rest of the day.

On the third day of Nisan,[46] two hours before the end of the night,
the *šešgallu* was supposed to wash himself in the water of the river
before saying a long prayer and, as on the previous day, have the
temple officiants enter so that each one could carry out his customary rituals. Three hours after the sun had risen, he had to see to the
preparation of two figurines, representing two figures whose names
are not mentioned, made of precious wood and covered with sheets
of precious metal: their dimensions and configuration were noted,
as was their use three days hence. To do this the *šešgallu* summoned
the craftsmen connected to the temple—the jeweler and the wood-
worker—to whom he gave the necessary materials (taken from the
temple storerooms): precious stones and gold, as well as rare wood,
and, to remunerate them for their work, he gave them pieces of
mutton.

On the fourth day of Nisan[47] there were the same morning ablutions of the *šešgallu,* who was then supposed to draw the curtain in
the cella that hid the images of Marduk and his wife Zarpanit, to
whom, each separately, he said a prayer, opening, as usual, with the
words: "Powerful master of the Igigi gods, exalted among the great
gods" and "Powerful, goddess, (most) exalted of the female divinities." After which he went into the great courtyard of the temple
and, as if to stress the cosmic significance of the temple, blessed the
Ésagil three times while calling it "Iku star; Ésagil, image of Heaven
and Earth!" He then opened the doors so that the various officiants—
kalû and cantors—could come to perform their customary rituals.
Then, once the "little evening meal" was served to the gods and completed, he recited the *Epic of Creation* in its entirety to Marduk. This
recitation further stressed the true sense of the universal and cosmogonic festival.

On the fifth day of Nisan,[48] even earlier than the preceding days,
there were the same ablutions of the *šešgallu,* who, wearing a linen

tunic, was to say a prayer to the two gods. The content of each prayer, in Sumerian, was cited in its entirety, and they were presented, as elsewhere, in the manner of litanies, with "refrains" at the end of each line, such as "My Lord, be calm" and "whose name is My Lady." It was then, as on the preceding days, that the members of the clergy were brought in to see to their duties.

Two hours after sunrise, once the meal was served to Bêl and his wife, the *šešgallu* was to summon an exorcist to sprinkle lustral water, thereby purifying the temple, while ringing a bronze drum and bringing in a censer and a torch. The *šešgallu* himself remained on the side during this ceremony. After which he similarly had the section of the temple reserved for Nabû and his wife Tašmêtu purified. The customary residence of those gods was the temple of the city of Borsippa in Babylonia, twenty-five kilometers southeast of Babylon; but (Nabû being the son of Marduk) they participated in the festival, no doubt in the form of their cult statues, which had been transported that very day (?) from where they usually resided. After sprinkling water from the Euphrates, anointing all the sections of the adjacent doors with cedar oil, and fumigating with incense, the *šešgallu* gave the order to an executioner to "behead a sheep," with whose body he "wiped" the temple to purify it, before an exorcist went to the river and, facing west, threw the body filled with impurities from the sanctuary into the water; the executioner did the same with the head. After which the executioner and the exorcist left the city to remain outside it while Nabû was visiting there. The *šešgallu* himself, under the threat of impurity, was to stand in the wings during these lustral ceremonies. A gold canopy was then erected, and Marduk, who was assisted by two divinities, Kusu and Ningirim, specialists in exorcisms, was asked to chase "all evil" from the temple.

Then came a detailed service at table, prepared for Bêl and his wife. Before presenting it, there was another short address to Marduk. Then—an important event—after everyone else had been dismissed, the king himself was brought into the cella, face-to-face with the statue of Bêl. Here is the literal rendering of the passage that followed:

> When he (that is, the king) reaches [the presence of the god Bel], the [*šešgallu*] priest shall leave (the sanctuary) and take away the scepter, the circle, and the sword [from the king]. He shall bring them [before the god Bel] and place them [on] a chair. He shall leave (the sanctuary) and strike the king's cheek. He shall place

the . . . behind him. He shall accompany him (that is, the king) into the presence of the god Bel. . . . he shall drag (him by) the ears and make him bow down to the ground. . . . The king shall speak the following (only) once: "I did [not] sin, lord of the countries. I was not neglectful (of the requirements) of your godship. [I did not] destroy Babylon; I did not command its overthrow [I did not .] . . the temple Esagil, I did not forget its rites. [I did not] rain blows on the cheek of a subordinate. . . . I did [not] humiliate them. [I watched out] for Babylon; I did not smash its walls.". . .[49]

At that moment, as if to reassure him, the *šešgallu* addressed a speech to the king, of which the beginning is destroyed, and what comes afterward is in fragments:

". . . Have no fear . . . which the god Bel. . . . The god Bel [will listen to] your prayer . . . he will magnify your lordship . . . he will exalt your kingship. . . On the day of the *eššešu*-festival, do . . . in the festival of the Opening of the Gate, purify [your] hands . . . day and night. . . . [The god Bel], whose city is Babylon . . . , whose temple is Esagil . . . whose dependents are the people of Babylon. . . . The god Bel will bless you . . . forever. He will destroy your enemy, fell your adversary." After (the [*šešgallu*] priest) says (this), the king shall regain his *composure*. . . . The scepter, circle, and sword [shall be restored] to the king. He shall strike the king's cheek. If, when [he strikes] the king's cheek, the tears flow, (it means that) the god Bel is friendly; if no tears appear, the god Bel is angry: the enemy will rise up and bring about his downfall.

When (these things) have been done, at *sunset*, the [*šešgallu*]-priest shall tie together forty reeds—each three cubits long, uncut, unbroken, straight—using a palm branch as the bond. A hole shall be dug in the Exalted Courtyard and he shall put (the bundle into it). He shall put (in it) honey, cream, first-quality oil. . . . He shall . . . a white bull [before the hole]. The king shall [set all this afire] with a burning reed. The king [and the *urigallu*-priest shall recite] the following recitation.

O Divine Bull, brilliant light which lig[hts up the darkness], . . .[50]

What follows is lost, but it is at least probable that the white bull was sacrificed in front of the flaming trench.

For the five or six days that remained of the festival we have only very sparse and indirect information. Thus, by virtue of the ritual of the fourth day of Nisan, we know that they must have "broken and thrown into the fire" the two figurines prepared that day. We also believe that in a specific room of the temple a court of divinities must have been assembled (i.e., their statues and images) and, reflecting the royal government councils, under the presiding king of the gods, Marduk, they deliberated in order to "fix the destinies" of the sovereign and the people, indeed, of each subject, for the rest of the coming year. These decisions were immediately inscribed by Nabû, who was both the son of Marduk and the secretary of the gods (and in the late period the patron god of writing), onto the "Tablet of Destinies," which the king of the gods kept in his possession.

Most important (with a connection that is not very clear given what precedes), a ceremonial procession transported Marduk and his entire divine court to a sanctuary outside the walls, which was universally and traditionally called the Temple of Akîtu (there was one near every large city). The name of the temple is derived from a very old seasonal festival with a rather complicated history (the name may be pre-Sumerian), which was later connected, at least in part, to the celebration of the New Year we are examining here. The statues of the gods were carried on palanquins along a traditional route. The journey took place in seven stages over one or two days' time. The itinerary included crossing the Euphrates by boat, each god having its own sacred vessel. We do not know whether the crowd followed the procession, which is likely, or whether people were kept away from it.

It seems that once the procession arrived at the sanctuary of Akîtu, an essential event occurred there, one of the highlights of the festival. A few scattered allusions suggest this: with Marduk alone in the central room, the ritual commemorated and in some way served as a reenactment of Marduk's famous victory over Tiamat, the ancient original mother of the gods, as was told in the *Epic of Creation,* a victory thanks to which he rose to the first place among the gods, created the world, and then mankind. We know no more than this.

Then the gods were naturally taken back to their respective dwellings in Babylon, and Nabû and Tašmêtu to Borsippa. Thus the festival was completed, until the next New Year.

It must be evident, and this is why we are justified in lingering on the subject a bit longer, that the celebration was not only of a particular solemnity but of a specific density. It was political, perhaps, but above all religious, one of those moments in a religion when everyone, each in his own way, feels both more joyful and closer to his gods. Insofar as we can judge, given the current status of our knowledge, everything fundamentally revolved around the image of a uni-

versal new beginning: the renewal of the king's power but above all
of the great adventure of the creation of the world and of humanity, following the formidable victory that had won Marduk his elevation. It was as if, in the minds of those people, everything was essentially extremely fragile and perishable, constantly dependent on
the sovereign activities of the gods, to such a degree that only their
intervention, constantly renewed, could prevent things from per-
ishing and disappearing. The world truly began again with the New
Year, in a succession of annual cycles, and this is an aspect of the religious vision of the ancient Mesopotamians to be remembered—it
was no doubt more an amorphous feeling, linked to their profound
conviction of total dependence, than a rigorous, defined theory. The
exceptional magnificence of those dozen great days, and the cold
and dry rubrics cited and summed up above, at least invite us to rediscover, through imagination and sympathy, that popular overflowing of religiosity and joy, of enthusiasm and release, of paroxysm
and devotion. All members of society, in one way or another, again
found themselves around their gods, pulled from their gloomy daily
lives and preoccupations, their work and their troubles, to lavish
only admiring and confident attention on the masters of the world.

This was how the Great Festival of the New Year unfolded, at least
in Babylon. Other cities had their own versions, although it is not
clear that they paid the same attention to Marduk and to his epic.
And even in Babylon, it is conceivable that before the end of the second millennium and the exaltation of Marduk, the ceremonies could
have been different. But we know nothing for certain. Thus, with the
usual reservations, we rely on the Babylonian ritual, which no doubt
in its own way developed an idea that was much more ancient and
more general: that is, the arrival of the New Year constituted a new
beginning, granted by the gods for the continuation of universal affairs and human destinies.

Piety

It is now time to look at this important aspect of religiosity and religious practice. Although we do not have any direct knowledge of
it, we have seen how festivals, and primarily major festivals, might
easily have unleashed a certain public fervor, which could have been
manifested in a massive and unavoidable participation in the liturgy
by the populace out of motives perhaps more of curiosity, of educa-

tion, and of relaxation than of true piety. But to my knowledge no document speaks of this outright or at length: most people did not know how to write and thus did not record their thoughts for posterity, leaving that exercise to the literate professionals, who were not very concerned with teaching us about the masses and do not appear to have been interested in what we are looking at here.

However, we do know a bit more about personal devotions. Apart from the peasants and shepherds, isolated in their fields and pastures and rarely frequenting the cities or towns, we have a small idea of the *uomo qualunque*'s attachment, not of course to "theology," but to common religious practices. Except in personal names, where part of the name addressed a deity as "father" or "mother," the people did not normally express personal devotion to the gods. Here, however, is one piece of "advice" that a "father" supposedly gave to his "son" to instill what we call "good principles" in him, and in that way to help him create a successful life for himself on the prevailing scale of values:

135 Every day worship your god.
Sacrifice and benediction are the proper accompaniment of
  incense.
Present your free-will offering to your god,
For this is proper toward the gods.
Prayer, supplication, and prostration
140 Offer him daily, and *you will get* your reward.
Then you will have full communion with your god.
Reverence begets favour,
Sacrifice prolongs life,
145 And prayer atones for guilt.[51]

This was indeed a matter of daily personal religious practices, which principally involved offerings, words, and pious attitudes. An almost constant devotion was thus recommended and possible, indeed normal, and one did not need to await great occasions that only occurred infrequently. But that advice did not fly high: it did not preach a true and disinterested attachment to the gods, which was, moreover, unimaginable in that land; rather, it viewed devotion to the gods as *beneficial,* reflecting a hedonistic life that was above all geared for success. Viewing religious practice as a sort of "investment" is an attitude encountered almost universally, even in religions that we consider more "lofty."

The same notion occurs in the famous piece called *Ludlul (The*

Poem of the Righteous Sufferer), in which a man, suddenly, inexplicably plunged into the worst misfortunes (even if he describes them in a somewhat rhetorical manner), deploring his cruel experience, recalls his always irreproachable attitude toward the gods:

> 12 Like one who has not made libations to his god,
>   Nor invoked his goddess at table,
>   Does not engage in prostration, nor takes cognizance of bowing down;
> 15 From whose mouth supplication and prayer is lacking,
>   Who has done nothing on holy days, and despised sabbaths,
>   Who in his negligence has despised the gods' rites,
>   Has not taught his people reverence and worship,
>   But has eaten his food without invoking his god,
> 20 And abandoned his goddess by not bringing a flour offering,
>   Like one who has grown *torpid* and forgotten his lord,
>   Has frivolously sworn a solemn oath by his god, (like such a one) do I appear.

This is a true list of devout practices and routines, and the author continues in the same tone:

> 23 For myself, I gave attention to supplication and prayer:
>   To me prayer was discretion, sacrifice my rule.
> 25 The day for reverencing the god was a joy to my heart;
>   The day of the goddess's procession was profit and gain to me.[52]

Thus knowing, in his soul and conscience, that he has in everything shown the devout behavior his religion expected of him, he does not understand why the gods have treated him so harshly. The principle *do ut des* obviously appears to have been fundamental in that religiosity. It is therefore clear that individual piety had its place. And the counterproof would be provided, if need be, by the (rather rare) descriptions of the "impious":

> In your mind you have an urge to disregard the divine ordinances.
> . . . the sound rules of your goddess.[53]

The degree to which every individual's entire life—at least the lives of those who intended to lead them in conformity with religious obligations—could be, in theory, subjected each day to devout restrictions is reflected in those directories of daily existence that we have found in our texts: the menologies. They are collections that usually span the entire year—month after month and day after day—whose principal concern, in that land so saturated with divination and a preoccupation with the future, was no doubt (starting in the second millennium at the latest) to mark the days that were favorable or unfavorable to human affairs, although we do not know very much about the criteria involved. Starting from there, and following a development whose continuation escapes us, those lists were enhanced with daily notices concerning everything deemed necessary to ensure a happy future: in other words, everything necessary for a person to lead an existence that not only exhibited respect and service to the gods but was above all *successful*.

When a date was mentioned ("such and such a month"; "such and such a day of that month"), the general nature of the day was added in a telegraphic style: favorable/lucky or unfavorable/ill-fated; the name of the god whose patronage was applicable to that day; its liturgical definition (feast day, vigil of a festival, festival of a certain god); the specific festive offering to make; if necessary, special prescriptions for the ill-fated days or for the recitation or the nonrecitation of the formula of the *šigû*, a sort of avowal of sins, with an "act of contrition"; or perhaps the rituals and practices advised for that day (libation, prostration, "benediction"). Then followed the prohibitions for that day, with their consequences in the event of transgression; and finally, the food offerings to the god to be honored on that day. Here are a few excerpts from one of those directories:

1 Month of Nisan, the first day. Devoted to Enlil.
Ill-fated day. Worrisome for the ill:
the doctor must not touch them.
Nor will the diviner formulate a divinatory decision.
5 This day is not suitable for whoever wishes to achieve his desires.
Neither fish nor leeks will be eaten, under risk of misfortune.
If one washes one's clothes
10 one will have a satisfied heart. An offering of food
(is to be presented) to Enlil and Ninlil,
as well as to Šamaš and to Nusku, who will accept it (that is, who will follow up on the request implied in that gift).
. . . .
21 3 Nisan. Vigil devoted to Marduk.
If one takes a wife, one will have good health and contented heart.
. . . .
38 The 5th . . . : do not go to trial; you will lose.
. . . .

42   The 6th . . . : recite the formula of confession and contrition
     (*šigû*).

. . . .

II.11 The 13th . . . :   devoted to Sîn and to Mah.
       If you take a wife, you will not have a contented heart:
       you will lose face for it.
       You must present an offering and a "benediction"
       to Sin, to be blessed for it.[54]

Some of these menologies were reserved for the king, for whom
they listed daily obligations and taboos: he no less than his subjects
was held to an observance, all the more strict and minutial in that
his role put him more immediately in rapport with the gods and
rendered him more directly responsible for the luck and misfortunes of his people. The correspondence of the last kings of Assyria
informs us about this devout and credulous submission, which could
impose a true yoke of constraints or prohibitions on the sovereign,
and about the anxiety with which rulers resorted to exorcists, diviners, and astrologers of all kinds. Observing that Mars was retrograde
before entering into the constellation of Scorpio, an astrologer
warned the king that this was an ill-fated presage and that it was thus
forbidden for him to go through the door of his palace.[55] Could the
son of Esarhaddon (680–669), Šamaššumukin, pay a visit to his father without supernatural danger befalling him? Yes, responded the
specialist consulted: because the astral situation was completely favorable.[56] On a given day, the sovereign was reminded that he was
supposed to be "shaved" (his hair or his beard?).[57] And the smallest
events were reported to him by a multitude of specialized observers,
scattered, each at his post, throughout the entire kingdom, and
upon whom the king strongly depended. Just about any phenomenon could constitute an unfavorable presage, against which he had
to guard himself:

> On the 7th of Kislev a fox entered the Inner City, and fell into a
> well in the garden of Assur. It was hauled up and killed.[58]

Thus the entire life of every human, insofar as he accepted that
net of religious obligations and prohibitions, could be tied up, a bit
like that of the king, through a learned and complex etiquette: a person was pious, as he was supposed to be, if he respected those obligations; a person was not pious if he failed to recognize them. We
will later understand the risks and the perils of such negligence. But
for the time being it is enough to say that Mesopotamian religion

truly offered its faithful the opportunity for individual devotion, piety, and religious practice that, if they accepted it, more or less covered their entire existence. We have no source to inform us about the proportions of those who accepted and those who were indifferent: the "pious" and the "impious." Since the subject is not discussed very often, we can justifiably imagine that such a devout preoccupation played, for the "elite" among the people, only a subsidiary role and did not have a powerful daily impact on the common consciousness: there was thus no strictly religious anxiety, and the shame of "sin" was something else entirely.

At least, in weighing all our accounts, we can be certain that such pressure, even reduced, was uniquely exerted along the lines of that "centrifugal" religiosity: there was no hint of an emotional attachment, of tender searching, of authentic love, but only an attitude of reverence, of respect, of prostration, of fear, rooted in the profound conviction of a condition of servitude, both zealous and modest, with regard to the gods.

There is a final, weighty, question to be asked here: did *morality*, honest and righteous behavior, have an authentic religious and cultural value, a place in the practice of religion, a direct influence on the gods? We have never found any response, in all of our documentation, to such a question, a question that we ask ourselves from our own religious and "biblical" point of view.[59] The ancient Mesopotamians never overtly concerned themselves with or imagined such preoccupations, which are so familiar to us. This must have been one of Moses' great revolutions in Israel: to replace the purely material maintenance of the gods with the single and sole "liturgical" obligation in life to obey a moral law, thereby truly rendering to God the only homage worthy of him.

Among the Mesopotamians there was no evidence of such an attitude. They had, of course, like everyone else, their "moral code," which, if not explicitly detailed or conscious, was at least sufficiently known and integrated into their culture. But the reason for following it, beyond the guarantee of a good social order, was, as will be understood later, only to avoid the disadvantages that came from forgetting or ignoring it: the observance of moral laws did not stem from piety but from prudence, precaution (for "success"!). It had absolutely no role in the cult to the glory and benefit of the gods; rather, its sole purpose was to ensure a healthy balance sheet for one's own existence. The only way one could serve the gods and render homage to them was by providing them with opulent goods and services through one's daily work and by serving them or by having them served by the appropriate person; all of this was, as the Mesopotamians believed, agreeable and indispensable to the gods, and it was for the preparation, manufacture, and delivery of those goods and services that human beings had been created and put on Earth. Once that fundamental duty had been fulfilled, each person was free, and the gods expected nothing more from them, although a person might naturally be inclined to expect the gods to return some deserved favor—*do ut des*. We have already stressed that such a point of view is one of the specific differences between the religion of ancient Mesopotamia and other established religions.

The "Sacramental" Cult

Under this name, adopted here for lack of a more adequate term and without the slightest intent to compare, we shall now look at the ceremonial that was carried out, not directly and primarily for the honor, service, and satisfaction of the gods, as in the "theocentric cult," but for the benefit of human beings.

The two realms in which such benefit was sought were, on the one hand, a certain knowledge of the future and, on the other, the elimination of what we call "suffered evil"—not moral evil, evildoing, malice, but everything in our existence that intervenes to upset, sadden, or make our lives painful. The first was sought through practices of *divination;* the second through acts of *exorcism.* For everything appears as if the gods, not having had any reason to be angry a priori at humans, who were in fact indispensable to the gods, and whom the gods had created for the "maintenance" of their lives, behaved toward humans like good-natured "bosses." And to help humans live, the gods provided the double benefit of communicating, at least partially, what could happen to their "servants" and of intervening, at their request, to eradicate the disadvantages, suffering, and misfortunes that might befall them.

Divination

Just about everywhere in the world, in the past as today (we need remember only the bizarre fad of astrology, which seduces even minds that are otherwise quite solid, indeed learned!) people are naturally anxious, primarily about what awaits them, if not about what un-known, secret, mysterious, elusive force more or less conditions their lives: they want to know that force. The ancient Mesopotamians thought that their gods were inclined at least in part to satisfy their curiosity, since, as masters of the world and its workings, the gods were believed to have foreseen and planned everything before car-rying it out, and they could freely reveal and announce it as they saw fit.

They had two means at their disposal to do this. They either re-vealed it through direct discourse and "by word of mouth": this was "inspired divination." Or, following an original method devised by those ingenious Mesopotamians, the gods manifested it on the model of written discourse: by "inscribing" it in their own way; this is what I have called "deductive divination." The two processes, each in its own way, were equally rooted in a mythological vision of the gods and their behavior; this is why the processes must be consid-ered religious.

INSPIRED DIVINATION

"Inspired divination" as such left very little place for the free inter-vention of humans: everything visibly derived from the gods' initia-tive, even if the means to solicit and direct it might have been found. It therefore happened that a divinity, often identified by its name, de-pending on its whim or plans, sometimes spontaneously unveiled something secret, especially about the future. To do this the divinity chose an intermediary, a sort of go-between (this is roughly what was meant by one of the Akkadian terms that designated the "receiver" of such a message: *âpilu*), man or woman, young or old, known or obscure, who was leading either a normal life or more often a more or less marginal life, even showing a tendency toward "delirium" and "prophesying" (in Akkadian, *maḫḫû* or *muḫḫû*). The god com-municated the message he wanted to pass along directly to that in-termediary, perhaps in a dream or in a "vision" or through a sort of ill-defined "inspiration," which might have unleashed a harsh ex-plosion of words and gesticulations from the confidant. The mes-sage might have been immediately clear, but it could also be vague, expressed in a specific language, emphatic, ambiguous, and required an interpretation, which was then obtained from specialists. We do not know very much about those exegetes: perhaps they resembled the "explainers of dreams" (šâ'ilu and, above all, in the feminine form, šâ'iltu, for women often appear to have been preferred in matters pertaining to communication with the supernatural).

We should above all point out that our documentation (which is rather sparse regarding inspired divination in Mesopotamia) for the time being is pretty much restricted to two territories and two periods: to Mari in around 1780, in letters addressed to King Zimri-Lim from various vassals or from functionaries who wrote to him from their posts; and to Assyria in around 650, in collections of prophesies. Here, then, are a few excerpts from these documents from both sources, just enough to give an idea of the functioning of inspired divination.

Addu-dûri, the superintendent in the palace of Mari, wrote in these terms to Zimri-Lim (who was not at home):

> After the [disappearance] of [your] father's house in truth I never had a similar dream. . . . In my dream, I had entered the temple of Bêlet-ekallim: but (the statute of) Bêlet-ekallim was not there! And even the statues (of the other gods) usually placed in front of her were not there! At that sight I started to cry for a long time. I had this dream in the first part of the night. Later I had another: Dada, the priest of Ištar-bišrâ, was standing at the gate of the temple of Bêlet-ekallim, while a hostile voice did not stop crying: "Return! Dagan! Return! Dagan!" [60]

Another piece of news was communicated to the same person by his agent in the city of Sagarâtum (a day's walk north of Mari):

> A prophet of Dagan came to find me to tell me: "So, what am I going to eat that belongs to Zimri-Lim?" I thus gave him a lamb that he devoured raw before the Great Door. Then he gathered the Ancients before that same Great Door and announced to them: "There is going to be an epidemic!" [literally, the last word alludes to sick people "devoured" by illness, just as the announcer had "devoured" his lamb]. Therefore, demand from the different cities the restoration of sacred goods [an allusion to an obscure affair of sacrilegious theft], and may whoever (in order to take them) indulged in violence be banished from his city! For the salvation of your lord Zimri-Lim, you will clothe me in a suit of clothes!" I therefore clothed him in a suit of clothes! At this hour I am writing down this message to send it by the present person to My Lord! The prophet did not pronounce this oracle in secret, but in the middle of the Gathering of the Ancients. [61]

And here is another letter to the king from another functionary:

> [A certain] prophet came to find me, some time ago, concerning the restoration of the Great Door. He was all upset, and he said to me: "Undertake this work!" At present, the very day when I am sending My Lord the present tablet, he came back to tell me, forcefully: "If you do not restore this door, there will be piles of bodies, and you will never escape the consequences!" This is what he said to me.[62]

The following missive is from Zimri-Lim's wife, Queen Šibtu, who remained in the palace in the absence of her husband:

> In the temple of Anunit, in the city, a young servant girl of Dagan-malik [an unknown] began to prophesy while saying: "If you pay no attention to me, O Zimri-Lim, I will create carnage for you! I will deliver your enemies to you! And I will put my hand on my thieves" [an allusion to an affair of sacrilegious theft, as above, about which we know absolutely nothing].[63]

Finally, the following message is addressed to someone close to the king, who is to announce sad news to him:

> A prophet had had an "ecstasy" concerning the girl whom the Queen brought into this world: this daughter of My Lord did not live: she died today. . . . The same day, a certain Irra-gamil (unknown) also had had an "ecstasy" and had declared: "She will not live!" Before the king arrives in Mari, tell him that his little girl is dead, so that he will be informed! We fear that he will be profoundly upset by this news.[64]

The passages cited below, taken from collections of oracles addressed to Esarhaddon (680–669) would have been pronounced in the name of first-level divinities by various figures, otherwise unknown, called "vociferators" (*raggimu; raggimtu* in the feminine form), who must have played the role more or less of the *âpilu* and the *ma/uḫḫû* of Mari:

> [Esarh]addon, king of the lands, fear [not]!
> What wind has risen against you, whose wing I have not broken? Your enemies will roll before your feet like ripe apples.
> I am the Great Lady; I am Ištar of Arbela, who cast your enemies before your feet. What words have I spoken to you that you could not rely upon?
> I am Ištar of Arbela. I will flay your enemies and give them to you.
> I am Ištar of Arbela. I will go before you and behind you.

> Fear not! You are paralyzed, but in the midst of woe I will rise and
> sit down (beside you).
> By the mouth of Ištar-la-tašiyat of Arbela.[65]

> Words of Ištar of Arbela to Esarhaddon, king of Aššur: "As if I had
> done nothing for you! As if I had given nothing to you!
> Have I not beaten your enemies? And your adversaries, enraged
> against you, have I not entrapped them like butterflies?"[66]

The following is in the name of the greatest god of Assyria:

> Myself, Aššur, I have heard your complaint, and I descended, in all
> majesty, from my Great Door of Heaven (to respond to it). I will set
> myself to it and will make all your enemies be devoured by fire. . . .
> I will make enormous hail (?) fall upon them! I will massacre them
> and will fill the river with their blood! Let them think of this and
> let them beware! I am Aššur, the lord of the gods, am I![67]

The one who was believed to have received divine revelation was
therefore more or less mysteriously viewed as only a sort of intermediary: he either transmitted the message to whoever was concerned;
or the publicity of his experience was enough to alert the local authorities, who, playing their role, had only to report it to those concerned or to the king.

It was the king himself, the master of the land, who, at least if we
believe our documents, appears to have been preferentially chosen to
receive those hints that were revealed about the future or a mystery.
Whether it concerned the announcement of fortunate or unfortunate events, admonishments or warnings against threatening absolute or conditional dangers, or encouragement or promises, equally
absolute or conditional, for a better future—all these tableaus appear in our documentation to have more often concerned the chief
holder of power in the land, in other words, the interests of the entire land.

Behind the scenes of these revelations it is difficult not to sense the
activities, open or on the sly, of some "pressure groups," as we call
them today; most likely, given the context, "the clergy," who were
necessarily implicated in these theocentric affairs, and who might
have had an interest, even in all good faith, in directing or influenc-
ing the conduct of the sovereign. The prophet who so brutally demanded the restoration of the Great Door (of the palace? of a temple?
of the city?), going so far as to promise, in case of disobedience,
"many corpses" as a result—in the name of what interests was he
speaking (unconsciously, no doubt, but under what more or less

subtle or indirect pressures?)? Even if he was speaking on his own behalf and by virtue of his own mythology, he was convinced of the supernatural nature of his experience. Behind inspired divination an entire sphere of meddling in the exercise of power was thus hidden, accessible to a small number of individuals in the wings.

This did not exclude the good faith of those principally involved nor those who inspired them, if there were indeed conspirators. In the presence of a "mentality" and of a worldview so far from our own, we must not, however, naively give in to our own way of thinking and feeling, to our own rationalism and psychological analyses, which are valid above all for us alone. All religions of all time know a similar mixture of credulity and machinations, of promoting a will from On High and of the veiled pursuit of less lofty interests. Whatever its secret mechanisms, conscious or not, may have been, inspired divination was deeply integrated into religious belief and practice in Mesopotamia and elsewhere, throughout time.

Other factors naturally came into play, beginning with the intimate conviction of the individuals possessed by those revelations and of their audience that they were truly in the presence of a supernatural intervention. They did not, moreover, transmit only "political" messages, as is shown in the case of those two "prophets" who had foreseen and announced the death of the king's little daughter. In the future that was unveiled there was thus a place for personal destiny, and not only for that of the land and of the king. If we possessed more complete and richer documentation, we would certainly have the opportunity to discover more evidence of this, thus putting inspired divination in its true, perhaps more all-encompassing, place.

We can nevertheless question the meagerness of our documentation (some fifty pieces, at most). If discovering the future through prophets was unknown or seldom practiced in Mesopotamia as a whole, and was essentially restricted to two adjacent territories of indisputably Semitic dominance—Mari, primarily West Semitic, and Assyria, which, far to the north, seems to have escaped the initial Sumerian influence—then we might be tempted to consider that such a divinatory practice was particular to Semitic religiosity, especially since we find its equivalent, with many common traits, in other cultural regions unique to the West Semites, as evidenced in the Bible. This might explain why the Babylonians so clearly and so lastingly preferred to call upon deductive divination.

DEDUCTIVE DIVINATION

Unlike inspired divination, evidence of deductive divination is found directly in writing only in Mesopotamia, where we have recovered thousands of texts attesting to it. All the other ancient cultures who employed deductive divination—notably the Hittites of Asia Minor in the middle of the second millennium, the Etruscans, then the Romans, a few centuries later, and the Egyptians in Hellenistic times—according to the evidence owe their use of it to the Mesopotamians. It was no doubt in Mesopotamia that deductive divination saw the light of day in the third millennium, and as a quintessential local product, it endured in full strength until the very end of that civilization.

In fact, deductive divination is rather amazing. In order to introduce it and to demonstrate its mechanism it is preferable to refer directly to original texts. Deductive divination is ordinarily limited in cuneiform literature to long *lists* (again!) that are sometimes interminable *ad nauseam*—of many thousands of propositions, all uniformly constructed on the same grammatical model of a "protasis" (conditional), which contains a "presage," followed by an "apodosis" (response to the protasis), in which the resulting oracle is noted. Here is a short sample, taken from a "treatise" where the oracles—almost always relating to the future—were derived from presages relating to the appearance of newborns at the time of their births:

51. If a woman gives birth to a "body"—pestilence; that man will die before his time.

52. If a woman gives birth to a male idiot—troubles; scattering of the house of the man.

53. If a woman gives birth to a female idiot—the house of the man will . . .

54. If a woman gives birth to a male dwarf—troubles; the house of the man will be scattered.

55. If a woman gives birth to a female dwarf—correspondingly.

56. If a woman gives birth to a boy cripple—the house of the man will suffer.

57. If a woman gives birth to a girl cripple—the house of the man will be scattered; ditto (i.e. will suffer).

60. If a woman gives birth to a blind child—the land will be disturbed; the house of the man will not prosper.

63. If a woman gives birth to a deaf child—that house will prosper outside (of its city).[68]

And so forth.

What do these declarations mean? The list above meant that each
of those abnormal appearances of a newborn revealed a specific future, either favorable or unfavorable, for an individual or a land: if a
baby was stillborn, one was to expect an epidemic; a dwarf, drought;
and so on. This future fate was not communicated directly by a god
or "by word of mouth," as in the case of inspired divination; but
the gods, creators of all unusual things and presiding over the destiny of each individual, had in some way closely connected that fate
with a specific, abnormal, notable phenomenon in which each person could determine and *deduce* it. That is why I have called this
divinatory method of revealing the future "deductive." The ancient
Mesopotamians imagined that every anomaly or peculiarity was
purposeful and employed by the gods to announce a determined
future.

This belief was facilitated, if not suggested, by their own type of
writing. They had invented it shortly before the end of the fourth
millennium,[69] as an auxiliary to and a support for their accounting
practices, in which they found themselves constrained by the perpetual movement of great quantities of goods that were the result of
their know-how and zeal, as well as of the wealth of their land, perfect for grain farming and raising sheep and goats. The brilliant idea
at the origin of the rather prodigious invention of writing was that,
lacking the ability to place the merchandise itself in their accounts
and desiring to note the contents of and to remember every transac-
tion, they began to portray it by sketching rather evocative and uniformly recognizable drawings: sketched using a few lines, a horned
head replaced a unit of large livestock; a pubic triangle, a woman; a
star, that which was found On High; and a profile of a mountain,
the foreign territory behind it. This first writing could naturally only
refer to concrete and rough-hewn realities, a bit like the language
that we call "pidgin": "Me want bread!" It was just as rudimentary
and of limited use but was sufficient, all the same, for what needed
to be recorded. The process was intellectually all the more striking,
no doubt, in that it supported an ancient conviction unique to the
local culture, that is, the link between the true identity of things and
their expression: to draw a fish or a head of grain, just as to simply

say their names, was indeed to "achieve"—to give existence to—that fish, to that head of grain. Writing, like speech, was "realistic."

Even if writing was rather quickly perfected and people learned to transcribe not only things, material realities, but the *words* that expressed them in the common language, and consequently to record that language—the only perfect and ideal means of communicating thoughts—in its entirety, everything leads us to believe that in Mesopotamia thinkers were profoundly marked by that basic correlation between "producing" and writing. In his own way the scribe *made,* or *produced* what he wrote down. We can thus much more readily understand the emergence and perseverance of that strange practice of deductive divination only if—for it was born not *with* but *out of* writing—we connect it to writing in its initial state: *the writing of things.*

In ancient Mesopotamia it was thus imagined that the gods, creators of everything, each day *wrote* "in relief," if I may say so, through their *making* of things. Creating things was the writing of the gods, for they made objects the bearers of a definite meaning, of a message they wanted to communicate to humans. We know nothing about the origins of the divination that was based on those convictions unique to the ancient Mesopotamians, but we have many enlightening indications that they were indeed struck by the profound analogy between creation and the writing of a divine message. They called the starry sky, which contained astrological revelations concerning the future, "celestial writing," as if the gods had arranged the stars in order to form them into significant configurations. And every oracular consultation involving the examination of the entrails of a sacrificed animal began with an address by the diviner, asking the patron of divination, the god Šamaš, to "be present in [the stomach of] this ram, place (in it) a firm positive answer, favorable designs, favorable, propitious omens by the oracular command of your great divinity, and may I see (them)." [70]

Without claiming to be able to guess what the lack of documents hides from us—the true conditions surrounding the birth of deductive divination—it is undeniable that the analogy between it and the essential writing process at its origins sheds light on both a justification for deductive divination and the driving force behind it. The gods were imagined to "write" things and, like all those who write, to deliberately have a message passed through those things, a mes-

sage that preferably involved an activity of great interest to humans, an activity that humans, unlike the gods, were incapable of fully undertaking: the unveiling of the unknown and, above all, of the future (we will later specify in what sense). It sufficed to "read" the objects thus created, to examine them, to reflect upon them in order to "decipher" them, just as it sufficed to examine and decipher a cuneiform tablet in order to read it and thus understand what its author wanted to say. Through deductive divination the future was not pronounced by the gods themselves speaking to a human *medium*, it was inscribed in things that they created. Humans had only to read the future in them, to decipher it, to deduce it, like any written message.

To do that, as in writing itself, a "code" was indispensable: it was necessary to know all the possible meanings of all the "signs." We know that to learn to read and write demanded many years of study and practice, so that reading and writing constituted a true profession. The same was true for divine and divinatory writing, but its practice was systematized in a completely different way and was reserved for other professionals.

The specialists in deductive divination, the diviners, were called *bârû* in Akkadian, or "examiners." They were not "seers" but were supposed to *scrutinize* the divinatory messages from every angle, so to speak, in order to decipher the divine cryptograms within them. They evidently did not go to the trouble to leave us anything explaining the "code" they used, and we have found only fragments of it here and there. Moreover, it is very likely that they never really needed such a "manual." To learn their profession they above all had "treatises."

This is what we call those endless lists mentioned above. The *bârû* scholars must have begun, in the second half of the third millennium and outside the Sumerian sphere of influence (the language of deductive divination was always Akkadian, and therefore that "science" was presumably developed among the Semites of the land, a new indication of the Semitic interest in knowledge of the inaccessible), to patiently collect all sorts of "presages" and the "oracles" of the future that could be perceived through those presages. It is likely that their research was first inspired by "empirical" observations of good or bad twists of fate, both individual and collective, that followed unusual, aberrant, or unique events, and which they were

thus tempted to attribute to a specific wish among the gods, such as the unexpected death of an important figure shortly after the appearance of a monstrous animal. Following such observations their attention must have been drawn to the common or analogous elements that linked two occurrences: for example, the discovery of a liver comprised not of one but of *two*, normally single anatomical parts and, later, the disputing of the throne by *two* competitors. It thus very quickly occurred to them that the second event was not simply forecast by the first but in a certain sense was *included* in the first by the gods and was thus announced in it.

"Treatises" were then born out of that research, the writing of which must have begun in the beginning of the second millennium, and whose content was gradually and systematically expanded to all classes of reality, all equally the objects of the efficient activities of the gods and, consequently, all able to contain and convey their messages. There were, therefore (we are the ones proposing all these scholarly names), treatises of *astrology* (the movements and relative positions of the stars), of *chronomancy* (chance occurrences and coincidences of events as related to the calendar), of *tocomancy* (the appearance of newborn humans and animals), of *physiognomy* (the appearance of the human body and also of the human temperament and character), of *extispicy* and notably of *hepatoscopy* (the examination of entrails, especially the liver, of sacrificed animals), of *oneiromancy* (dreams), of the *hazards* and multiple encounters *of daily life;* and even more. In each of these lists, presages were meticulously and rigorously classified, each followed by the oracular statement concerning the future that it promised.

These collections were not created to enable diviners to find an answer to every question raised about the future through multiple presages. The *bârû* normally did not consult them for specific interpretations. An interpretation was, *in concreto,* usually not easy to establish and necessitated calculations and balancing, while taking into account all the decipherable data as well as the quality of the consultant and of the *hic et nunc* presentation of things. The treatises, which were read and reread, if not learned by heart, in that culture of casuistic pedagogy, played the role of our grammatical paradigms and arithmetic tables: unable to formulate abstract and universal "principles" and "laws," the ancient Mesopotamians used those treatises as guidelines to acquire *the meaning* of things, to learn how a

given presage was to be interpreted as either a good or bad omen—
and it was from that knowledge that a *bârû* knew how to read those
divine messages and to give his clients a suitable response.

The future thus unveiled was not, however, an "absolute future,"
one that would unfailingly occur, but one that we should call a "ju-
diciary future." It indicated the *decision* that had been made about
a certain future, like the decision of a judge who declares a certain
punishment or of a king who bestows a certain advantage. We will
later see that the divine decisions communicated through deductive
divination, like the decrees of a sovereign and the sentences of a
judge, were susceptible to appeal and to change.

Deductive divination was therefore a "science." But it was also,
and perhaps above all, a *religious practice,* because everything related
to the gods, who were responsible for the countless mysterious messages that life presented to people and, through such messages, revealed a fragment of our future to us.

It must be made clear that although the general method of de-
coding the many categories of presages was basically the same, they
were not all dealt with in the same way. Some concerned the private
lives of common people, revealing the futures unique to each one
of them, whereas others concerned Mesopotamia itself or, what
amounted to the same thing, the sovereign. In time a sort of popular deductive divination was conceived that was placed in the hands
of all and sundry, although we cannot be sure how widespread it
was. For example, a woman faced with a decline in her partner's
amorous interest, and who wanted clarification concerning his sexual capabilities or his faithfulness, was counseled to show a pig a figurine in her own image accompanied by one representing her lover.
If the animal approached them, it meant there had been an accident,
a "blow from Ištar," as they said, that was easily curable; but if the
pig turned its back, the situation was more serious and more difficult to cure: the unfortunate man had been bewitched.[71]

THE DIVINERS

At least in serious cases one could usually resort to a professional diviner, the *bârû,* who, when consulted by an individual, could indeed
detect a public danger in that person's affairs and warn those concerned. In a short letter from around 700, the author (whose name

is unknown), obviously a *bârû,* recalls a passage from the treatise of tocomancy, before coming to the specific affair that has fallen into his hands:

> If an anomaly's feet are 8
> (and) its tails 2—
> a prince will
> seize universal kingship.
> He is a weaver.
> Tam-danu is his name.
> He says: "When my sow
> gave birth,
> its (the piglet's) feet were 8 (and) its
> tails 2.
> I pickled it in salt,
> and placed (it) in the house."
> (report) of Nergal-etir.[72]

Astrological presages, which were visible everywhere in the sky, and which required precise and knowledgeable observations, required specialized *bârû,* who were called something like "doctors in astrology" (literally, "scribes specialized in the treatise of astrology"). They were probably expensive, given their specific knowledge and their importance, and they played a somewhat official role, which must have excluded them from being involved with more mundane subjects. They were in the service of the king, who distributed them throughout the land as observers and above all as gatherers of information, to keep the king up to date about anything they noted of political importance: epidemics, bad harvests to anticipate; danger of revolts; threats from enemies on the borders, all deduced from the reciprocal positions and movements of the stars. The royal correspondence from the time of the Sargonids (720–609) gives a vivid portrait of them, showing them responding to the questions the sovereign raised, warning him of certain dangers, or reassuring him. Although they report their observations in great detail and their reflections and conclusions, and refer to written treatises[73] and to oral traditions among professionals, they never explain how they reasoned or whether, as is probable, their duties were more or less infused with a religious attitude.

The same uncertainty surrounds the specialists in the various other realms of deductive divination. How did individuals consult them (like Tam-danu mentioned above, who warned his *bârû* of the birth of a phenomenal piglet at his home, obviously in order to find out what such an unusual occurrence might mean)? How did the operations of divinatory "deduction" and deciphering unfold, and what were their results? How were those conclusions received and remunerated? We know almost nothing about all that.

The best documented cases are those of the professionals of extispicy and hepatoscopy. The importance and the notoriety of their disciplines, which were already considerable (more than others, it seems) at the beginning of the second millennium, continued to grow as time went by, even if, focusing on the first millennium, one might wonder to what degree astrology, which was considerably developed, would or would not have bowed before them, at least on the public and political level. We discover that the diviners, increasingly aware of the complexity of things, gradually sought to combine the results of the two great systems of divination by explaining that "the signs in the sky just as those on the earth give us signals" [74] and that it was thus necessary, to be thorough, to take both into account, following complicated calculations.

We have several hundred accounts of extispicy. It involved the slaying of a lamb, a sheep, or a barnyard fowl, opening it up, and examining the condition of its entrails to find anomalies of number, position, or anatomy and then to balance all the many divinatory responses obtained through such observations to determine how it all related to the future. Here is the translation of one of these pieces. It is from the time of Esarhaddon (680–669), who questioned the *bârû* in order to discover whether an earlier diagnosis (similarly hepatoscopic) concerning the health of his mother, Naqia, the widow of Sennacherib, was correct, and whether consequently it was necessary to continue to hope and to follow the treatment that was previously ordered. Such documents also reveal a great deal of information concerning political and daily life, especially of the elite classes, who were probably the only ones rich enough to pay for such expensive consultations. The questions asked reveal many details, such as the thousand and one problems of all kinds with which a sovereign was confronted. But the way they were formulated, which was always more or less fixed, quite clearly reveals, as we will see, more than one trait of the *religious* ceremonial of divination.

The diviner thus began with an invocation to the "Great Master of Divination," the god Šamaš, the light from whom nothing escaped. The diviner conveyed to Šamaš the question asked by the client and requested "a clear and plain response," all the while recalling the dozen impediments that might render it uncertain or null and void (we do not know why such caveats were repeated, but it was at least a good precaution in the event of failure!).

> Šamaš, great lord, give me a firm positive answer to what I am
>   asking you!
> Niqia, mother of Esarhaddon, king of Assyria, who is now ill,
>   and on whom the "hand" of god Iqbi-damiq was placed in
>   extispicy—
> *will it pass by unto* sacrificial sheep and oxen?
> If she is ill with this disease,
> is it decreed and confirmed in a favorable case, by the command
>   of your great divinity, Šamaš, great lord? Will he who can see,
>   see it? Will he who can hear, hear it?
> Disregard that a clean or an unclean person has touched the
>   sacrificial sheep, or blocked the way of the sacrificial sheep.
> Disregard that an unclean man or woman has come near the
>   place of the extispicy and made it unclean.
> Disregard that an unclean person has performed extispicy in this
>   place.
> Disregard that the ram (offered) to your divinity for the perfor-
>   mance of the extispicy is deficient or faulty.
> Disregard that he who touches the forehead of the sheep is
>   dressed in his ordinary soiled garments, (or) has eaten,
>   drunk, or anointed himself with anything unclean.
> Disregard that I, the haruspex your servant, have eaten, drunk, or
>   anointed myself with anything unclean, changed or altered the
>   proceedings, or jumbled the oracle query in my mouth.
> Let them be taken out and put aside!
> I ask you, Šamaš, great lord:
> Be present in this ram, place (in it) a firm positive answer, favor-
>   able designs, favorable, propitious omens by the oracular com-
>   mand of your great divinity, and may I see (them).
> May (this query) go to your great divinity, O Šamaš, great lord,
>   and may an oracle be given as an answer.[75]

Everything here shows the degree to which those operations of de-ductive divination, performed by the ex officio *bârû*, were immersed in a pious and rigid ceremonial and a truly religious spirit. We have fragments of the ritual of the *bârû* that provide a general prescrip-tion for what we have just seen detailed in a concrete example. And we also have prayers, primarily to Šamaš and to Adad, who were con-sidered the patrons of deductive divination, as well as to other super-natural figures, in particular to the stars, which to a certain degree shared a divine nature. And because the stars, surrounded in nocturnal silence and mystery, were seen as divine entities, the diviners took advantage of that belief to confer an august and moving (or to sum it up in one word: religious) character to the decipherment of the stars' divine messages. We shall cite one such prayer here, not only to illustrate the profound religiosity of deductive divination, sentiments that still touch us today, but also to breathe in the great serenity, the serious piety, and the noble poetry of its lines:

1   The nobles are deep in sleep,
      the bars (of the doors) are lowered, the bolts(?) are in place—
      (also) the (ordinary) people do not utter a sound,
      the(ir always) open doors are locked.
5   The gods and goddesses of the country—
      Šamaš, Sîn, Adad and Ištar—
      have gone home to heaven to sleep,
      they will not give decisions or verdicts (tonight).
      Night has put on her veil—
10 the palace is quiet, the countryside does not utter a sound—
      (Only) the (lonely) traveler calls to the god (for protection)
      (and even) the one for whom the (divine) decision (is
         sought) remains asleep—
      Šamaš, the just judge, the father of the underprivileged,
      has (likewise) gone to his bedchamber.
15 May the great gods of the night:
      shining Fire-star,
      heroic Irra,
      Bow-star, Yoke-star,
      Šitaddaru, Mušḫuššu-star,
20 Wagon, Goat-star
      Goatfish-star, Serpent-star—[76]
      stand by and
      put a propitious sign
      on (the exta of) the lamb I am blessing (now)
25 for the extispicy I will perform (tomorrow)![77]

Exorcism and Magic

Magic and exorcism should be distinguished. Exorcism had absorbed ancient magic and was, like magic, governed by an infinitely broader and more urgent problem than simply the unveiling of the future and the unknown: it was employed for the elimination of "suffered evil." The ancient Mesopotamians, involved less, it seems, in a positive search for what we call happiness, of which they almost never speak, and through a sort of fatalism, or a deep-seated resignation

toward the common fate that their "inventors" and sovereign masters had assigned to them, appear to have believed that life in itself
was sufficiently advantageous, as long as it could be rid of the disadvantages that tainted it: illnesses; calamities, both personal and collective; downfalls; pains and heartbreaks; large and small worries.
Death was the exception: however cruel one felt it to be, it was considered, not an (avoidable) "evil," but an (unavoidable) "destiny."
Gilgameš learned this at his own expense, through his long and
difficult experience.

First of all, how were those evils accounted for? It was indeed necessary to pinpoint their origin if one wished to find a remedy for
them. If it was easy to recognize the immediate cause of a number
of them—"Last year I ate garlic; this year my inside burns," as was
said in a proverb[78]—the great and essential personal question that
everyone always asked and that demanded enlightenment at all
costs was "Why me? Why was it necessary that this chain of causali-
ties occurred *hic et nunc* to me, specifically to me?" This attempt to
explain suffered evil, the processes of which have changed throughout time and place, gave rise to two successive systems: first *magic;*
then *exorcism,* which to us appears much more important and religiously essential.

THE MAGICAL EXPLANATION OF EVIL

A number of indications lead us to believe that the most archaic explanation of evil resembled a small-scale model of the aforemen-
tioned explanation of the origins of the world. The gods were viewed
as rather indulgent and were not held responsible for those annoy-
ing and cruel accidents in life that could easily diminish our zeal in
our service to them. Such accidents were attributed to imaginary beings who still vaguely resembled humans, or something close to
human, but were necessarily superior to us and inferior to the gods.
Through innate evilness, these beings attacked people as irritable
ruffians would, without any other motive than their bad temper,
thereby bestowing upsets and misfortunes upon humans and poi-
soning their existence.

We may assume that a specific being was imagined for a specific
evil from the fact that the Mesopotamians had no generic term to
designate those malevolent beings as a whole, such as dingir/*ilu* to
refer to the gods. There was no term in either Sumerian or Akkadian

for "demons" or "devils" or anything that resembled them, only specific names for mysterious and noxious beings, some borrowed from repressive and traditionally harsh institutions such as "jailer/policeman" (gala/*gallû*). We do not know much about most of these monstrous, fearsome, dangerous, and evil anthropomorphous or zoomorphous beings (udug/*utukku,* á.sàg/*asakku,* gedim/*eṭemmu,* etc.; the oldest of these terms were borrowed from the Sumerians, like many of the names of the gods). Names were even borrowed from disastrous forces such as illnesses, the same name evoking the effect and the personalized cause: fever was caused by Fever; epilepsy, by Epilepsy, and so on. The Akkadians not only Akkadianized the Sumerian terms but later added their own to the mix (*aḫḫâzu,* "Gripper"; *mamîtu,* "Perjurer"). Since the primary language of magical and exorcistic documents, unlike those of divination, was Sumerian, it is very likely that these evil personnel, like many divinities, originated with the Sumerians, to whom magic and exorcism would then belong, at least in part, whatever their possible precedents or borrowings might have been.

The only possible reason that could be given to explain attacks by "demons" (as *we* would say), was their wantonness and pure malevolence, for the attacks could not be explained through any provocation on the part of their victims. Such was the "magical" explanation of evil.

THE EXORCISTIC EXPLANATION OF EVIL

A number of scattered facts, dating from the middle of the third millennium, alert us to a profound change in this exegesis of misfortune, one that was probably drawn out over centuries. The magical system, at first independent and the only one known, was gradually absorbed by the strictly religious system, which, to clarify everything that occurred here on Earth, knew only the single power and intervention of the divinities, before whom even the strongest demons could only bow down and submit themselves. The misfortune and pain of humans were of course attributed to multiple "evil forces," but those forces were gradually recognized as being incapable of persecuting and harming people without having first received orders from the gods, of whom those demons were only the "executors." But how could sadism be imputed to the gods, who were always tacitly and undeniably recognized as just and even benevolent? It was thus necessary that a reason for the unleashing of the evil inflicted by "evil forces," but commanded by the gods, be found in *the person.*

An immemorial conviction comes into play here, one that we easily attribute to the Semites (it was universal to them, not only in Mesopotamia but everywhere): the fundamental metaphor used to represent the gods and their power was the earthly political authority, the king. The gods governed all people and, like kings, but on their own divine scale, decreed the obligations and prohibitions that marked out all of social life. It followed that all the prescriptions that ruled human existence—as much on the strictly religious level as on the political, administrative, and "moral" ones, including those folkloric constraints inherited from a distant, forgotten past and those obscure routines that everyone respects without knowing why— were believed to emanate from the "governmental" will of the gods. Similar to defying the king's orders, ignoring those of the gods, consciously or unintentionally, on a serious or a venial point, indeed, not even just by oneself, but—in that land which admitted familial and collective responsibility—by those close to one, implied "negligence" or "disdain" with regard to the august divine authors of those rules, a "revolt" against them and their authority—in a word, a "sin." To convey such a concept the terms *arnu* (sin), *ennêtu* (fault), *ḫiṭîtu* (lacking), *gillatu* (hostile action), and *šêrtu* ("punishable action") were used. The unusual number of these synonyms eloquently points to Semitic influence, as Sumerian had only, as a vague equivalent, moreover rather rarely used, nam.tag.ga, "contest," "revolt."

Sin, the disobedience of divine will, of which we have lists of dozens of examples in all realms of behavior, was at the very center of the religious consciousness of the Mesopotamians beginning at the latest at the turn of the third millennium, and it remained there until the very end. It appeared almost everywhere, in particular in prayers, alongside mention of the gods' "anger" (*kimiltu, uzzu,* etc.), which it provoked:

1   Éa, Šamaš and Marduk, what are my iniquities?
. . . .

16   Release and remove the iniquities of my father and mother!
. . . .

19   May my guilt be distant, 3,600 leagues away,
20   May the river receive it from me and take it down to its
       depths.
. . . .

29 My iniquities are many: I know not what I did.
    · · · · · · · · · · · · · · · · · ·
148 I have continually committed iniquities, known and
     unknown.
     · · · · · · · · · · · · · · · · · ·
154 Though my iniquities be many, . . .
155 Though my transgressions be seven . . .
156 Though my sins be many . . .[79]

Such declarations often recur: those above are drawn from a collection in which the confessions of guilt and the cries of repentance
were believed "to appease the wrath of the gods."Parents, stricken
or perplexed on the occasion of the birth of their child, would even
name the child in an echo of that same obsessive question: *Mîna-
arni*, "What is my sin?" *Mîna-ahti-ana-ili*, "What sin have I committed against a god?" (understood as "to find myself thus stricken").

"Sin" was the primary reason for suffered evil: it was in order to
punish that sin, as was deserved, that the gods—like kings delegat-
ing their police during a time of disorder—had assigned "demons"
and "evil forces" to bring misfortune upon the guilty ones. The only
explanation for the evils in life was sin. Thus the exorcistic system
resolved the "problem of evil." It was a mythological solution all the
more universally accepted in that it was simple, coherent, and, as
we will see later, also accompanied by a remedy.

However, it does not appear to have satisfied everyone. The a pos-
teriori reasoning that it most often implied, in the absence of any
memory of a consciously committed sin was that "If I am unhappy
it is because *I must have* sinned!" Such a conclusion might easily
awaken a feeling of the injustice of the gods if, when faced with a
misfortune, that is, a particularly severe "punishment," one could
reproach oneself only for peccadilloes in the course of a basically
honest and righteous life, and one knew obvious scoundrels who
had been singularly blessed with good fortune and happiness.

This bitterness toward and latent criticism of the solution exorcism advocated to explain the problem of evil was so well diffused,
at the very least within the educated class, that it became a literary
theme, at least from the beginning of the second millennium. Since
that time we have uncovered rather abundant and telling remnants
of at least three or four works, let us call them "theological essays,"
devoted to that aporia, about which we should say a few words. Only
the first was composed in Sumerian. Each, in its own way, presents

"a man" before "his god" who is conscious of having remained just and righteous, in spite of some peccadilloes, which were moreover inevitable ("Never has a sinless child been born to its mother"),[80] as it was so easy to transgress in a thousand ways the countless barriers from every direction that restricted behavior. The man complains to "his god," his personal god or the one toward whom he was turned at the moment, for having been stricken by penalties that were far too heavy. He therefore asks for pardon and for the restitution of his lost happiness. In fact, the gods he implores agree, in the end, to return to the plaintiff a sufficiently happy life free of all the misfortunes that had been inflicted.

The third of these "essays" (dating from the second half of the second millennium) is a monologue of around five hundred lines, normally distributed over four tablets, that we sometimes refer to by its first few words (*Ludlul bêl nêmequ,* "I will praise the lord of wisdom") and sometimes as *The Poem of the Righteous Sufferer.* This composition apparently attempts to unveil the ultimate reason for inflicted evil and for the pardon granted by formulating a solution to the problem of evil that is different from the one offered by traditional exorcism. Here is how it is introduced:

> 1   I will praise the lord of wisdom, solicitous god,
>   Furious in the night, growing calm in the day:
>   Marduk! lord of wisdom, solicitous god,
>   Furious in the night, growing calm in the day:
> 5   Whose anger is like a raging tempest, a desolation,
>   But whose breeze is sweet as the breath of morn.
>   In his fury not to be withstood, his rage the deluge,
>   Merciful in his feelings, his emotions relenting.
>   The skies cannot sustain the weight of his hand,
> 10 His gentle palm rescues the moribund.[81]

In other words, there was something more decisive here than simply putting forward "sin" to explain suffering and evil: there was first of all the absolute freedom of the gods, who had, in the end, like the sovereigns here on Earth, only their completely autonomous will to justify all that they did, even against us. And in that, too, they were like kings: supremely independent but with a variable mood—sometimes furious and fearsome, sometimes good-natured and smiling (political experiences and memories must not have been lacking!). Evil was thus explained by that very balancing, which conveyed the rulers' complete authority. It was enough therefore to patiently await the "return" of their benevolence: this attitude, forgetting the earlier cruelty, would necessarily restore the happiness that the gods had at first destroyed. In sum, the author of the *Ludlul,* who only formulated in plain language what his two predecessors had implied without explicitly saying so, obviously does not in the least deny the central importance of "sin" (like them, he even mentions it here and there) to explain evil/punishment. But he aims to deflect attention from that problem in order to advocate above all a disposition of the heart and of life: resignation, fatalism, and patience. "After the rain comes good weather!" he seems to say, more concerned with a truly religious, rather than a rational, attitude.

The author of the fourth and final piece in the same vein, which we call the *Theodicy,* a dialogue, as it were, from the turn of the second millennium, clearly, although without saying so, shares such a view. After having his "patient," who is speaking to a "sage," a great lover of truisms, utter the most biting truths in all of Mesopotamian literature concerning the unbearable way in which things occur, in general, here on Earth, under the indifferent eyes of the gods, he continues:

> 70 Those who neglect the god go the way of prosperity,
> While those who pray to the goddess are impoverished and
>   dispossessed.
> In my youth I sought the will of my god;
> With prostration and prayer I followed my goddess.
> But I was bearing a profitless corvée as a yoke.
> 75 My god decreed instead of wealth destitution.
> A cripple is my superior, a lunatic outstrips me.
>
> . . . .
>
> 243 I have looked around society, but the evidence is contrary.
> The god does not impede the way of a devil.[82]

At the end he presents his protagonist as unexpectedly, without a reason being given, prepared to have every confidence in the same gods that he had just so vehemently denounced, suddenly assured that they would release him from his misfortune—regardless of all that he had advanced against that theory earlier.

Even if we think that such fatalism does not reveal great intellectual qualities, we must recognize that it does reveal true progress in religious thought. The author of the *Ludlul,* and the other authors as well, refused, in sum, to hinder the sovereign freedom of their gods through logical reasoning. They preferred to submit to the gods' all-powerfulness and independence. Without undermining or thwarting it in the least, they allowed the explanation of evil through sin to retain its value, but in their sentiment—their *religious* sentiment—that explanation faded before the humble acceptance of the gods' decisions, whatever they might be, before their sovereignty, before our necessary patience, before the hope that their indulgence and natural goodness would ultimately win, in any case for those who had not acted in a truly reprehensible way. In this sense these "essays" marked an important religious innovation. One cannot really say that they advanced *absolute* divine transcendence (which would have been unthinkable in a polytheistic environment) before which no one could do anything other than accept and admire, even at one's own expense, as notably the authors of Job and Ecclesiastes would later do in Israel, but their method of addressing the problem of evil tended in that direction—from even farther away and apparently naively.

THE MAGICAL THERAPEUTICS OF EVIL

Magical therapeutics was necessarily derived from mythological representations. Magic considered evil to be the unforeseeable result of the actions of "evil forces." Therefore, those forces had to be targeted in order to compel them to "let go." The image people had of demons (which, to our knowledge, no one ever attempted to mythologically "specify" beyond a few fantastic and frightful traits) was immersed in a conception of the world that was in part irrational or, shall we say, "fairylike." Things had a multitude of obscure connections among them, one thing being able, for example, to represent and thus to replace all the individuals of its species: a scorpion was *the* Scorpion, and thus every scorpion; the image or the figurine of an individual, his name, or something that had been in contact with him *was* the individual; and mysterious contacts enabled a defect, or an evil, to pass from one object to another, as if by contagion.

Moreover, a person (at the very least certain people who were endowed, at birth or otherwise, with powers and particular secrets: let's say "sorcerers") could act upon things by imposing his dual natural capacity on them to alter, create, or neutralize his environment: his *hand*, manipulation, through the use of instruments or products defined and believed to be efficacious, could transform things or destroy them; and his *voice*, "incantation," imposed his will upon them and made them obey him, for they were sensitive to that. With experience and in time a true "anti-evil technique" was developed that enabled, if not everyone, then at least a few individuals, not to do evil (such people were included among the evil forces), but to repel the mysterious evil enemies of mankind and in that way to eradicate the misfortunes they caused. Such a system of defense against evil is called "magic."

This system was organized into formulas, procedures, and rituals, all adapted to the effects one wished to obtain from them or to the disadvantages one wished to repel, through the calculated use (even if its logic escapes us, so far removed are we from these imaginings) of oral and manual rituals, indeed, preferably the two together, as oral rituals gave all their meaning to manual rituals, and manual rituals materialized the strength and the effectiveness of oral rites.

We have ample documentary proof that such a system functioned in ancient Mesopotamia, at first all alone, then more or less engulfed or supplanted by exorcism or relegated to "popular practices," which the official religion had no reason to protest. Relevant texts are often in very elliptical and ambiguous language full of images and obscure allusions that are strange and undecipherable. Here are two examples. First is an incantation (here, this is indeed the proper word) against the effects of a scorpion bite. It is in Sumerian, dates from around the middle of the third millennium (therefore its language is quite difficult), and has been found both in Mesopotamia proper and in Ebla:

> "This Scorpion (representing the entire species), its tail is pulled off" (this was the elementary manual ritual to neutralize the animal: both the present evil that it had just inflicted and all later stingings of all possible scorpions). (What follows is an oral ritual: these words flattering both THE scorpion to coax it and demonstrating it henceforth without harmful effects, powerless): "Its body is made of gold! Its tongue [= its stinger] and its body (because its tail had been pulled off) are henceforth like a hand and an arm (separated)!"

Thus were the evil of the sting and its outcome eliminated.[83]

Another incantation was addressed to an evil demon, which was not even named. Naming was considered unnecessary since its victim had not the slightest doubt about its identity:

1   Let him eat his fury like the beast eats grass!
     And may the evil he has caused lose its force!
     . . . .

5   May he be able to cover his face (with shame, or impotency?)
     And may his speech again become as ineffective as when he
         was born![84]

We even find very short oral rituals that are reduced to a sort of
conjuration: an order given to noxious forces to passively obey the
powerful orders of the "sorcerer" and to carry off with them the evil
they had brought: "I entreat you! Be entreated!"

Sometimes an oral ritual did not need to be formulated, as the manual ritual was sufficiently effective by itself. Thus, to circumvent the
ill fortune that was to be expected from an encounter on a path either with a prostitute who was unavailable due to her having her period or with a pottery reject (viewed as bad luck), a failed vase cast
away, it sufficed, in the first case, to touch the breast of the woman,
thus opposing the evil effect of the *blood* with her *milk,* and, in the
second case, to seek out a "failed man," the image of the incomplete
and evil vase (i.e., one of the well-known, effeminate men),[85] the appearance of which would cancel out the effects of the pot.

THE EXORCISTIC THERAPEUTICS OF EVIL

As has been pointed out, the use of strictly "magical" defenses, without completely disappearing, became somewhat overshadowed in
the third millennium (it was still noted in Fâra and Ebla around 2500)
by the exorcistic "reform" movement, whose system from then on
was extraordinarily developed and maintained until the very end:
the vast amount of literature that has remained from almost every
century and found in almost all sites is testimony to this. While in-
tegrating magic into its religious and theocentric vision, exorcism
conserved the manual rituals of magic but completely reoriented
them: instead of maintaining their self-sufficiency, they henceforth
served only to offer the gods—the only ones who could intervene—
a sort of theatrical mimicry, a gestural program within the framework of which the gods had only to inject their will and their power
to make them effective and successful. In other words, the gods
then enjoined the "demons and evil forces" in the gods' service to
suppress the evils they had inflicted, following divine orders.

In accordance with its doctrine, exorcism focused its rejection of
evil on the responsibility of man, the sinner, vis-à-vis the gods; on the
repentance he was to express to them; and on the gods' will to erase

both the offense against them and the punishments that offense had provoked. The manual rituals could remain as they were; it was the oral rituals that, from north to south of the land, changed the meaning of the whole operation. It was no longer a matter of the victim or the "sorcerer" authoritatively "entreating" the demons through incantations to disappear along with their evil effects. Rather, the gods were implored through oral rituals that were formulated quite differently, so they would intervene and give the order to the tormenting evil forces to henceforth cease and desist in their punishments. In the magical regime the gods never appeared; in the exorcistic system they occupied center stage: everything was concentrated on them.

Here is a short account, and an example, of an exorcism ritual. It once again involves the painful and dangerous effects of a scorpion sting, which had, moreover, the effect of weakening its victim against the risks of existence: in other words, it constituted an "evil omen." The ritual, of which we have a few duplicate copies—proof that it was used regularly—first prescribes the necessary materials, notably:

> A bundle of seven reeds, to be used as a torch ["Seven," since the dawn of time, has been one of those numbers innately endowed, we do not know why, with a specific efficaciousness]. Then: the scorpion will be placed [the one responsible for the evil or another one, believed to be just as guilty and able to replace the other effectively] on the burning torch, until it is consumed. During that time one will recite, over the sting, the prayer as follows: "O wolf in the attic! Lion in the pantry! [Thus the author of the evil was flattered, as it was always better to cajole it to have a better hold over it.] Its 'horns' [the anterior legs, so characteristic] are used like those of a wild buffalo! Its tail is bent like that of a powerful lion. It was Enlil who built such a construction. The building that he has thus raised, let him demolish its precious bricks ('of lazulite'), and may his little finger erase everything! [Thus Enlil is asked to completely destroy the animal like a brick building that he had built, and, again, to flatter Enlil, the building is said to be made of precious bricks.] Then, let the flowing water carry everything away in its eddies. [It is thus tacitly advised, as a supplementary precaution, to throw into the river what remained of the creature:] let the current take it away, and may a salutary hand [that of Enlil!] descend to rest on its victim!" Such is the formula to calm the effects of the sting of a scorpion![86]

Thus the system of exorcism gave birth to an unbelievable increase in the number of such specific and ritualized procedures and operations which we call "exorcisms," whose goal was to suppress all the imaginable evils that might be imposed on human beings by the actions of demons and evil forces that had been ordered by the gods (who did not themselves intervene in those cases: the king did not perform the duties of his police!), who had been justifiably irritated by the "sins" of the victim and were motivated to punish severely to maintain good order. Since death was not, as we have stressed, an avoidable evil, one never fought against it; but all the misfortunes, illnesses, pain, sorrow, and suffering of the human condition could be, and in fact were, the objects of such exorcisms, of which ample specialized collections were composed, sections of which, if needed, could be pulled in "rapid copies, for immediate use."

There was thus an entire exorcistic realm of medicine, different from the more rational one based on empiricism. Exorcisms were similarly composed and assembled into collections along with other sources which, rather than battling against a current suffering or misfortune, were meant only to prevent the infinitely varied evils that were divinatorily foreseen. It is here that we begin to understand: the future unveiled by deductive divination was thus not something that was absolute and irrevocable but was only a decision made *hic et nunc* by the gods who communicated it. And like all the decrees of the sovereign and the decisions of judges, it was susceptible to reprieve, appeal, or revision. The exorcisms prepared with the intent of having the gods reverse their sentence were called *namburbû*, an Akkadianized term from the Sumerian nam.búr.bi, "(rituals of) dissolution (of evil presages)." Their purpose was thus practically coexistent within the divinatory universe; in certain "treatises," following each unfavorable oracle there are the appropriate *namburbû* to nullify it. And we have indications that the collections of *namburbû*, no doubt "open" and indefinitely augmentable, covered more than a hundred and thirty tablets: a rather admirable amount and variety!

Not only—and we will return to this—did exorcism constitute an important religious recourse, but it offered all the elements of an ample, multiform ceremonial. Many of its compositions were rather short: we read one example above. Here is another, somewhat longer, that provides a glimpse of the unfolding and general formulation of an exorcism, for the language and the style of these rituals were necessarily formalized. It concerns the dark presage that was presented to a family by the birth of a premature, sickly, misshapen, monstrous fetus, which was called an *izbu*. Here, first, is the opening paragraph, in which we can admire how all envisionable cases are judiciously foreseen to render the use of the ritual as extensive as possible.

If, in the house of the one concerned, there arrives a misshapen birth, either a farm animal, large or small, or a cow or a goat or a horse or a dog or a pig or a human—in order to avert the misfortune promised by this phenomenon, so that it touches neither the person concerned or his house:

Then comes the ritual of exorcism designed to counter the evil:

One will go to the banks of the river and will erect an enclosure of reeds, inside of which one will spread some "garden grass" [the name of a plant thought to be lustral; one thus created a space protected from any supernatural danger and inside of which at least part of the ritual could unfold without risk or supernatural obstacle]. Then one will construct a small, rough altar out of reeds there, on which one will place seven breads of offering, beer, dates, and *sasqu* flour; one will fill an incense burner with *burâšu*-juniper; and will fill three jugs of beer, to be placed [. . .]; *pannigu* breads, ear-breads; a grain [= 4 centigrams] of silver and a grain of gold. [To "butter up" the gods to whom one was going to speak, it was necessary to perform this act of "service" for them, in other words, to prepare at the very least a small meal for them, accompanied by an expensive gift. After which, one dealt with the misshapen object, the cause of all the hubbub, which had been preserved, since it was going to be at the center of the apotropaic ceremony, and was to be wheedled and above all "tricked" so that it did not suspect the fate that was being prepared for it: it was thus also given gifts before being placed on a board and sent off, as on a raft, for a simple voyage.] One will then place at the head of the misshapen object a pin (?) of gold, and after having attached a breastplate of gold to a piece of red wool, it will be attached to its chest. Then one will place on top of the "garden grass" the misshapen object thus presented. Then, after having the one concerned kneel, he will be made to recite the following: [This is the prayer to the gods, the oral ritual that constituted the essence of the exorcism. It was addressed to one of the most implored divinities in the course of these ceremonies: the god of justice, as well as of the sun]. Prayer: "O Šamaš, Judge of the Heavens and the Earth, Lord of Right and of Equity, Ruler of regions of On High and of Below! O Šamaš, it is in your power to give life to a dying man, to deliver the prisoner! O Šamaš, I have come to you! O Šamaš, I have sought out your presence! O Šamaš, I have turned toward you! Deliver me from the misfortune foretold by this misshapen object: let it not reach me! May that misfortune flee far away from me, so that day after day I may bless you, and that whoever sees me (thus delivered by you) forever sings your praises!" This should be recited three times [Re-iteration was believed to reinforce efficacy, in the exorcistic as much as in the magical domain.]

[There followed an additional oral ritual, addressed to the divine personality to whose powers one was going to resort for this par-ticular part of the ritual: "Divine River," for the "Flow of the Wa-ter," "River," had, in the eyes of the ancient Mesopotamians, a cer-tain divine nature and appropriate supernatural powers] . . . And facing River, one will say this to it: "O Holy River, you are the cre-ator of everything. [One then presented to it, by his name and his patronym, the one who needed its help:] "So and so, son of so and so, whose personal god is such and such and whose personal god-dess is such and such [these indefinite pronouns, which often ap-peared in the text of rituals, highlighted the applicability to all sub-jects], prey to the danger of a misshapen object, of ill omen, is in fear and terror! Take away from him the misfortune announced by this misshapen object! May such a misfortune not approach him, not come to meet him, not reach him! May that misfortune flee far away, so that day after day he may bless you and that whoever sees him (delivered by you) forever sing your praises! Through Éa and Asalluḫi [the great patrons of exorcism], make that misfortune go away [in these circumstances, this involved the *izbu* itself, which one was going to confer to River so it would swallow it up], and may your banks not allow it to freely escape [to thus return to land, still just as venomous]: make it descend into your depths [in other words: make it sink to the bottom!]! Take away this misfortune and grant the one concerned joy and life!"

Then came the actual ritual to expel the "evil":

Having recited this three times, the one concerned will be purified with water, with tamarisk, with *maštakal,* with *šalâlu* reed, and with "little palms." Then the misshapen object will be placed in the wa-ter with provisions and gifts. [The only thing left to do then was to put things back in place, completely removing all traces of the cer-emonial; the "evil," subtle and powerful, was always assumed to be capable of escaping, at least in part, the measures of annihilation, to once again exercise its ravages.] And when the apparatus of the cer-emony is taken down and one has prostrated oneself, the one con-cerned will be able (safe and sound) to return home. [But before then, to be cautious] "one will make a necklace out of carnelian beads, lazulite, serpentine, "spotted stone," "very spotted stone" [?], shiny silex, breccia, and "little breccia" [?], and one will put it around his neck for seven days. And the misfortune announced by the misshapen object will then be completely dissolved.[87]

Some of these exorcisms, in order to successfully face the more fearsome evils, had been developed into interminable "liturgies" with complicated manual rituals and multiple prolonged and solemn oral rituals. A famous one was called *Šurpu*,[88] "Combustion," and was directed against the interventions of an evil force that is rather mysterious to us and whose name was "Perjury," *Mamîtu* in Akkadian. In it one resorted to the seven- and even eightfold combustion of various objects that one imagined to have at first "taken," through contact, the evil of the victim. Included among the oral rituals [in some three hundred fifty columns on three tablets] was a sort of "confession" of all the sins imaginable that the victim, who could not remember distinctly, *might have committed.* The person concerned, who undoubtedly had to assume the costs of the religious service, appeared alone, and there is no mention of an entourage or any sort of companion—the person was called "the man," which might also be understood, depending on the case, as "the patient." He was always explicitly identified and presented to the gods by his complete name—we saw an example of this above.

Given the king's responsibilities and the supernatural dangers that threatened him more than anyone else, he was the object of many exorcisms, sometimes created for him alone. Perhaps part of a king's schedule was reserved for undergoing exorcisms, as is suggested by one of the many letters that his staff exorcists wrote to Esarhaddon (680–669)—who was, it is true, particularly pious:

> We have rites to perform ton[ight]: I shall perform one against "Loss of Flesh," and Urad-Ea another one before Enlil. We shall go to the *qirsu*.
>
> Yesterday I performed the ritual of *Bit [r]i[mki]*. I made a burnt-offering and we executed a purification ritual.
>
> I have appointed an exorcist for the chanter who is here, and gave him the following orders: "For six days do likewise, performing the purification ritual after this [fashion]."[89]

We do not know whether a ruler was obliged to attend all those devotions in person, but we might presume as much, at least for the most important rituals, those that concerned him most directly in the most consequential matters. In any case, we can assume that his exorcistic schedule was very full.

Dictated above all by circumstances (to take care of someone seriously ill, it was of course necessary to go to the bedside), *the place* of the exorcistic "sacramental" ritual was obviously not the temple, except when it concerned intervening during an ongoing liturgy, or any other type of sacred place, which were reserved, as we have seen, for the actual divine worship service. The exorcist himself, before beginning his ceremonies, prepared the space, which was purified and protected from evil influences and inside which he could operate without danger. Depending on the prescriptions of the ritual, a ritual could be performed on the banks of a river, on a steppe, or elsewhere outside, even at night, under the watch of the stars, as well as in the home of the "patient."

The *time* of this sacramental cult was naturally not determined by the regular liturgical calendar—again unlike the "service to the gods." It depended on the urgency of a patient's case or on other, variable criteria. But, no doubt depending on complicated calculations, of which we know nothing, by resorting to deductive divination—notably astrology and chronomancy—the ancient exorcists determined "propitious moments" *(adannu)* for the successful outcome of their exorcisms: "If it is performed then, it will be successful!" It goes without saying that success was never guaranteed—as is true of all promises made on some imaginary speculation. But failures never discouraged anyone, and there were a thousand explanations to explain a failure, beginning with a lapse in a ritual, the untimely intervention of some glitch, or the imperfect execution of some formula. Moreover, "backup exorcisms" were expressly anticipated for cases when a first operation might not give the anticipated results. In these matters, which were concrete and specific, everything no doubt depended on the personality and the "profession" of the official representative of the exorcistic discipline.

THE EXORCIST

The exorcist (in Sumerian, lú.maš.maš; in Akkadian, *âšipu,* from a root which appears to have referred to "exorcism" itself: that *sui generis* activity which, through special procedures, sought to obtain from the gods pardon for a sin and the relaxation of its punishment), the principal, indeed the only officiant, exercised a truly delicate and complex profession. The exorcist was experienced in diagnosing the patients who came to see him; he was also capable of choosing the formula that was exactly fitting and of organizing and directing its execution at the "propitious moment." He had to have been simul-

taneously a diviner, a psychologist, a doctor, a perspicacious confidant, and a liturgist. We have recovered a tablet (from the beginning
of the first millennium) that bears an impressive list from the professional library of an exorcist: several hundred works that covered all
relevant knowledge and activities. The exorcist was thus necessarily
well educated, and we have much proof of this. Once he chose the
most appropriate formula for the situation, he made the preparations for and presided over the entire ritual: he gathered the materials necessary for the manual rituals and used them appropriately;
he recited the oral rituals, including those in which he had to present himself as commissioned and endowed by the gods with all
necessary special powers; he made the patient repeat the oral part
that fell to him; he supervised the patient as to the repeating of exorcistic elements, as well as of certain words and gestures; and he
followed up with him after the ceremony, equipping him with am-
ulets and protective advice. The exorcist was the most important
member of the clergy in matters pertaining to the sacramental cult—
moreover, we are practically aware only of him!

As we have seen, the exorcist took part in a number of ceremonies
of the divine cult itself, in particular those involving "purifications,"
but we are not systematically informed as to his role in those cases.
Apparently, it was in the sacramental part of the cult that he above
all exercised his talents. Even if these exorcistic practices were far
from the majesty, the pomp, and the magnificence of the service to
the gods, if they did not move the officials or the crowds as the great
feast days did, and if they did not follow, throughout the year, a
strict liturgical calendar, we can believe, given the importance of a
universal recourse against "evil" (not only do innumerable documents point to this, but we can imagine that every day countless patients must have resorted to exorcism), that even if the exorcists'
place in the the clerical hierarchy was rather modest, the exorcists
were, in the end, as solicited and active as the priests of the "great
liturgy."

Once exorcism had replaced outdated magic and came under the
patronage of Éa and his son Marduk, who in that role was called
Asalluḫi, from the name of an ancient god connected to him, exorcism certainly occupied an unequaled place in the "inner" lives of
ancient Mesopotamians. The average person was practically excluded from the daily worship activities of the temples and was isolated in his life and everyday work. His need for help from the gods

apparently formed the essential aspect of his contact with the divine, the essence of his *actual* religion. The *minores* of their world—not to mention that wild and uncultivated group of humanity isolated in their fields and their steppes, like the "animals" of La Bruyère—had scarcely any opportunities, even in the cities, to take part in the strictly religious activities of the liturgical year, with the likely exception of the collective relaxation and joy of the great festivals. Exorcism provided everyone with the opportunity to express their dependency vis-à-vis the gods; to recognize the gods' grandeur and power as well as their activities on Earth; to benefit from their indulgence and from their pardon; to experience and to manifest gratitude toward them and to present modest offerings to them, thereby bringing together their innate vocation as servants and providers of their masters On High. Moreover, in addition to the possibility of foreseeing the future and the secrets of suffered evil, the hope that they might be relieved of their misfortunes and their pain brought about, or continued to bring about, a favorable personal contact with the gods, and such beliefs revitalized and maintained individuals' religiosity.

The sacramental cult—divination and exorcism—thus represented the true foundation of the religion of the *minores,* that is, of the great masses of the population, leaving the upper class alone in a position to know and to practice the religion in more depth.

CHAPTER SEVEN

Influence and Survivals

Influence

During its peak at the end of the fourth millennium and for centuries to come, the brilliant sun of Mesopotamia shed its light on the world around it. This was especially true since, located in the center of the Near East, from the earliest times it was connected through commerce, war, or politics to states and cultures of neighboring lands—entities that we only began to hear of at the end of the third millennium. Although those cultures might have provided Mesopotamia with not only the raw materials it lacked but also visual images, ideas, and discoveries, Mesopotamia was, and remained for a long time, in a position to contribute much more, even if the documentation available to us makes it almost impossible to know the specifics of that contribution. Let us at least cite the prodigious gift Mesopotamia offered the world, a gift that simultaneously implies inestimable teaching abilities and a profound transformation of the vision of the world and the culture around them: at the beginning of the third millennium Mesopotamia conveyed the original writing system that it had invented and developed to the Elamites in the southeast and, a few centuries later, to the peoples of Mari and Ebla in the northwest, while history waited for it to be disseminated everywhere before the ingenious simplification of the alphabet. Shortly after the middle of the second millennium, it was not by some small chance that this same writing system, in spite of its complexities and the Babylonian language written with it, was the vehicle of international diplomatic correspondence throughout the Middle East, as far as arrogant Egypt.

And what about Mesopotamia's religion? It is well agreed that divinities, primary sentiments, basic beliefs, and even essential practices could not have been materials for exportation: people do not change their gods easily! But when it concerned the great questions that people necessarily asked their masters On High, those concerning origins, the why and how of the universe surrounding them, humankind's existence, and the problems that never cease to arise in a person's life, the myths and rituals that a religion's pious imagination easily combines in response to those questions have always circulated, by word of mouth, like goods from hand to hand, assuming the beneficiaries accepted, absorbed, and adapted them to their own religious representations and convictions.

To give at least one idea of this influence, of that potential dependence of other oriental religions with regard to ancient Mesopotamia, without undertaking an exhaustive investigation, which would scarcely be appropriate here or even seriously conceivable, let us at least take a look at the religious system of the Semitic people of Israel, beginning in the twelfth century B.C.—in other words, at the Bible, which constitutes an account of those people and which has become, in the end, one of the foundations of our civilization, thus the more fascinating to us.

Anyone who has any familiarity with the Bible and with the beliefs of the ancient Mesopotamians cannot help being struck by their overlapping and convergences, on more than one point. For example, using a different vocabulary, since their languages were not the same—one is in Hebrew, the other in Akkadian—both represent the same scenario concerning a person's fate once he died and was buried: the Hebrew *nepheš* exactly reflected the Akkadian *eṭemmu*, the "phantom." After death both the *nepheš* and the *eṭemmu* were believed to be detached, in a certain sense, from the body in which until then they had had only a latent and as if virtual existence; their only other refuge was the immense and sinister underground abysses, which the Hebrews called *Šé'ôl*, the equivalent of the Mesopotamian *Arallû*, their "Great Earth" and their "Land of No Return," where for the shadows of the dead "there is no work, nor device, nor knowledge, nor wisdom" (Ecclesiastes 9:10), but only an endless torpor. It is, however, not at all certain that such a "mythology of death" was born in Mesopotamia: it is possible that here, among the Hebrews and among still others (up to the ancient Greeks, from Homeric times),[1] we are witnessing a very ancient foundation of representations that came from who knows where, earlier than any written tradition.

And yet, in a perhaps more firmly positive direction, in the Bible, as in Mesopotamia, we are continually struck by the same notion:

that is, that human existence is governed in everything by the supernatural world, which plays the role of sovereign, and which watches over the good behavior of its subjects. Everything that, positively or negatively, directs our lives responded to an express will, an explicit "command" from above. And to go against that command was to become guilty of a "revolt," of a "disdain," of a "sin" against the gods, thereby exposing oneself to "punishment" from them.

Such coincidences, and there are still more, are intriguing: might ancient Mesopotamian religion and thought have had some close relationship with those of other peoples of that time and, notably, with the ancient Israelites, the authors of the Bible? To dispel any doubt and to determine with some competence whether and to what degree the religious "beacon" of Mesopotamia shed its light on the minds and hearts of peoples as far as Palestine beginning at least in the final days of the second millennium, we must carefully distinguish what Israel might have already had from its traditional Semitic culture that it shared with the Mesopotamian Semites, and what those latter might have communicated to the Israelites pertaining to their own Mesopotamian heritage which they had developed by themselves.

The ontological superiority of the divine over the human, the perpetual directing intervention of the On High in our lives, the gods' role as "lawmakers" and regulators of our behavior, and their unleashing of their vengeful punishments if we "sin" against them, as well as the tableau of death and the afterlife and a few other common visions, quite likely came out of a cultural heritage specific to what we might call the Semitic "mentality." It was as specific to those people as the structure of the language that conveyed it and was thus, like their mentality, present wherever the members of that specific and culturally coherent "family" were gathered, along with everything else that makes up a culture: a certain worldview, a unique way of feeling about things and estimating and grading their worth, an esthetic, defined tastes and revulsions, and all those hereditary representations and routines that are received at birth from one's parents and environment and that will be passed on to one's own children. The Mesopotamians, despite any influence the Sumerians might have had on them in this regard, patiently formed those traditional givens in the course of their long history; and the other Semitic populations, each grouped in their own locales, did the same, just as they separately developed within a given framework the precision and wealth of their own individual languages. These are commonalities of kinship, of family—and not necessarily of teaching and borrowings. The likely influence of the Sumerians was felt in other areas and does not appear to have truly and profoundly affected those cultural traits.

When we find ourselves, here and there, in the presence of more elaborate constructs, which nothing in itself requires or renders inevitable, and which cannot be explained as coming from a naive and spontaneous traditional perspective, we are forced to detect complex constructions, learned and duly established reflections, which were thus not received from birth but were indeed constructed and transmitted from the oldest to the most recent, from the most to the least experienced, from the richest to the poorest, with a preferential source, at least, being the ones among whom one notes such complexities first, from a certain distance in time.

For example, on four or five occasions in various books of the Bible, all later than the sixth century, one finds, regarding the creation of the world, allusions to a formidable battle between the Creator and "the Sea," personalized and accompanied by gigantic dragons, who are beaten down along with it. Thus the author of Psalms 74:13–17 calls upon God in these terms:

> Thou didst divide the sea by thy strength: thou breakest the
>   heads of the dragons in the waters.
> Thou breakest the heads of Leviathan in pieces, and gavest him
>   to be meat to the people inhabiting the wilderness.
> Thou didst cleave the fountain and the flood: thou driedst up
>   mighty rivers.
> The day is thine, the night also is thine: thou hast prepared the
>   light and the sun.
> Thou hast set all the borders of the earth: thou hast made sum-
>   mer and winter.

On the one hand, the relationship between the creation of the world and a gigantic victory of the Demiurge over the Sea and its fearsome associates in itself has nothing obvious or restrictive about it and, in fact, has not the slightest connection with other biblical representations. On the other hand, all these passages were composed after a certain class of Israelites had been in Mesopotamia for a long time during the great exile (sixth century). We are thus quite reasonably led to believe that those Israelites would have encountered, appreciated, and adopted, in their own way, the mythological representation of the creation of the world they found there, undeniably created in the land and elaborated, in particular, in the *Epic of Creation* as the result of the immense victory of the demiurge Marduk over the terrifying forces of the Sea (Tiamat), the original mother goddess, and her army of enormous monsters and dragons. The Israelites would thus have at that time received (under what circumstances, we naturally do not know) an idea, an image: an explicative myth about the origins of the universe, which they did not themselves have (there is no mention of such a myth earlier or elsewhere in the Bible) and which they might have adopted and adapted for their own religious convictions, before making it their own in the new biblical presentation, which was deemed acceptable. The demiurge in Israel was no longer Marduk, the god of Babylon, but Israel's own god, the single god, Yahweh, who, to create the world, had annihilated all the other immense divinities.

Israel, ever since Moses (around 1250), had its own intolerant and exclusive religious representations. Unlike the Mesopotamians and alone among all other peoples around them, Semites and non-Semites alike, the Israelites were resolutely *not* polytheistic but recognized only a single god, Yahweh. And they refused to see that god, or any other, in some image or human likeness whatsoever: they vigorously rejected any anthropomorphism. The authors of the Bible were thus very happy to receive new images and myths from outside their land, including from Mesopotamia, provided they could pour them into their own religious mold, adapting them to their religiosity and to their particular view of God.

There is a revealing example that can easily shed light on both the dependency and the independence of the authors of the Bible in the above cases with regard to Mesopotamian religious ideology. It concerns their adoption, use, and transformation of the famous and central myth *Atraḫasîs* to present the origin of humankind and human history in the first chapters of Genesis. As in the Babylonian tale, man was created, certainly not by the divinities that were mentioned in that myth (Enki/Éa and the goddess Mammi), but by Yahweh alone, the single god of Israel, and thus the single creator of everything. And man was created not to labor on behalf of the gods, in order to provide and procure them with everything they needed to live opulently and tranquilly, for Yahweh needed *nothing;* man was created simply "to till the ground" (Genesis 2:5). He was made out of clay; but Yahweh, having neither usable divine flesh nor blood, had not molded that clay "with the flesh and blood of a god" of second rank: he simply gave it life through an immaterial gesture, by "breathing" life into it (Genesis 2:7). Later (Genesis 6:1ff.), jumping ahead to the end of this story, to the Flood, if Yahweh decided to annihilate mankind, it was not because their noisy throngs were preventing him, like Enlil, from sleeping, for Yahweh did not sleep and had no need for sleep; but simply because, concerned above all about mankind, about the justness, righteousness, and honesty of their lives, he wanted to wipe out that initial, completely corrupt population. Here is another difference between Yahweh and Enlil: it was Yahweh himself, in his desire to see humanity continue, who prepared a man—a just man—to serve as his new stock. There can hardly be a more brilliant or consequential example (although in the end it was the version in the Bible and not that of *Atraḫasîs* that finally won out) of how, through its religion and mythology, Mesopotamia shed its light around it through time and place, thereby leaving us strong and powerful images of our origins, or how the cultural fabric it had woven from its religion and mythology became our own, after it had been reworked and radically transformed from within by stronger religious concepts and imaginations that were ultimately more fruitful and more durable than its own.

Survivals

Around the middle of the first millennium Mesopotamia and its world began slowly to decline to their demise. At that time Mesopotamia had lost, and had no chance of recovering, its political independence, which until then had been the firm cement of its culture and religion, as well as of its ability to disseminate them.

Cyrus the Great integrated Mesopotamia, along with all its territory, into the huge Persian Empire. Two centuries later Alexander the Great seized Babylon and its lands, which were once again, after his death, incorporated into another foreign organism, the empire of the Seleucids. Two centuries later, without having contributed anything to it, the Seleucids lost Babylon, which fell into the hands of the Parthians, before very quickly being erased from all memory and sinking into a long night of oblivion.

If we are to believe the mass of cuneiform documents, daily life in Mesopotamia hardly changed; there were no sudden or profound ruptures. Changes occurred as if on the sly, over long periods, without fanfare: they never leap out at us. Until the middle of the Seleucid Period, not only did the life of the temples with their opulent daily rituals and the rhythm of their solemn festivals follow their course unchanged, but those who were involved on a daily basis, whom we encounter everywhere, bear the same personal names as their ancestors, undeniable witnesses of the longevity of their sentiments and beliefs with regard to the gods whom they worshiped: Anu, Enlil, Éa, Sîn, Šamaš, Adad, Ištar, Nanaya, Marduk, Nabû, Nergal, Ninurta, Papsukkal, and a few others. They were still invoked as "munificent," "benevolent," "generous," "protective," "masters," "creators," "givers of life" and "of favors," and "who pardon sins." Everything here strongly attests to the stability of representations, of benevolent attitudes and of religious practices.

However, under the unchanged surface one senses things evolving, without haste and as if in the shadows: "Under the straw the water flows," as the old scribes of Mari used to say.[2]

Foremost, Mesopotamia was gradually to lose its own language, that indispensable support of an autonomous culture. Aramaic, a recent Semitic formation, was imported at the end of the second millennium by nomadic hordes who at first lived apart, in "the steppe," and rarely frequented the towns or the villages except to attack and raid them. Aramaic had the undeniable advantage, which was obstinately disdained and rejected by the learned of the land, of being written by means of the extraordinary graphic simplification of the alphabet, which would ultimately rally the entire world around it. It was so influential that the Achaemenids, to ensure a connection between so many diverse peoples living in their empire, made Aramaic the official, international language. Aramaic therefore began slowly but steadily and patiently to usurp Akkadian in the land. In time Akkadian endured the fate that it had itself imposed on Sumerian fifteen centuries earlier: it became reduced to the language of "scholars," of religion, of science, of the upper cultivated classes, whose representatives were increasingly fewer in number and increasingly self-contained and isolated from the masses.

Greek culture complicated the picture. A certain number of its representatives lived and worked at the Persian court. Following Alexander, Greek influence spread, and the Greek language was adopted in refined circles, by the masters of culture. It was not by chance that

Berossus, a contemporary of Alexander and "priest of Marduk in Babylon," decided to present *in Greek* the venerable traditions, customs, and beliefs of his compatriots. A certain cultural class thus retained the sense of holding onto an ancient, opulent, and incomparable cultural heritage, and the glorious past of the land was not yet annihilated.

But the culture was no longer viewed in the same way: not only did the loss of its original language weaken its impact, but in time its content was no longer understood as it used to be. The first "commentaries" on ancient myths date from the first millennium: works that were once "transparent" increasingly had to be explained, a result of and contributing to a loss in understanding. Ancient myths, the texts of which were always faithfully recopied and consequently disseminated, were no longer considered to be explanatory. They had become distant memories of "ancient history," "traditions," and motifs, themes for explication.[3] Moreover, it had been some time since such myths had been composed, people being content to present them as so many illustrations of rituals or of liturgical activities. Even the view of the gods changed. A more frequent, more immediate contact with foreign divinities than occurred before seems to have revived an ancient penchant for syncretism, which had long been active in the land. The traditional well-known recognition in Mesopotamia of the supernatural nature of foreign divinities sometimes suggests that in that polytheistic world they above all saw *divine functions* (sovereignty over the world; its creation and its government; justice; the animation and moderation of various great mechanisms of nature and culture; etc.) rather than *divine figures*. These functions were carried out by figures whose names and appearances might vary (e.g., Kamulla was Éa among the Kassites, and Laḫura-til was Ninurta among the people of Subartu) and were thus to be considered secondary, as illustrated at the end of the *Epic of Creation:*

> Let the black-headed folk be divided as to gods,
> But by whatever name we call him, let [Marduk] be our god.[4]

Hellenism crystallized and reinforced those already ancient beliefs which were gradually implanted and tacitly developed into the religion of the land. And Berossus makes use of them in his tale of the Flood when he replaces the name of the ancient supernatural ruler of the gods, Enlil, with that of old Kronos, as Herodotus had already

done in *The Persian Wars* (I, 181) when he made Zeus the equivalent
of Marduk. And it was following the same logic, when Berossus was
presented with strange allegations regarding his rendering of the creation myth from the same epic—"The woman cut in two by Bêl/
Marduk, and from one-half of which he had made the Earth, and
from the other, Heaven"—that he explains: "But that was speaking
of Nature through metaphor."[5] In other words, the contents of
myths were emptied of their initial religious significance, becoming
examples of a, shall we say, neutral, "philosophical," and rational
view—in the Greek fashion. We do not know how the common
man, the "simple faithful," understood and felt about these changes,
but it is clear that the religiosity of the *majores,* the educated, those
who could still recopy, read, and understand the ancient myths and
rituals, must have assimilated a sort of diffuse "pantheism" that
blurred the differences in divinities and primarily exalted their divine nature. When the last of those old scholarly minds disappeared,
leaving behind only a few memories and a few not easily accessible
translations of their old stories of the gods, the age-old religion of
Mesopotamia disappeared with them.

But was it completely and forever dead? Or did a fragment of it survive? It is too difficult to believe that such a vast, powerful, and deep-
rooted system, one that was so firmly constructed and "reasonable,"
was, in that way, completely swallowed up, along with everyone involved, in a few dozen or hundred years. A few Mesopotamian deities reappeared here and there in the course of the first centuries of
our era. They were invoked, but represented rather vague, more or
less mysterious and obscure concepts, in gnostic writings. There were
notably Nebo (Nabû), Nergal, and a few others, but not the major
gods (Anu, Enlil, Éa, Mammi, etc.), who were apparently erased from
memory, as if they incarnated the old religion of which they had so
long remained the support columns, and as if they were unable to
survive its crumbling. However, such an assertive, adventurous, and
provocative personality as that of the shameless patron of "free love,"
Ištar, left much of herself in her Greek and Roman homologues: Aphrodite and Venus. Finally, a great myth also endured until much later,
no longer due to its strictly religious content but as a speculative "position," an explicative "principle" of things: close to half a millennium *after* the beginning of our era, Damascius, a Neoplatonic phi-
losopher who lived in Athens and who held forth on the "Problems
and Solutions about the First Principles" still cited quite correctly,

probably from some old Aramaic translation unknown to us, the first words of the obsolete *Epic of Creation* to stress that unlike other "thinkers," the Babylonians never mentioned a unique principle of things but had imagined two.[6]

Thus we see the crumbling and disappearance of that ancient religious system which, ever since "the night of time," even before history, had accompanied and given life to the ancient Mesopotamian civilization from which it had come.

Although we lack indigenous testimony, which is nonexistent, and for good reason, the flood of Hellenistic and Roman documents nevertheless reveals a long, even brilliant, although restricted, survival of Mesopotamian civilization. Everyone knows that Alexander the Great's conquests in the lands of the Mediterranean world brought about a formidable revolution in thought and feeling there. From Asia Minor to Egypt, Syria, and Persia, the assembled forces of Greek reflection and knowledge encountered venerable exotic and fascinating traditions everywhere they looked: very ancient thinking, experiences, and constructs that had accumulated over the years from unexpected and unheard of cultures, in models that were still more or less uncommon and new, and in which were reflected unusual ancient wisdom that was both attractive and exploitable.[7]

Out of all this, and during the centuries that followed those encounters, a true multiform religious explosion occurred. The discovery of ancient oriental deities that had until then been confined to their own lands, of their images and personalities, both original and unknown, and of the strange myths and unique rituals surrounding them—those of the Great Mother of Phrygia, the seductive Egyptian Isis, the Syrian Ba'als, and the secrets of Iranian dualism—successively gave rise here and there to new religious systems that for a time fed the minds and hearts of those around them.

One of these systems, undoubtedly the most remarkable, which had a truly grandiose, universal, and durable destiny, was a true *astral religion*. It existed everywhere in the Mediterranean world and ruled there a long time until its apogee in imperial Rome. Its divine personnel was made up of celestial bodies: the Sun, the Moon, the planets, the stars, the constellations, and in particular those that made up the zodiac, were considered to be authentic divinities, who, from their celestial domain, dominated the world, directed it, and illuminated it with their splendor. Their power, which was manifest as much in the phenomena of nature as in the existence of humans, was absolute; their decisions, without appeal. Each entity harbored prerogatives, abilities, and virtues within itself that defined and personalized it, and which it irradiated to objects and people, imprinting them with their destinies, of which the stars were the absolute masters in everything.

This destiny could be known by *deducing* it from the appearance or absence of certain stars in the sky at any given moment, from their movements, from their mutual approaching, through which they informed people of their wills and decisions, bearing not only on the world—the land and its rulers—but on every person. Only by studying and following the unchangeable and duly established rules known only by the experts, the appearance of the sky, the visibility or the disappearance, the placement or the movement of the stars at the moment of a person's birth, the moment when the stars took control of him, was one in the position, not to conjecture, but to conclude, to *deduce* with scientific rigor from those observations the infallible trajectory of the subject: his *destiny* established by those celestial and invariable divinities. The rule of the stars thus imposed a total fatalism: one could, thanks to them, know one's future, but no one could escape from it. The world was essentially ruled by a sort of universal law that was above everything, that irresistibly governed everything, and from which nothing could be removed, an inflexible law—"Fortune" (Tyche), "Destiny" (Heimarmene), "unbendable Necessity" (Ananke)—that bent everything to its decisions. Rather less a movement of fear and recoil before this pitiless power, religious sentiment had changed here into a sort of boundless admiration of those all-powerful stars, of that supernatural starry sky, sparkling, brilliant, the contemplation of which was enough to incite avid enthusiasm as well as a complete ecstatic submission.

Of course, in such a doctrine it was out of the question to expect to bend *Necessity:* prayer and cult thus in themselves had no place there and were supplanted by complete abasement to supreme wills. But religions and mythologies always touch the heart more closely than they do the mind and are therefore never completely logical, and in at least common religious practice, alongside such desperate determinism, there slipped in prayers, rituals, pious recipes, words, and gestures, more or less adjusted to deal with all the circumstances of life, and which purported to act, not on the gods, but on things: a kind of "sorcery" or "magic" or "exorcism" in that it was most often to the stars themselves that people appealed in order to obtain the favorable outcome that was hoped for.

The astral religion even penetrated and—following its own vision of things—strongly transformed the beliefs and myths concerning the meaning of death and of what came afterward, as well as the very makeup of humankind. The human was not, as had been thought, simply a body, a carnal mass: to animate and enhance him he above all had a "spirit," in itself independent from the body, a "soul" existing by itself, created foremost by the divine stars in their celestial dwellings, one of those layers in the sky that were assigned to each of them. At birth the soul descended to join the material body, itself formed on Earth. As it descended toward its earthly goal, the soul crossed through successive circles belonging to the various stars, thereby acquiring at the whim of those stars, the qualities, the peculiarities, and the talents unique to them which they thus bestowed to form and to define the soul's personality. At the other end of existence, at the time of death, freed from its carnal attachments to the body, which then returned to matter, the soul returned to its celestial homeland, gradually becoming more enriched by the luminous and beatific attributes that were conferred upon it by the sovereign stars according to their goodwill until it was lost among them, endlessly to contemplate them in the incomparable spectacle of the sparkling and magnificent starry sky and settled forever in that blessed state. As we can clearly see, even though it contains remnants of other ancient religions—Mesopotamian—it is an original and complete religious system, coherent and logical, capable of inspiring and teaching: it ruled over the minds of the land for a few centuries, having, in truth, everything it needed to satisfy them.

A number of texts from that time, more or less opaque and obscure, original or obviously apocryphal, explained the workings and principles of that religion and encouraged belief in and devotion to it. They all focus on that which formed the depths and the essence of the system, out of which everything else emerged: destiny that was assigned and known in advance and unfailingly concluded, *deduced*, from the position of the stars and from other indications of their wills that they were believed to provide. In other words, astrology was so fascinating, so attractive, so advantageous, and, at the same time, so certain and so clear that it was rapidly transformed from simple observation and calculation into a true *science*, and from a science into

a *faith* and a *religion*—from a system of knowledge into a supernatural construct, one able to join both the heads and hearts of people,
and to direct them, with the caution of the greatest minds of the
time, indeed, of the main philosophy of that time, that of the Sto-
ics, who had integrated astral religion into their own system and vision of the world.

Where did it originally come from? It has sometimes been suggested that Egypt might have made the greatest contribution, and
that it might in fact have been there that the Greeks first learned of
it. It is no doubt not a coincidence that a few bibles of the astral religion were composed in Alexandria under the names of legendary
figures, such as the revelation of Nechepso-Petosiris or that of Hermes Trismegistus, "Thrice-Greatest Hermes." But Egypt, since the
dawn of time, was traditionally never really interested in astrology,
and astrology could therefore not have been born there: Egypt only
received it, like other riches, as other lands did, from Mesopotamia.
In what we have just read and summarized about astral religion, it
is impossible, if we recall everything we have learned up to now, not
to repeatedly notice many reflections of what we now know to be
unique to the Mesopotamian religion, elements that have been
stressed each time they have appeared.

In its land of origin, in Mesopotamia, astrology was not an isolated discipline but one of the realms of a religious practice that was
in some way universal: deductive divination, which gathered some
of its "presages" from the positions and the movements of the stars
("If the planet Venus is late in the firmament, before disappearing:
the rains will cease"),[8] while others were derived elsewhere ("If a
woman gives birth to a stillborn baby—pestilence"). In this form of
indigenous and increasingly practiced astrology—as in all of deductive divination—the celestial bodies were not the *actors,* the *causes,*
but only the *announcers* of the unveiled future: they *warned of it,*
they *did not bring it about.*

The destiny that the stars revealed in this way was not imagined
to be fixed and unavoidable. In Mesopotamia a great number of formularies—of "exorcisms," as we call them—had been calculated,
drawn up, and put into circulation; their goal, following some threat
of an ominous future, was to obtain from the gods a "change into
good of the evil at first foreseen." Because the "evil" was like a verdict,
or sentence, from a judge, that sentence could always be appealed,
commuted, or annulled.

In other words, astrology, at its point of departure in Mesopotamia, was diametrically different from the rigid and fatalistic discipline that developed into the "astral religion" as practiced on the model described above. In the beginning, astrology was a part of a system, and then it became another system in itself. Its structure was superficially the same: the future unveiled by the stars. But in Mesopotamia, let us repeat, the future was only *unveiled,* and not *caused* or *unbendably imposed* by the stars. To go from the first to the second belief it was necessary to divinize the stars: instead of being simple subjects and instruments of the gods, they became not only true gods but great gods, equipped with absolute powers over the world and all things.

We cannot deny that celestial objects, at least in religious representations, touched the divine and thus had something divine about them, somewhat like other supernatural beings such as certain "forces" in the world—fire, rivers, mountains, as well as "demons" and other nuisances, and like our saints. Not only, as they are defined in the *Epic of Creation* (V:2), were they "images" or "reflections" *(tamšilu)* of the gods, like the gods' shadows placed on the screen of the sky; but in order to explain the existence, the unfailing eternal itinerary, and the always impeccable revolutions of all those celestial bodies, the Mesopotamians, since the darkness of time, had mythologically placed at each one of their sides—if we may say so—a "patron divinity" who was more or less connected to them. Thus the Moon had Nanna/Sîn to animate and rule over it; the Sun had Utu/Šamaš; the planet Venus, Inanna/Ištar; and the Auriga, Enmešarra. Such inseparability was believed, at least in popular belief, to cause something of the attributes, the prerogatives, the powers, and, in short, the divine character of the divine patron to rub off, so to speak, onto each individual celestial body.

It is a fact that in liturgical documents the name of a star was sometimes replaced with that of the god who was the master of it. As unfailing objects of a supernatural nature, people made offerings to them, and prayers, which sometimes still move us, were addressed to them. The stars were also considered to be intermediaries between the gods and humans and were assigned to deliver human beings' desires and requests to the gods:

> Star of the Waggoner, his god sends you to the man, and the man sends you to his god! I therefore deputize you to intercede on my behalf with my personal god.[9]

They were believed to have superhuman powers, such as that of rendering medications prepared under their nocturnal watch more active and powerful.

Such a "shifting" seems to have occurred, not in the reasoning of "theologians," but in the imagination and common religious practices of the masses, which would apparently have gradually forced the theologians' hand. It is therefore possible that at least in the common religion in Mesopotamia people gradually forgot, or blurred, the ontological distance between those august elements of the universe and the divine world, even if the official religion maintained that uncrossable chasm. Thus people might have been led to more or less "divinize" the stars entirely, even if, in the original astrology, they had never been considered anything but the instruments and the "written messages" of the gods.

Although there is nothing concrete to suggest this, was that step made in Mesopotamia itself? Or did it occur far from Mesopotamia's immediate and corrective influence? We have not the slightest idea. It is nevertheless more likely, perhaps, that the transfer, the exporting, of Mesopotamian astrology at least favored a "change of nature" in the stars, which were henceforth considered no longer as mere signs of a change in things but as the all-powerful and divine authors of all change.

The fact is that although ancient Greek religion never considered the celestial bodies as such as objects of its devotion, its myths, or its cult, they were presented as being endowed with a true divine nature beginning in the middle of the first millennium. In Plato's *Epinomis* (of which the true author is believed to be his disciple and secretary, Philippus of Opus), written around 350, and perhaps following on the heels of Pythagorism, while referring to the "Barbarians," in whom it is not difficult to perceive the distant "Babylonians" (986), the author invokes and defends "the divine order of the stars" (981), "that should be celebrated as authentic divinities, or, at the very least, as images of the gods, prepared by the gods themselves" (983). Such were the divine stars, the astral divinities, which would, in a few centuries, arrive at the very heart of a great and overwhelming religion.

If we needed additional proof of the Mesopotamian origins of astrology, thus transformed, magnified, and universalized into the astral religion, we can simply recall the name that was given to its propagators, the first great astrologers, the principal officiants and apostles of that religion, who burgeoned in the Hellenistic and above all Roman eras. They were called "Chaldeans"—as one might say "Babylonians," indeed "priests of Babylon," as Herodotus already expressed in *The Persian Wars* (I:181). The name of this Aramean tribe, after the beginning of the first millennium, changed in meaning and henceforth designated those who had been born in Babylonia. Later, and elsewhere, it became synonymous for the term "astrologer" and, in short, "apostle of the astral religion," without considering the land of origin of the one so designated. It was thus indeed from Mesopotamia that the first specialists in astrology, still genuine but on its way to being transformed, had arrived, loaded with old secrets of the Mesopotamian religion.

It is quite possible that they imported other secrets with them as well, those linked more or less closely to their religion and their profession, beginning with those "prayers," manipulations, rituals, and formulas that enabled their creators and the first Mesopotamian users of them to appeal to the gods to act upon events, in particular on those revealed and expected through deductive divination, with astrology in the lead, so they might "transform from bad to good" the destiny thus uncovered. We have found evidence of some illogical practices in the astral religion (but could there have been any rigorous logic in that system—in any religious system at all?), practices that conveyed the hope of deflecting the unbearable fatalism of the stars. In their original Mesopotamia, such practices were only so many exercises of the "sacramental cult," in the form of requests for pardon, types of appeals presented to the gods in the hope of convincing them to commute, reduce, or cancel the too severe initial sentences. Following the natural evolution of things, it is highly likely that no doubt beginning in their native Mesopotamia and even more so once they were uprooted, those exorcisms became simple recipes, simple formulas acting *ex opere operato*, self-sufficient "secrets" upon which religions are often fed, especially "popular" and debased religions. Through those practices, as well, Mesopotamia largely survived in Hellenistic and Roman religiosity.

Although we have just scratched the surface of the world after Mesopotamia, after being steeped for this short time in the vast and age-old Mesopotamian religion, we notice that the world, perhaps even more so on the religious level, was full of Mesopotamian fragments of all kinds, of which a complete inventory has not yet been drawn up.

Conclusion

Like all the parameters of our culture, religion is one of the greatest resources we have for living: not only does it channel a profound sentiment about our nature, but it alone can explain the unbearable secrets and absurdities of brutal facts and neutralize their hostility. It can even bring us a certain joy in life.

After having examined it here at length, over its three millennia of existence, and having drawn something like a finished diagram, if not a portrait, of it, who now could deny that the ancient Mesopotamians organized and deployed an intelligent religious system? That system was at first composite, founded on the exchanges and the accommodations of two cultures (at least!) in symbiosis, with distinct characteristics and completely diverse from the start—Sumerian on the one hand, Semitic on the other. Later, it remained only in the hands of the Semites, who were profoundly marked, of course, by their first teachers but were henceforth left to themselves, as devout followers. They steered their religion through many stages in its evolution, developing it reasonably and gradually in perfect harmony with their own way of being, living, seeing, and thinking.

The religious system harmonized with their image of the body, the head, and the heart. In the Mesopotamians' representation of that "supernatural order of things" which their religious sentiment mysteriously and vaguely conveyed to them, they saw a uniform, greater, stronger, more clairvoyant, and endlessly exaggerated reflection of themselves and of their society. But that analogy never erased their awareness of an uncrossable ontological distance separating them from their gods; nor did anything ever threaten the feelings that linked them to the gods.

As if to further stress that radical distance, and while representing the gods' role in the world and in the lives of each individual, the Mesopotamians chose the most telling, the most striking, and to them the most unforgettable fundamental metaphor: the earthly political power that was familiar to them—monarchic and "pyramidal," with, at the top, a single and uncontested chief and beneath him an entire gamut of lesser authorities, more powerful the closer they were to the summit.

Thus they hierarchized the initially rather confused multitude of their divinities, even if it meant making a few exceptional rearrangements to deal with occasional bends in the road that occurred with a secular balancing of their devotion. Thus they also sought, and very quickly and no doubt lastingly found, clever and multiple responses to the insistent questions endlessly raised by their own existence and purpose in life, as well as those of the universe and even of the gods, by resorting to the imaginary, ingenious, and all-powerful interventions of their divinities. The rich mythological literature that Mesopotamia has left behind—a pale reflection of all that was ever written down and above all discussed—attests to the Mesopotamians' curiosity but also to their vivacity of spirit and their religious intelligence.

In this way, not only by virtue of the affirmed ontological superiority of their gods, whose inscrutability no one could overcome, but also by virtue of the gods' role as masters and governors of the world, they recognized the gods' sovereign privilege of complete freedom of decision and action. All the expressions and all the demonstrations of the gods' will were thus accepted within the same "civic" spirit, as it were, like the orders of the kings by their subjects: without discussion, without protest, without criticism, in a perfect and fatalistic submission, with the clear consciousness that one does not resist that which is stronger. The gods were considered too clever, too equitable, and too irreproachable for them ever to be called arbitrary or for their decisions ever to be questioned. In that land, even in words, no one ever really rebelled against the most pitiless of all decisions: our universal condemnation to death.

As for all the ills, problems, and misfortunes that befall us, the ancient Mesopotamians introduced a logic, a rationality, a justification, by presenting them as the "punishment" for our disobedience to the will from On High, for our "sins" against the sovereigns of the world. It is true that, in this regard, as in the presence of other enigmas to which, for lack of anything better, they had attributed more than one response, they seem later to have preferred to invoke—still in perfect accord with the metaphor of political power—the sovereign liberty of those who held absolute power, who were capable, the gods as well as the kings, of abrupt, gratuitous, and inexplicable changes of heart and were sometimes driven to destruction and ruin and sometimes to benevolent and well-meaning dispositions, for which it was only necessary, when plunged into misfortune, to patiently await. Thus, everything we see around us, all that happens to us, was explained, rendered acceptable, and rid of its incoherence or its apparent injustice.

It was never believed—there was no reason to do so—that the gods, even though some of them, by virtue of their very roles, were in fact to be feared, were themselves inspired by any hostility toward humans. After all, were not humans at the very least quite useful if not indispensable to the gods? The earthly subjects' primary role was to obey their king and his representatives and also to ensure the luxury of their material lives; likewise, the gods were believed to have "invented" humans so that they might work and provide all the goods and services the gods needed for a pleasant existence, so the gods would be free to deal with the concerns of governing the world. Religious practice in Mesopotamia, what we call the "cult," was reserved for that "service to the gods," carried out with zeal, with splendor, with pomp, as was appropriate to those lofty figures. In spite of his humility and his insignificance, the human thus had an essential mission in the workings of the world, an august, ennobling one: from his position he contributed to the entire order of the universe.

That function did not go beyond the realm of "work" and of "service." When the latter had been accomplished, things were in balance, and the gods did not expect any effort of moral rectitude from a person, which would have brought nothing to the gods. A person's behavior concerned only himself: without faults, without disobedience to the gods, without disdain for their orders, in other words, without "sins," such "good" behavior at least spared him the gods' vindictive anger and the misfortunes that it unleashed. In that religion there were only relationships between humans and gods that were in some way "economic" and "of service": an affectionate attachment, truly cordial personal relationships, were not even imaginable. Not being of the same order as the gods, each person lived on his own scale, and it does not seem that the ancient Mesopotamians suffered from any feeling of day-to-day drudgery, since it was simply part of the order of things.

Nor does it seem that such a religious perspective—the destiny of labor, of submission, of servitude—which the Mesopotamians never sought to upset, as we would undoubtedly not fail to naively attempt to do today—led them to any real pessimism, bringing on discouragement and despair. A religion is not meant for that, and without shouting it from the rooftops, they must necessarily have liked the life that their gods had made for them. They above all applied themselves to being successful in it, even if, in our opinion, such an exclusive ideal seems very down-to-earth, far from any grandiose and exalting horizon. There were evidently many joys in that religion, which the devout admit to on more than one occasion. Most often experienced calmly and without fanfare, those joys occasionally appear in short paroxysms, as in those moments of common joy, excitation, and enthusiasm that the people seem to have experienced during the magnificent ceremonies of the liturgy and, even more so, during the great festivals.

Moreover, to enhance human lives, the gods, like good "bosses" who provide a few reassuring and useful benefits for their employees, had given humans two abilities that facilitated their existence and, subsequently, improved their "service." They notably granted humans the ability both to know, through divination, the future that the gods had assigned to them and, using the procedures of exorcism, to rid themselves of the ills of all sorts that might befall them.

Of course, neither divinatory operations nor exorcistic practices were de facto infallible; but the failures, necessarily frequent, scarcely seem to have weakened the confidence people had in them or discouraged people from using them. But what was important was, not the actual success of those practices, but the *possibility of success:* the hope that they inspired, the suppression of despair, which would have made human life a locked and stifling, confining space. To be sustained, our lives have an absolute need for illusion. And the Mesopotamians' religion indeed offered them a certain amount of hope.

As for the afterlife, that inevitable indefinite drowsiness that awaited them all, it seems not to have overly concerned them, as they were unable to do anything about it.

Having seen a few extraordinary pieces of evidence it seems at least possible, if not probable, that the religion allowed an elite group of more demanding, more penetrating, more profound, more frankly devout minds to glimpse—just barely!—an unsuspected and wider religious horizon, to have a higher notion of the supernatural, as we have sensed (perhaps too influenced by our own religious representations and routines) in those timid and vague attempts—for lack of anything better!—of henotheism; in that obscure expectation of a universal "destiny," or "necessity"; in that anticipation of possible progress toward an even better affirmed transcendence—everything oriented, from afar, of course, and unknowably, if not *ex eventu*, toward a new and powerful religiosity which was in fact unveiled and flourished only later and elsewhere, after the death of the old local system, and in particular in the astral religion of Hellenistic and Roman times.

The venerable religion of Mesopotamia, in its structure, its achievements, its successes, but also primarily in its potentialities and its promises, was in truth intelligent, open, and reasonable. It was a rich phase and is a wonderful remembrance of our human past.

NOTES

Preface

1. This book would not have been possible without the encouragement, the help, the knowledge, and the friendship of E. Vigne and his team (S. Simon and B. Peyret-Vignals), who worked very hard on it. I hope the reader will thank them as much as I do.

2. See J. Bottéro, *Mesopotamia: Writing, Reasoning, and the Gods* (Chicago, 1992), p. 95 n. 4.

Chapter 1: Religion and Religions

1. J. Bottéro and S. N. Kramer, *Lorsque les dieux faisaient l'homme: Mythologie mésopotamienne* (Paris, 1989), pp. 79ff.

Chapter 2: Mesopotamia and Its History

1. Bottéro and Kramer, *Lorsque les dieux faisaient l'homme*, pp. 198ff.

2. And perhaps at the beginning of the *Epic of Gilgameš*, with the primitive and uncultivated Enkidu (*Epic of Gilgameš* I:82–93).

3. Bottéro and Kramer, *Lorsque les dieux faisaient l'homme*, p. 199.

4. Bottéro, *Mesopotamia*, p. 69.

5. Ibid.

6. In particular the poem of *Atraḫasîs*, or *The Supersage* (see B. R. Foster, *From Distant Days: Myths, Tales, and Poetry of Ancient Mesopotamia* [Bethesda, 1995], pp. 52–78), and the *Epic of Gilgameš*.

Chapter 3: Sources

1. In particular see the following chapter and the documents cited on pp. 138ff.

2. A. L. Oppenheim, *Ancient Mesopotamia: Portrait of a Dead Civilization* (Chicago, 1964), p. 172.

Chapter 4: Religious Sentiment

1. F. Thureau-Dangin, *Rituels accadiens* (Paris, 1921), pp. 108ff. Numbers placed in the margins of poems or inserted within prose texts are there to aid the reader to locate the passages cited within various editions.

2. See translation in Bottéro, *Mesopotamia,* p. 209.

3. C. A. Benito, "'Enki and Ninmah' and 'Enki and the World Order'" (Ph.D. diss., University of Pennsylvania, 1969), pp. 114–15.

4. B. R. Foster, *Before the Muses: An Anthology of Akkadian Literature* (Bethesda, 1996), vol. 2, p. 596.

5. R. F. Harper, ed., *Assyrian and Babylonian Literature: Selected Translations* (New York, 1900), pp. 430–31.

6. Šamaš, who set every evening in the west and rose every morning in the east, was imagined to retrace his steps after mysteriously passing underneath the Earth during the night.

7. Foster, *Before the Muses,* vol. 2, pp. 536–38.

8. Ibid., p. 612.

9. Foster, *From Distant Days,* pp. 241–45.

10. R. Otto, *Le sacré* (Paris, 1949), pp. 54ff.

11. *Epic of Gilgameš* IV:1–34.

12. E. Ebeling, *Keilschrifttexte aus Assur religiösen Inhalts* (Leipzig, 1919), vol. 1, no. 158, ii:42.

13. E. Cassin, *La splendeur divine* (Paris, 1968).

14. A. K. Grayson, *Assyrian Rulers of the Early First Millennium* B.C., vol. 2, *858–745 B.C.* (Toronto, 1996), p. 227.

15. Cited in R. W. Rogers, *The Religion of Babylonia and Assyria: Especially in Its Relations to Israel* (New York and Cincinnati, 1908), p. 151.

Chapter 5: Religious Representations

1. The literal translation of these two Sumerian words—é (house) and a (water)—is only a "popular etymology," without any semantic or historical value.

2. Bottéro and Kramer, *Lorsque les dieux faisaient l'homme,* pp. 644ff.

3. Ibid., p. 653, VII:44.

4. M. Krebernik, "Die Götterlisten aus Fâra," *Zeitschrift für Assyriologie* 76, no. 2 (1986): 168ff.

5. It is true that there was at least one good reason to place her very high up and not far from An(u): she was traditionally recognized as his hetaera, his Aspasia: his "hierodule."

6. See R. L. Litke, *A Reconstruction of the Assyro-Babylonian God-Lists AN:ᵈA-NU-UM and AN:ANU ŠA AMĒLI,* Texts from the Babylonian Collection, vol. 3 (New Haven, 1998).

7. The *(m)* following Anu is purely morphological.

8. A. Finet, *Le code de Hammurapi* (Paris, 1983), p. 31, I:1–15.

9. Bottéro and Kramer, *Lorsque les dieux faisaient l'homme,* p. 640, VI:39ff.

10. The origins and the root meaning of this name escape us. Perhaps it had something to do with the "Westerners," *Martu,* the Sumerian name of the Semitic Amorites?

11. Bottéro and Kramer, *Lorsque les dieux faisaient l'homme,* pp. 602ff.

12. Foster, *Before the Muses,* vol. 2, p. 598.

13. P. Jensen, *Texte zur assyrisch-babylonischen Religion* (Berlin, 1915), p. 118, no. XX.

14. In the documents of the *Epic of Creation* recopied in Assyria, the name of Marduk had been systematically replaced by that of Aššur: a new and remarkable example of syncretism.

15. Foster, *From Distant Days,* p. 14.

16. Ibid.

17. Lambert, *Babylonian Wisdom Literature,* pp. 77ff.

18. Ibid., p. 41.

19. Foster, *From Distant Days,* p. 14.

20. Bottéro and Kramer, *Lorsque les dieux faisaient l'homme,* p. 537, I: 206ff.

21. Ibid., p. 639, VI: 13ff.

22. *Epic of Gilgameš* XI: 1ff., 189ff.

23. Ibid., p. 113.

24. Ibid., I: 46.

25. L. W. King, *Babylonian Boundary Stones* (London, 1912), passim.

26. Foster, *From Distant Days,* pp. 132ff.

27. Ibid.

28. A. Livingstone, *Mystical and Mythological Explanatory Works of Assyrian and Babylonian Scholars* (Oxford, 1986), pp. 94ff.

29. Foster, *From Distant Days,* pp. 52 ff., I: 352ff.

30. S. N. Kramer and J. Maier, *Myths of Enki, the Crafty God* (New York and Oxford, 1989), pp. 57ff.

31. Foster, *From Distant Days,* p. 55, I: 93ff.

32. Ibid., I: 360, II: 5ff.

33. Ibid., II: 44ff.

34. Bottéro, *Mesopotamia,* pp. 188ff.

35. *Epic of Gilgameš* VI: 6.

36. Foster, *From Distant Days,* p. 349.

37. Bottéro and Kramer, *Lorsque les dieux faisaient l'homme,* pp. 105ff.

38. Foster, *From Distant Days,* pp. 9ff.

39. Ibid., p. 39, VI: 39.

40. Ibid., p. 37, V: 125.

41. E. F. Weidner, *Handbuch der babylonischen Astronomie* (Leipzig, 1915), vol. 1, p. 51.

42. Foster, *Before the Muses,* vol. 1, p. 377.

43. *Cuneiform Texts from the Babylonian Tablets . . . in the British Museum* (London, 1896–), XXV: pl. 50; see also Livingstone, *Mystical and Mythological Explanatory Works,* pp. 30ff., 44.

44. Litke, *Reconstruction of the Assyro-Babylonian God-Lists,* pp. 20–23.

45. Bottéro and Kramer, *Lorsque les dieux faisaient l'homme,* pp. 602ff.

46. The text makes no mention of Enlil, not because his existence was denied, but since the purpose of the entire epic was to explain why Enlil had been replaced by Marduk, they preferred not to mention Enlil at all.

47. Bottéro and Kramer, *Lorsque les dieux faisaient l'homme,* pp. 472ff.

48. Ibid., pp. 487ff.

49. A. Sjöberg, *Der Mondgott Nanna-Su'en in der sumerischen Überlieferung* (Stockholm, 1960), vol. 1, pp. 167:11, 81:22.

50. Foster, *Before the Muses*, vol. 1, pp. 376, 379.

51. Livingstone, *Mystical and Mythological Explanatory Works*, pp. 82ff.

52. Wayne Horowitz, "The Babylonian Map of the World," *Iraq* 50 (1988): 147ff.

53. *Epic of Gilgameš* X.

54. A. Shaffer, *Sumerian Sources of Tablet XII of the Epic of Gilgameš* (Ann Arbor, 1963), microfilm, p. 99.

55. Bottéro and Kramer, *Lorsque les dieux faisaient l'homme*, p. 531:1–16.

56. Ibid., pp. 480ff.

57. Ibid., pp. 481ff.: 12ff.

58. S. N. Kramer, *Mythologies of the Ancient World* (Chicago, 1961), p. 123.

59. Bottéro and Kramer, *Lorsque les dieux faisaient l'homme*, pp. 488ff.

60. Ibid., p. 486.

61. Ibid., p. 495.

62. Ibid., p. 493.

63. English translation in Foster, *From Distant Days*, pp. 9–51.

64. Lambert, *Babylonian Wisdom Literature*, p. 87:262, 263.

65. Foster, *From Distant Days*, p. 34:55.

66. Ibid., p. 34:57.

67. Bottéro and Kramer, *Lorsque les dieux faisaient l'homme*, pp. 678ff.

68. Ibid., pp. 497ff.

69. Mention is often made of these deliberative councils and assemblies of the gods, which were always based on the model of the government of human beings. See, e.g., *Epic of Creation* I:55, 132, 149, 153; III:132 (Foster, *From Distant Days*, pp. 9–51).

70. Foster, *From Distant Days*, p. 31; IV:122.

71. Bottéro and Kramer, *Lorsque les dieux faisaient l'homme*, pp. 389ff.

72. H. Zimmern, *Beiträge zur Kenntnis der babylonischen Religion*, vol. 2, *Ritualtafeln für den Wahrsager . . .* (Leipzig, 1901), pp. 178ff.; no. 61, ii:7.

73. Kramer and Maier, *Myths of Enki*, pp. 57–68.

74. Bottéro and Kramer, *Lorsque les dieux faisaient l'homme*, p. 277:14. In another myth (ibid., p. 261:118ff.), she makes a loincloth out of the m e to protect herself from rape, but in vain.

75. S. M. Burstein, *The Babyloniaka of Berossos* (Malibu, 1978), p. 33a.

76. T. Jacobsen, *The Sumerian King List* (Chicago, 1939), passim.

77. Lambert, *Babylonian Wisdom Literature*, pp. 121ff.

78. Bottéro and Kramer, *Lorsque les dieux faisaient l'homme*, pp. 527ff.

79. "The Babylonian Model of the Biblical Genesis," *L'histoire* 164 (March 1993): 14ff.

80. The initial w of this word, which rendered the g of the Sumerian equivalent gedim, was later removed, leaving only the Akkadian *eṭemmu*.

81. Bottéro and Kramer, *Lorsque les dieux faisaient l'homme*, p. 537, I:212ff.

82. Foster, *From Distant Days*, pp. 9–51.

83. Bottéro and Kramer, *Lorsque les dieux faisaient l'homme*, pp. 188ff.

84. Ibid., pp. 564ff., no. 46.

85. Ibid., pp. 502ff., no. 39.

86. C. Virolleaud, *L'astrologie chaldéenne: Šamaš* (Paris, 1907), p. 11, viii:20.

87. F. Nötscher, "Omina: Die Omen-Serie *šumma âlu ina mêlê šakin*," *Orientalia* 39–42 (1929): 172ff.: 21.

88. *Epic of Gilgameš* X:286–309.

89. Cited in Foster, *From Distant Days*, pp. 78–84.

90. Ibid., pp. 78–79.

91. Bottéro and Kramer, *Lorsque les dieux faisaient l'homme*, pp. 437ff.

92. O. Gurney and P. Hulin, *The Sultantepe Tablets* (London, 1964), vol. 2, no. 400:45ff.

93. *Epic of Gilgameš* X (cited from the Old Babylonian version).

94. B. Alster, *The Instructions of Suruppak* (Copenhagen, 1974), p. 43.

95. Lambert, *Babylonian Wisdom Literature*, pp. 103, 105.

Chapter 6: Religious Behavior

1. The Sumerian equivalent of *ziqqurratu*—ù.nir—is not often found; the ziggurat must therefore be later than the time of Sumerian dominance.

2. J. Bottéro, *Mythes et rites de Babylone* (Paris, 1985), p. 183.

3. A. Sjöberg and E. Bergmann, *The Collection of the Sumerian Temple Hymns* (New York, 1969), p. 29, no. 16.

4. E. Sollberger and J. R. Kupper, *Inscriptions royales sumériennes et akkadiennes* (Paris, 1971), p. 174:IVA4b.

5. Lambert, *Babylonian Wisdom Literature*, pp. 60ff.

6. R. H. Charles, *The Apocrypha and Pseudepigrapha of the Old Testament* (Oxford, 1913), vol. 1, pp. 601–3.

7. G. Dossin, "Un rituel du culte d'Ištar provenant de Mari," *Revue d'assyriologie* 35 (1938): 11.

8. J. S. Cooper, *The Curse of Agade* (Baltimore and London, 1983), p. 33.

9. W. W. Hallo, "A Sumerian Amphictyony," *Journal of Cuneiform Studies* 14 (1960): 103, text no. 15.

10. Thureau-Dangin, *Rituels accadiens*, pp. 75ff.

11. Ibid., p. 81.

12. Ibid., p. 84.

13. J. Bottéro, *Textes culinaires mésopotamiens* (Winona Lake, Ind., 1995).

14. Charles, *Apocrypha and Pseudepigrapha*, vol. 1, p. 660.

15. M. Streck, *Assurbanipal*, vol. 2, *Texte* (Leipzig, 1916), pp. 304ff.

16. A. L. Oppenheim, *The Interpretation of Dreams in the Ancient Near East* (Philadelphia, 1956), p. 301, type D:20ff.

17. King, *Babylonian Boundary Stones*, p. 125.

18. W. F. Leemans, *Ištar of Lagaba and Her Dress* (Leiden, 1952), pp. 1ff.

19. J. Bottéro, "Les inventaires de Qatna," *Revue d'assyriologie* 43 (1949): 1ff., 137ff.

20. Bottéro and Kramer, *Lorsque les dieux faisaient l'homme*, pp. 128ff.

21. Streck, *Assurbanipal,* vol. 2, pp. 250ff.

22. Foster, *From Distant Days,* p. 283.

23. A. Falkenstein and W. von Soden, *Sumerische und akkadische Hymnen und Gebete* (Zurich and Stuttgart, 1953), pp. 59ff. and 361: no. 1.

24. Kramer and Maier, *Myths of Enki,* "Hymn to Enki with a Prayer for Ur-Ninurta," pp. 89–92.

25. Engur and Lalgar (see below) are both of unknown origin and root meaning but are synonyms for Abzu (also spelled Apsû), the freshwater that extended everywhere under Earth and represented the domain and residence of Enki/Éa.

26. See n. 25.

27. The names of various instruments, about which we do not know a great deal, appear in these verses.

28. Kramer and Maier, *Myths of Enki,* "Enki and Eridu: The Journey of the Water-god to Nippur," pp. 69–72.

29. Foster, *From Distant Days,* pp. 238–41.

30. Ibid., pp. 247–48.

31. This was the common epistolary style at the time. The sender and the recipient were ordinarily not expected to know how to read and write, so the sender had his "secretary" inscribe the message on the tablet, which the bearer of said tablet would then communicate to the recipient.

32. J. J. Stamm, *Die akkadische Namengebung* (Leipzig, 1939), pp. 54ff.

33. Thureau-Dangin, *Rituels accadiens,* pp. 118ff.

34. Ibid., pp. 10ff.

35. Bottéro and Kramer, *Lorsque les dieux faisaient l'homme,* pp. 275ff.

36. M. Çiğ, *Puzriš-Dagan: Die Puzriš-Dagan-Texte der Istanbuler archäologischen Museen* (Helsinki, 1954), vol. 1, p. 92, no. 300.

37. J. Bottéro, *Archives royales de Mari,* vol. 7, *Textes économiques et administratifs* (Paris, 1957), p. 11, no. 29.

38. S. Parpola, *Letters from Assyrian and Babylonian Scholars* (Helsinki, 1993), p. 200, no. 253.

39. S. N. Kramer, *The Sacred Marriage Rite: Aspects of Faith, Myth, and Ritual in Ancient Sumer* (Bloomington, Ind., and London, 1969), p. 77.

40. Ibid., pp. 92–93.

41. R. H. Pfeiffer, *State Letters of Assyria* (New Haven, 1935), p. 158, no. 217.

42. Ibid., p. 156, no. 215.

43. The prayer in question is bilingual: in Sumerian on one side, and in Akkadian on the other.

44. J. B. Pritchard, ed., *Ancient Near Eastern Texts Relating to the Old Testament* (1950), p. 331.

45. Ibid.

46. Ibid.

47. Ibid., p. 332.

48. Ibid.

49. Ibid., p. 334.

50. Ibid.

51. Lambert, *Babylonian Wisdom Literature*, pp. 104ff.

52. Ibid., pp. 38ff.

53. Ibid., pp. 76ff.

54. R. Labat, *Hémérologies et ménologies d'Assur* (Paris, 1939), pp. 50ff.

55. Parpola, *Letters*, p. 9, no. 8:24ff.

56. Ibid., p. 157, no. 193:9ff.

57. Ibid.

58. Ibid., p. 105, no. 127:7ff.

59. J. Bottéro, *Naissance de Dieu: La Bible et l'historien* (Paris, 1986), p. 14, n. 1.

60. Bottéro, *Archives royales de Mari*, p. 10, no. 50:3ff. Translation cited in Bottéro, *Mesopotamia*, p. 111.

61. J. M. Durand, *Archives épistolaires de Mari* (Paris, 1988), vol. 1, pt. 1, p. 434, no. 206.

62. Ibid., p. 450, no. 221 *bis*.

63. Ibid., p. 422, no. 214.

64. Ibid., p. 451, no. 222.

65. S. Parpola, *Assyrian Prophecies*, State Archives of Assyria, vol. 9 (Helsinki, 1997), pp. 4–5.

66. S. A. Strong, "On Some Oracles to Esarhaddon and Ašurbanipal," *Beiträge zur Assyriologie* 2 (1894): 629, l. 15.

67. Ibid., p. 628.

68. E. Leichty, *The Omen Series šumma izbu* (New York, 1970), p. 36a.

69. Bottéro, *Mesopotamia*, pp. 67ff.

70. I. Starr, *Queries to the Sungod: Divination and Politics in Sargonid Assyria*, State Archives of Assyria, vol. 4 (Helsinki, 1990), pp. 192ff., no. 190.

71. R. D. Biggs, *Šà.zi.ga: Ancient Mesopotamian Potency Incantations* (New York, 1967), pp. 46ff., no. 27.

72. Leichty, *Omen Series*, p. 11a.

73. The author of the letter just mentioned, probably a diviner himself, cites a pertinent passage from the *Treatise on Tocomancy*. Compare with Leichty, *Omen Series*, notably VI:19ff. passim.

74. A. L. Oppenheim, "A Babylonian Diviner's Manual," *Journal of Near Eastern Studies* 33 (1974): 197ff.

75. Starr, *Queries to the Sungod*, pp. 192ff., no. 190.

76. These are all names of stars or constellations.

77. A. L. Oppenheim, "A New Prayer to the 'Gods of the Night,'" *Analecta Biblica* 12 (1959): 293ff.

78. Lambert, *Babylonian Wisdom Literature*, p. 243:56ff.; p. 249.

79. W. G. Lambert, "DINGIR. ŠÀ.DIB.BA Incantations," *Journal of Near Eastern Studies* 33, no. 3 (1974): 274–75.

80. S. N. Kramer, *Wisdom in Israel and in the Ancient Near East* (Leiden, 1955), pp. 170ff.

81. Foster, *Before the Muses*, vol. 1, p. 308.

82. Lambert, *Babylonian Wisdom Literature*, pp. 63ff.

83. M. Krebernik, *Die Beschwörungen aus Fâra und Ebla* (Zurich and New York, 1984), pp. 9ff.

84. F. M. T. de Liagre Böhl, "Zwei altbabylonische Beschwörungstexte: LB 2001 und 1001," *Bibliotheca Orientalis* 11 (1954): 82.

85. F. Köcher and A. L. Oppenheim, "The Old-Babylonian Omen Text VAT 7525," *Archiv für Orientforschung* 18 (1957): 71.

86. S. Maul, *Zukunftsbewältigung* (Mainz am Rhein, 1994), pp. 346ff.

87. Bottéro, *Mythes et rites*, pp. 44ff. This ritual was also published in *Orientalia* 34 (1965): 125ff.

88. Bottéro, *Mythes et rites*, pp. 163ff.

89. Parpola, *Letters*, p. 169, no. 212.

Chapter 7: Influence and Survivals

1. E. Rohde, *Psyché* (Paris, 1928), pp. 1ff.

2. Durand, *Archives épistolaires de Mari*, vol. 1, pt. 1, p. 424, no. 197:13ff.; and p. 426, no. 199:44.

3. Bottéro and Kramer, *Lorsque les dieux faisaient l'homme*, pp. 728ff.

4. Foster, *From Distant Days*, p. 42, VI:119.

5. Bottéro and Kramer, *Lorsque les dieux faisaient l'homme*, pp. 676ff.

6. Ibid., pp. 678ff.

7. Even if, ever since the book's initial appearance close to a century ago, we have a much better understanding of the value and the meaning of Mesopotamian sources, it is still essential to refer, in particular for all that concerns "astral religion," to the admirable and famous work by F. Cumont: *Les religions orientales dans le paganisme romain* (Paris, 1929), and specifically to chap. 7: "L'astrologie et la magie." See also H. Gressman, *Die hellenistische Gestirnreligion* (Leipzig, 1925).

8. C. Virolleaud, *L'astrologie chaldéenne: Ištar* (Paris, 1908), p. 3, ii:16.

9. Maul, *Zukunftsbewältigung*, p. 427a (62ff.).

BIBLIOGRAPHY

Readers may want to consult the following journals for articles on the topics discussed in this book: *Archiv für Orientforschung, Beiträge zur Assyriologie, Bibliotheca Orientalis, L'histoire, Iraq, Journal of Cuneiform Studies, Journal of Near Eastern Studies, Orientalia, Revue d'assyriologie.*

Alster, B. *The Instructions of Suruppak.* Copenhagen, 1974.

Benito, C. A. "'Enki and Ninmah,' and 'Enki and the World Order.'" Ph.D. diss., University of Pennsylvania, 1969.

Biggs, R. D. *Šà.zi.ga: Ancient Mesopotamian Potency Incantations.* Texts from Cuneiform Sources, vol. 2. New York, 1967.

Böllenrücher, J. *Nergal: Gebete und Hymne an Nergal.* Leipzig, 1904.

Bottéro, J. *Archives royales de Mari.* Vol. 7, *Textes économiques et administratifs.* Paris, 1957.

———. *L'épopée de Gilgameš: Le grand homme qui ne voulait pas mourir.* Paris, 1992.

———. *Mésopotamie: L'écriture, la raison et les dieux.* Paris, 1987. Translated by Zainab Bahrani and Marc Van de Mieroop under the title *Mesopotamia: Writing, Reasoning, and the Gods* (Chicago, 1992).

———. *Mythes et rites de Babylone.* Paris, 1985.

———. *Naissance de Dieu: La Bible et l'historien.* Paris, 1986.

———. *Textes culinaires mésopotamiens.* Winona Lake, Ind., 1995.

Bottéro, J., and S. N. Kramer. *Lorsque les dieux faisaient l'homme: Mythologie mésopotamienne.* Paris, 1989.

Burstein, S. M. *The Babyloniaka of Berossos.* Malibu, 1978.

Cassin, E. *La splendeur divine.* Paris, 1968.

Charles, R. H. *The Apocrypha and Pseudepigrapha of the Old Testament.* Vol. 1. Oxford, 1913.

Ciğ, M. *Puzriš-Dagan: Die Puzriš-Dagan-Texte der Istanbuler archäologischen Museen.* Vol. 1. Helsinki, 1954.

Cooper, J. S. *The Curse of Agade.* Baltimore and London, 1983.

Cumont, F. *Les religions orientales dans le paganisme romain.* Paris, 1929.

Cuneiform Texts from the Babylonian Tablets . . . in the British Museum. London, 1896–.

Durand, J. M. *Archives épistolaires de Mari.* Vol. 1, pt. 1. Paris, 1988.

Ebeling, E. *Die akkadische Gebetsserie Handerhebung.* Berlin, 1953.

———. *Keilschrifttexte aus Assur religiösen Inhalts.* Vol. 1. Leipzig, 1919.

Falkenstein, A. *Sumerische Götterlieder.* Vol. 1. Heidelberg, 1959.

Falkenstein, A., and W. von Soden. *Sumerische und akkadische Hymnen und Gebete*. Zurich and Stuttgart, 1953.

Finet, A. *Le code de Hammurapi*. Paris, 1983.

Fiore, S. *Voices from the Clay: The Development of Assyro-Babylonian Literature*. Norman, Okla., 1965.

Foster, B. R. *Before the Muses: An Anthology of Akkadian Literature*. 2 vols. Bethesda, 1996.

————. *From Distant Days: Myths, Tales, and Poetry of Ancient Mesopotamia*. Bethesda, 1995.

Grayson, A. K. *Assyrian Rulers of the Early First Millennium B.C.* Vol. 2, *858–745 B.C.* Toronto, 1996.

Gressmann, H. *Die hellenistische Gestirnreligion*. Leipzig, 1925.

Gurney, O., and P. Hulin. *The Sultantepe Tablets*. Vol. 2. London, 1964.

Harper, R. F., ed. *Assyrian and Babylonian Literature: Selected Translations*. New York, 1900.

Hooke, S. H. *Babylonian and Assyrian Religion*. London and New York, 1953.

Jacobsen, T. *The Sumerian King List*. Chicago, 1939.

Jensen, P. *Texte zur assyrisch-babylonischen Religion*. Berlin, 1915.

King, L. W. *Babylonian Boundary Stones*. London, 1912.

Kovacs, M. G., trans. *The Epic of Gilgamesh*. Stanford, 1989.

Kramer, S. N. *Mythologies of the Ancient World*. Chicago, 1961.

————. *The Sacred Marriage Rite: Aspects of Faith, Myth, and Ritual in Ancient Sumer*. Bloomington, Ind., and London, 1969.

————. *The Sumerians: Their History, Culture, and Character*. Chicago and London, 1963.

————. *Wisdom in Israel and in the Ancient Near East*. Leiden, 1955.

Kramer, S. N., and J. Maier. *Myths of Enki, the Crafty God*. New York and Oxford, 1989.

Krebernik, M., *Die Beschwörungen aus Fâra und Ebla*. Zurich and New York, 1984.

————. "Die Götterlisten aus Fâra." *Zeitschrift für Assyriologie* 76, no. 2 (1986): 161 ff.

Labat, R. *Hémérologies et ménologies d'Assur*. Paris, 1939.

Lambert, W. G. *Babylonian Wisdom Literature*. Oxford, 1960.

Langdon, S. *Die neubabylonischen Königsinschriften*. Leipzig, 1912.

Leemans, W. F. *Ištar of Lagaba and Her Dress*. Leiden, 1952.

Leichty, E. *The Omen Series šumma izbu*. New York, 1970.

Litke, R. L. *A Reconstruction of the Assyro-Babylonian God-Lists AN:ᵈA-NU-UM and AN:ANU ŠA AMĒLI*. Texts from the Babylonian Collection, vol. 3. New Haven, 1998.

Livingstone, A. *Mystical and Mythological Explanatory Works of Assyrian and Babylonian Scholars*. Oxford, 1986.

Maul, S. *Zukunftsbewältigung*. Mainz am Rhein, 1994.

Meier, G. *Die assyrische Beschwörungssammlung Maqlû*. Berlin, 1957.

Nötscher, F. "Omina: Die Omen-Serie šumma âlu ina mêlê šakin." *Orientalia* 39–42 (1929).

Oppenheim, A. L. *Ancient Mesopotamia: Portrait of a Dead Civilization.* Chicago, 1964.

———. *The Interpretation of Dreams in the Ancient Near East.* Philadelphia, 1956.

———. "A New Prayer to the 'Gods of the Night.'" *Analecta Biblica* 12 (1959): 293ff.

———. "A Babylonian Diviner's Manual." *Journal of Near Eastern Studies* 33 (1974): 197ff.

Otto, R. *Le sacré.* Paris, 1949.

Parpola, S. *Assyrian Prophecies.* State Archives of Assyria, vol. 9. Helsinki, 1997.

———. *Letters from Assyrian and Babylonian Scholars.* Helsinki, 1993.

Perry, E. G. *Hymnen und Gebete an Sin.* Leipzig, 1907.

Pfeiffer, R. H. *State Letters of Assyria.* New Haven, 1935.

Pinches, T. G. *The Cuneiform Inscriptions of Western Asia.* Vol. 4. 2d ed. London, 1891.

———. *The Religion of Babylonia and Assyria.* London, 1906.

Pinckert, J. *Hymnen und Gebete an Nebo.* Leipzig, 1920.

Pritchard, J. B., ed. *Ancient Near Eastern Texts Relating to the Old Testament.* Princeton, 1950.

Rogers, R. W. *The Religion of Babylonia and Assyria: Especially in Its Relations to Israel.* New York and Cincinnati, 1908.

Rohde, E. *Psyché.* Paris, 1928.

Shaffer, A. *Sumerian Sources of Tablet XII of the Epic of Gilgameš.* Ann Arbor, 1963. Microfilm.

Sjöberg, Å. W. *Der Mondgott Nanna-Su'en in der sumerischen Überlieferung.* Vol. 1. Stockholm, 1960.

Sjöberg, Å. W., and E. Bergmann. *The Collection of the Sumerian Temple Hymns.* Text from Cuneiform Sources, vol. 3. New York, 1969.

Sollberger, E., and J. R. Kupper. *Inscriptions royales sumériennes et akkadiennes.* Paris, 1971.

Stamm, J. J. *Die akkadische Namengebung.* Leipzig, 1939.

Starr, I. *Queries to the Sungod: Divination and Politics in Sargonid Assyria.* State Archives of Assyria, vol. 4. Helsinki, 1990.

Streck, M. *Assurbanipal.* Vol. 2, *Texte.* Leipzig, 1916.

Thureau-Dangin, F. *Rituels accadiens.* Paris, 1921.

Virolleaud, C. *L'astrologie chaldéenne.* Paris, 1905–12.

Weidner, E. F. *Handbuch der babylonischen Astronomie.* Vol. 1. Leipzig, 1915.

Zimmern, H. *Beiträge zur Kenntnis der babylonischen Religion.* Vol. 2, *Ritualtafeln für den Wahrsager.* . . . Leipzig, 1901.

INDEX

Abyss, 80
Achaemenid dynasty, 17–18, 20, 209
Adad, 54, 57, 185, 209; divination,
    184–85; power, 91
addresses, 138
Addu-dûri, 172
administrative responsibilities, 120–21,
    152
Advice of a Father to His Son, 112–13
afterlife, 105–10, 222. *See also* death;
    Netherworld
agriculture, 10
Akkadian language, ix, 209; creation
    myths, 56, 83, 98; lists of gods, 50;
    personal names, 38–39
Akkadian peoples, 9–11, 19, 27–28; de-
    scriptions of the gods, 47; historic
    era, 12–15; syncretism with Sumerian
    gods, 46–48
Akkadische Götterepitheta (Tallqvist), 45
Alexander the Great, 18, 95, 208, 209,
    212
alphabetic writing, 17–18, 203, 209
Amar-Sîn, 142
Ammiditana, 145–46
Ammiṣaduqa, 98
Amorites, 14–15, 19, 54
ancient triad of gods, 88
anonymity of texts, 25
anthropomorphism, 3, 6, 43, 207, 219;
    behaviors of the gods, 66–69; divine
    nature, 58–64; images of the gods,
    64–71; origins of the gods, 72
An/u, 30, 60, 209, 211; ancestors, 72–
    73; creation, 83–85, 87; heaven, 44,
    46, 79–80; hierarchies of the gods,
    48–51, 56–57, 68, 70, 88; hymns/
    prayers, 139–42, 146–47; Ištar/
    Inanna, 226n.5 (chap. 5); liturgy,

149–50; the m e, 94; meals, 128–29;
    mentioned in documents, 30, 54, 57,
    69, 85, 86; New Year celebrations,
    158; origins of the gods, 74–75;
    temple, 115; Uruk, 53
Anunna, 59, 142
Anunnaku/i, 55, 80, 99, 109
Anzû, 93
Aphrodite, 211
Apsû, 75, 78, 80, 85, 230n.25
arable land, god of, 46
Arabs, 96
Aramaic language, 209
Aramean people, 19
Arbela, 135
archpriests, 121–22
Aristotle, 3
Arsacids, 20
Asalluḫi, 198, 201
Ašnan, 44, 91
assembly of the gods, 92–93, 228n.69
Aššur, 57, 69, 76, 115, 174, 227n.14
Aššurbanipal, 131, 135
Assyria/Aššur, vii–viii, 17, 19, 54, 115;
    calendar, 151; monarchs' role in wor-
    ship, 168; prophecies, 172; sacred
    marriage, 157–58. *See also* Aššur;
    Esarhaddon
astral religion, 212–18, 222
astrology, 69–70, 168, 180, 182–83; ex-
    orcism, 200; religion, 212–18, 222;
    treatise on creation, 86
Atraḫasîs, 98, 101–102
Atraḫasîs, 55, 66, 207, 225n.6 (chap. 2);
    creation, 84; gifts to the gods, 126;
    human existence, 98–103; mortality,
    106
attitudes towards the divine. *See* reli-
    gious feeling/religiosity

Auriga, 216
authority of the gods, 37–38. *See also*
    government by the gods
Aya, 54

Ba'al, 212
Babylon, 15–16, 19–20, 53–56, 68, 88,
    115–17, 208; *Atraḫasîs,* 98; Chalde-
    ans, 218; divination, 176; Epistle of
    Jeremiah, 119; geography, 81; Nabû-
    apla-iddina, 132; Nebuchadnezzar II,
    135; New Year celebrations, 158–64;
    numerical valuation of the gods, 71;
    temples, 119
Babylonian language, 203
balance, 221
bârû, 179–86
behaviors of the gods, 66–69
Bêl. *See* Marduk
"Bêl and the Dragon," 130–31
Bêlit-ilî, 100
benevolence of the gods, 39–40
Berossus, 95, 210
Bible, 61, 98, 116, 130–31, 204–8;
    apocryphal works, 119; calendar,
    151–52; cosmology, 79, 80
boats for the gods, 134, 163
bodies of water, 63, 80, 206, 230n.25
Book of Daniel supplement, 130–31
Borsippa, 157
Bottéro, Jean, viii
Buddhism, 6

calendar, 150–54; divination, 180; ex-
    orcism, 200; New Year celebration,
    158–59
Canaanites, 14
catalogues of gods, 23, 48–55, 219–20;
    the m e, 94
celebrations, 123, 151. *See also* festivals
celibacy in the priesthood, 122
cellae, 116–17, 130, 160
center of the world, 96–97
ceremonies, 154, 222; exorcism, 194–
    200; extispicy, 183–84. *See also*
    liturgy
Chaldeans, 16–17, 20, 218
childbearing by female priests, 120, 122
Christianity, 6
chronologies, x; creation, 82; religious
    systems, 25

chronomancy, 180, 200
City of the Dead, 108
city-states, 13–14, 15, 19, 53, 74; calen-
    dar, 151; in prehistoric period, 8
clay modeling, 85; humans, 99–101,
    207
clothing, 125, 132–33; headdresses, 65,
    120; transgender, 123–24
clothing of the gods, 153
codes of conduct, 112–13
common people, 2, 54–56, 91; astral re-
    ligion, 217; divination, 171–85; exor-
    cism/magic, 185–202; feasts, 131;
    hymns/prayers, 136; religious behav-
    ior, 165–68; temples, 118–19
communication with the gods, 111;
    correspondence, 148–49, 230n.31
community of the gods, 45
companions of the divine, 116–17
conversion, 5
cooks, 124, 130
corporeal nature of the gods, 65–66
cosmogony, 75–77, 81–90, 203–4; *Epic
    of Creation,* 87–90; New Year celebra-
    tions, 158, 164
cosmology, 77–81
craftsmen, 124, 160
creation, 76, 83–90, 178, 206–8, 210–
    11
cultural heritage, 25–27, 105, 210; pre-
    historic era, 10–11; religion, 4–5, 13–
    14, 45–46. *See also* writing
Cumont, F., 232n.7
cuneiform, x, 12, 17–18, 23–24, 45
Cyrus the Great, 17–18, 20, 208

Dagan, 54, 57, 68, 96, 172
daily life, 165–70, 183–84. *See also*
    common people
Damascius, 211–12
Damgalnunna, 75
dancing, 123
death, 105–10, 186, 204, 220, 222; as-
    tral religion, 214; exorcism, 196; of
    the gods, 61–62
decimo-sexagesimal system, 70–71
decisions, god of, 44
deductive divination, 92–95, 176–81,
    218; astrology, 213–16; exorcism,
    196, 200
Deimel, A., 45

demons, 63, 187, 189, 192–94, 216
Der, 153
despair, 222
destiny. *See* fate
dialogues, 137
dingir, 45, 58, 64
divination, 92–95, 170–85, 222; astrology, 213–16; exorcism, 196
divine. *See* representations of the divine
diviners, 179, 182–86; exorcists, 200–202
divinity/divine nature, 58–64, 106
divinized mortals, 62
dreams, 180
drums, 150
dualism, Iranian, 212
Dumuzi, 62, 151; sacred marriage, 155
Dunnu, 75–76
duration of human life, 111
dwellings of the priests, 124

Éa, 46, 70, 80, 96–97, 209, 211, 226n.1 (chap. 5), 230n.25; creation of the universe, 31, 47, 75, 76, 83, 84, 85, 86, 207; death, 105, 111; evil, 101–2; exorcism, 198–99, 201; hierarchies of the gods, 50, 54, 57, 68, 87, 88; history of humanity, 99–102, 111; hymns/prayers, 146; mentioned in documents, 85, 86; sin, 188; temple, 115. *See also* Enki
Earth, 78–80
Ebla, 24, 151, 193–94, 203
economic role of the temples, 117, 125, 130–31
education, 54, 124, 201, 209, 211
Egypt, 176, 203, 215
Ékur, 73, 127, 133–34
Elamites, 96, 203
elements of the world, 91
end of the world, 95
Enegir, 134
Enki, 46, 66, 230n.25; creation of the universe, 31, 47, 59, 76, 83, 97, 207; death, 105, 111; Eridu, 53; evil, 101–2; government of humanity, 103; hierarchies of the gods, 49–50; history of humanity, 99–102; hymns/prayers, 139–44; the m e, 94; temple, 115. *See also* Éa
Enkidu, 11, 37, 225n.2 (chap. 2)

Enki/Éa's Part in the Creation of the Universe, 76
Enlil, 30–31, 70, 208, 209, 211; creation, 83–84, 86; evil, 101–2; exorcism, 199; hierarchies of the gods, 46–57, 88; hymns/prayers, 138–41; Kronos, 210; liturgical year, 152; Marduk, 227n.46; mentioned in documents, 31–32, 54, 86, 167, 195; Ninlil, 67, 76; Nippur, 53; ruler of the universe, 31–32, 46–57, 66, 72; sacred marriage, 156; syncretism, 96–97; temples, 115, 117, 127; *The Visit of Nanna-Sîn to Nippur*, 133–34; will of the gods, 93
Enlil and Ninlil, 67, 76
Enmešarra, 216
entrails, 178, 180, 183–84
Epic of Creation, 55–56, 61, 68–69, 75, 207, 210, 212; celestial objects, 216; cosmogony, 87–90; human existence, 102; Marduk, 47, 82, 87–90, 227n.46; new myths, 89–90; New Year celebrations, 160, 163; syncretism, 227n.14; universe, 79–80; will of the gods, 93
Epic of Gilgameš, 11, 37, 62, 225n.2 (chap. 2), 225n.6 (chap. 2); death, 105–6; hedonism, 111–12; Ištar, 67
Epinomis (Plato), 217
Epistle of Jeremiah, 119
Ereškigal, 108–9
Eridu, 53, 115, 118, 142–44; the m e, 94
Erra, 65
eršemma, 137
Erua-Sarpanitu, 147
Ésagil, 56, 117; New Year celebrations, 158–64
Esarhaddon, 153, 157, 168, 173–74, 183–84, 199
Etruscans, 176
evil, 101–2, 114, 164, 166, 168, 221–22; divination, 170–81; exorcism, 186–92, 194–200; magic, 185–87, 192–94
exorcism, 150, 161, 170, 185–202, 215, 222; astral religions, 213–14, 218; creation of the Earth, 85–86; phantoms, 109–10; of scorpion bite, 195–96; for toothache, 84–85
exorcists, 168, 199, 200–202
extispicy, 180, 183–84

family lives of the gods, 50–52, 68

Fâra/Šuruppak (site), 23, 72, 134, 194; catalogs of gods, 48–50; teachings about life, 112–13

fatalism, 191–92, 220

fate, 92–95, 103–5, 163, 167, 186, 204, 218; astral religion, 213–15; divination, 170–85

fear, 36–40, 169–70, 221; of the dead, 109–10

feasts, 130–31, 150; sacred marriage, 156–58

feeding of the gods, 125–31

female gods, 35–36, 46–47, 49, 64, 91, 108–9; Ašnan, 44; creation, 82–83, 100–101; Mamma/i, 54, 207, 211; Zarpanit, 160. See also Ištar/Inanna

female priests, 120–23, 137, 149–50; sacred marriage, 156–58

fertility, 63, 156–58

festivals, 123, 151, 153, 201–2, 209, 222; sacred marriage, 154–58

fetishism, 3

figures, 65

fire, 63

fire god, 91

fish, 125

Flood, 62, 81, 101, 102, 105–6, 208

floods, 66–67, 95

foreign gods, 96–97, 210

founder of the gods, 49

future, 167, 222; astral religion, 216; divination, 170–85. See also fate

future prophecy, 86

Genesis, 98, 102, 116, 207–8

geography, 80–81

Gibil, 91

Gilgameš, 37, 62, 67, 81; creation myth, 83–84; death, 186; hedonism, 111–12; immortality, 105–6. See also The Epic of Gilgameš

goddesses. See female gods

gods, 6, 55, 58–64, 96–97, 114, 209–10; evil and suffering, 187–92; family life, 68; food, 125–31; foreign, 96–97; henotheism, 40–42; pantheon, 45, 108; roles, 46–47, 59–61, 96–97, 210. See also female gods; names of specific gods

goodness, 39–40

government by the gods, 103–5, 188, 205, 220–21, 227n.69

grain, 44, 91

graves, 110

great exile of the Israelites, 206–7

Great Lady, 100

Great Mother, 212

Greek culture, 18, 20, 209–12, 215; astral religion, 217–18, 222

Gula, 64

Hammurabi, 15, 19, 54, 98, 145

Hammurabi's Code, 54

happiness, 111, 185

headdresses, 65, 120

heaven, 44, 46, 68, 78–80

Hebrew language, 14. See also Semitic languages

Hebrew people, 6, 204–8; calendar, 151–52. See also Bible

hedonism, 111–13, 165–66

Hell, 68, 78–79, 107–9. See also Netherworld

Hellenism. See Greek culture

henotheism, 40–42, 55–58, 222

hepatoscopy, 180

Hermes Trismegistus, 215

Herodotus, 210–11, 218

hierarchies: in the afterworld, 107–10; of the gods, 44–58, 219–20; in the priesthood, 121–22

hierodules, 122, 128

hieros gamos, 65, 123, 154–58

historical religions, 5–6; monotheism, 41–42

history, viii–ix, 12–18, 25–27, 98–103

Hittites, 176

holy days, 166

holy marriage, 123

homosexuality, 123–24

hope, 222

How Erra Wrecked the World, 65

human existence, 80, 95–113, 204–5, 207–8, 220; creation, 88–90; exorcism/magic, 185–92; happiness, 111, 185; Hebrews, 204–5; service to the gods, 100, 111, 124–26, 132–33, 169–70, 221–22; suffering, 101–2, 114, 164, 166, 168, 170–81, 186–200, 220–21 hymns, 22, 36, 117, 138; of dedication, 142–45; tigi, 139–42. *See also* prayers

Ice Age, 7
ideograms, 58
Igigi/u, 55, 59, 79–80, 99–100, 159–60
illness, 101–2, 172–73
ilu, 45, 58, 64
images of the gods, 22, 64–71, 116–17, 130; Babylon, 119; celestial objects, 216; New Year celebrations, 160–63; travel, 133–34; in wartime, 135
imagination, 4
immortality, 62, 105–6
impiety, 166
Inanna, 35, 50, 66, 151, 226n.5 (chap. 5); love/sexuality, 46, 49, 121–22, 216; the m e, 94, 228n.74; mentioned in documents, 35–36; sacred marriage, 155; temples, 115, 117; Uruk, 53. *See also* Ištar
Inanna and Enki: The Transfer of the Arts of Civilization from Eridu to Erech, 66, 94
incantation, 192–94
Infernal River, 78, 81
inheritance of the priesthood, 120
inspired divination, 171–75
intermediaries, 171, 174–75, 182–86
intolerance towards outsiders, 6
irrigation, 8
Išḫara, 64
Isimud, 142–44
Isin, 118, 139, 155
Isis, 212
Iškur, 49
Islam, 6
Išme-Dagan, 118
Israelites. *See* Hebrew people
Ištar, 35, 49–50, 54, 209, 226n.5 (chap. 5); clothing and jewelry, 132–33; feast, 131; hymns/prayers, 145–46; love/sexuality, 46–47, 49, 64, 67, 122–23, 211; meals, 128–29; mentioned in documents, 35–36, 59, 174, 185; Netherworld, 108, 151; rituals, 121; transgender clothing, 123–24; Venus (planet), 62, 216. *See also* Inanna
Ishtar's Descent into the Netherworld, 108
Jesus Christ, 6

jewelry, 132–33
Judaism. *See* Hebrew people
justice, god of, 33–34, 44, 49

Kalḫu, 16, 157–58
kalû priests, 121, 123–24, 137, 160
Kassites, 15–17, 19, 96
Ki, 84
kinship terms, 39–40
Kišar, 75
Kronos, 210–11
kudurru, 64
Kulla, 85
Kusu, 161

Lagaba, 132
Laḫar, 91
laments, 137
languages, 9–11, 13–18, 22, 209–10. *See also* specific languages
Larsa, 53, 134
legitimacy of religion, 2–3
lists: divination, 176–77, 179–81; of gods, 23, 48–55; the m e, 94
literacy of the priests, 122, 124, 209, 211
literature, 15, 22, 138, 152, 220
liturgy, 23, 28, 120, 128, 210; calendar, 150–54; exorcism ritual, 199; food, 128, 130–31; prayers, 136–38
livestock, 127
locations: of the gods, 68; of sources, 23–24; of temples, 115–16
love, 46, 49, 122, 155–56, 169. *See also* Ištar/Inanna
luck, 113, 168
Ludlul, 60–61, 118–19, 165–66, 190–92
Lugalbanda, 46, 62
lunar calendar, 71, 151

magic, 185–87, 192–94; astral religions, 213–14
Mah, 168
maintenance of the gods, 125–33, 154
Mamîtu, 199
Mamma/i, 54, 207, 211
Marduk, 31–32, 55–56, 66, 68, 69, 207, 209–10; Babylon, 53; birth, 59–60, 75, 87; body, 65–66, 76–77; creation of the universe, 79–80, 83; Enlil,

Marduk (*continued*)
227n.46; *Epic of Creation,* 56, 87–90,
163; exorcism, 201–2; Ḫammurabi's
Code, 54; henotheism, 56–57; human existence, 102; hymns/prayers,
146–48; liturgical year, 153; mentioned in documents, 32, 69, 168;
name, 226n.10 (chap. 5), 227n.14;
new myths, 88–90; New Year celebrations, 158–64; prayer, 135–36; ruler
of the universe, 47, 50, 55–57, 83;
sacred marriage, 157–58; sin, 188,
190; temples, 115–19; will of the
gods, 93
Mari, 24, 68, 151, 152–53, 209; divination, 172–75; writing, 203
marine origins of the gods, 74–75
marriage: *hieros gamos,* 123, 154–58;
priests, 120, 123
material needs of the gods, 125–33
the m e, 41, 94, 141, 144, 228n.74
meals, 128–31, 158; liturgy, 149–50
meaning, 177–81
medicine, 196, 201, 217
melammu, 61
memories of the dead, 110
menologies, 167–68
mental illness, 109–10
*Mésopotamie: L'écriture, la raison et les
dieux* (Bottéro), viii
metaphor, 211
Mîšaru, 44
monarchs, 54, 121, 157, 168; ceremoni-
als roles, 153–58, 161–62; death, 109;
divination, 173–75, 181–83; exorcism, 199–200; liturgical cult, 145–
46; maintenance of the gods, 118,
126; menologies, 168; models for the
gods, 67, 114, 132–34, 219–20
monotheism, 3, 41–42, 58, 77, 207; human existence, 102
moon, 212, 216
moon god, 32–33, 46, 49, 68, 70, 76, 91
morality, 169–70
mortality, 61–62
Moses, 6, 169, 207
mountains, 63, 80
Muhammad, 6
music, 22–23, 123, 131, 137; instruments, 230n.27; love songs, 155–56
mysticism, 37–38, 40

Myth of Anzû, 93
Myth of the Seven Sages, 9–11
mythology, 4, 210–11; astral religion,
217; of the divine, 58–77; of humanity, 95–113; of the world, 77–95

Nabû, 54, 57, 161, 163, 209, 211; sacred
marriage, 157
Nabû-apla-iddina, 132
naming. *See* onomastics
Nammu, 50, 75, 89
Namtar, 44
Nanaya, 209
Nanna, 32–33, 46, 49, 216; liturgical
year, 152; voyage to Nippur, 133–34.
See also Sîn
Naqia, 183–84
Nâru, 54
national gods, 57
natural phenomena, 44, 101–2, 216. *See
also* suffering
Nebo, 211
Nebuchadnezzar II, 17, 135
Nechepso-Petosiris, 215
Nergal, 34–35, 54, 57, 69, 108–9, 209,
211; hymns/prayers, 147; liturgical
year, 153
Netherworld, 34–35, 54, 107–10, 151,
153, 204; Anunnaki, 55
New Year celebrations, 123, 158–64
Nimrud, 16, 115, 157
Ninanna, 47
Ninazu, 54
Nin-égal, 133
Nineveh, 115, 153
Ningirim, 161
Ningirsu, 46
Ninlil, 54, 67, 76, 133–34; liturgical
year, 152; mentioned in poetry, 167
Ninsuna, 62
Nintinugga, 152
Nintu, 54
Ninurta, 46, 54, 57, 64, 96, 138, 209
Nippur, 53, 73, 115, 117, 118, 127,
142–44; calendar, 151; *The Visit of
Nanna-Sîn to,* 133–34
Nudimmud, 141, 143
number of gods, 45, 54, 55
numerical representations of the gods,
70–71, 73; tetrads, 49–50, 53, 57; tri-
ads, 57, 98–99

numinous nature of the gods, 36, 117, 149–50
Nusku, 57, 64, 167

offerings, 114–15, 194–95, 216. *See also* sacrifice
omnipotence of the gods, 91, 135, 191–92
onomastics, 99–100; descriptions of the gods, 47–48; foreign gods, 96–97; henotheism, 41; Marduk, 56; names of people, 38–39, 55, 57, 165; specific days, 167; temples, 117
Oppenheim, Leo, 26–27
oral traditions, 24, 72, 75; cosmogony, 81
origins of humans. *See* human existence
origins of religion, 4–5
origins of the gods, 52–55, 72–77, 81, 98–99
orthodoxy, 6
orthopraxy, 6
Otto, R., 36

Palestine, 151
pantheism, 3, 28, 45, 211
Pantheon babylonicum (Deimel), 45
Papsukkal, 46, 209
pardon, 190–91
parentage, 68, 72
Parthians, 18, 20, 208
pašīšu priests, 121, 123
patron gods, 216
Persia, 17–18, 20, 208
The Persian Wars (Herodotus), 210–11, 218
personal gods, 42, 91, 165; prayers, 148–49; sin and pardon, 190–91
personal names, 38–39, 55, 56, 93, 136
personnel of the temples, 115–19, 124
pessimism, 222
phantoms, 106–10, 204
Philippus of Opus, 217
Phoenicians, 96
physiognomy, 180
picto-ideographic writing, 12
piety, 164–70, 184–85
pilgrimage rituals, 133–34
Plato, 217
Poem of the Righteous Sufferer, The, 60–61, 118–19, 165–66, 190–92

poetry, 28–36; *Epic of Creation*, 56. *See also* prayers
political history, 13–18; prehistoric era, 8–9
political issues, 51–54; independence, 208
political role of religion, 90–95, 117, 154, 163, 175; government of humanity, 103–5
polytheism, 3, 6, 40–43, 58
power of the gods, 38–39, 111; creation, 82–83; henotheism, 40–42; the m e, 94
pragmatism, 113
prayers, 22–23, 135–49, 165; astral religion, 185, 213–14, 216; personal gods, 165; secret, 159; "with raised hand," 137
prehistoric era, 6–11, 19
presence of the divine, 116–17
priests, 54, 119–25, 154; Babylonian, 56; celibacy, 122–23; divination, 174; *Epic of Creation*, 56; exorcism, 200–202; literacy, 122, 124; liturgy, 149–54; meals, 130–31; sacred marriage, 157–58; women, 120–23
processions, 153, 163
procreation, 84
pronunciation guide, ix–x
prosperity, 156–58
prostitution, 122–23, 194
Psalms, 206
punishment, 147–48, 189, 205, 220–21
purification, 161, 201
Puzriš-Dagan (site), 127, 129, 152
pyramid of power, 50–52, 91, 219–20

Qatna, 133
Qingu, 61, 93, 102
qualities of the gods, 59–61, 92

rationalism, 211
recipes, 130
Les religions orientales dans le paganisme romain (Cumont), 232n.7
religious behavior, ix, 4–5, 23, 114–202; common forms of worship, 165–68; deductive divination, 176–81; divination, 170–85; exorcism/magic, 170, 185–202; liturgy, 149–54; maintenance of the gods, 125–33; prayer,

religious behavior (*continued*)
135–49; priests, 119–25; religious
feeling/religiosity, 164–70; social life
of the gods, 133–64; temples, 115–19
religious centers, 53
religious feeling/religiosity, ix, 2–6,
21, 28–42, 222; fear, 36–40; New
Year celebrations, 164; official images,
36; onomastics, 55–56; prayers, 138;
religious behavior, 164–70; sources,
28–36
religious psychology, 42
repentance, 138, 189
representations of the divine, ix, 3–4,
6, 22–23; fear, 36–40; goodness, 39–
40; hierarchies, 44–58; mythologies,
58–113; personal presence, 40; royalty, 114; transcendence of the gods,
40
revealed religions, 5–6, 41–42
rituals, 23, 114–15, 124, 209, 210; astral
religion, 213–14; baking, 129; exorcism, 194–200; liturgy, 149–54;
magic, 193–94; roles of priests, 120–
21, 123
roles of gods, 46–47, 210; foreign gods,
96–97
Roman culture, 176, 212; astral religion,
222
ruler of the gods, 49
rulers. *See* monarchs

sacramental activities; divination, 170–
85; exorcism/magic, 185–202
sacred marriage, 65, 123, 154–58
sacrifice, 156, 166; maintenance of the
gods, 125–26; New Year celebrations,
162; personal gods, 165
Sagarâtum, 172
Šamaš, 50, 54, 57; clothing, 132–33;
divination, 178, 183–85; exorcism,
197–98; government of humanity/
justice, 33, 103; hymns/prayers, 138;
mentioned in documents, 33–34,
59, 97, 167, 185; power, 91; sin, 188;
sun, 33, 44, 46, 59, 68, 216, 226n.6
(chap. 4)
Šamaššumukin, 168
Šamši-Adad, 54
šangû priests, 121, 123
Sargonids, 17, 20

Sargon the Great, 13–14, 19, 54
scholars, 120, 122, 124, 209, 211
schools, 124, 201
science, 214–15
Sea, 206
Seleucid people, 17–18, 20, 149–50, 208
Semitic languages, 9–11; ancestors of
the gods, 73–74; Aramaic, 209
Semitic peoples, vii–viii, 9–15, 19, 27–
28, 54, 96–97, 219; divination, 176,
179–80; evil, 187; Hebrews, 6, 151–
52, 204–8; prayer, 137; sacred marriage, 157; sexual roles of the priests,
122; transcendence of the gods, 61.
See also Akkadian people
Sennacherib, 183
sexuality, 67, 120–24, 194; sacred marriage, 154–58
Shu-Sîn, sacred marriage, 155–56
Šibtu, 173
Siddhartha Gautama, 6
šigû, 167–68
sin, 102, 146–47, 166–67, 188–92,
195–96, 205, 220–21
Sîn, 32, 46, 50, 54, 96, 209; mentioned
in documents, 32–33, 57, 59, 69, 168,
185; moon, 47, 68, 76, 216; power,
91; voyage to Nippur, 133–34. *See
also* Nanna
Sippar, 53
songs. *See* music
soul, 214
sources, vii, ix–x, 6, 21–28; divination,
176; Greek and Roman, 212; locations, 23–24; religious feeling/reli-
giosity, 28–36; writing, 12, 17–18
speeches, 138
stars/constellations, 62–63, 69–70, 79–
80, 178, 185, 231n.76; astral religion,
212, 216–17; divination, 180; liturgy,
150
statues of the gods, 65, 116–17, 130,
132; Babylon, 119; New Year celebrations, 160–63; travel, 133–34
Stoicism, 215
structure of religion, 1–6
success in life, 111–13, 169–70, 222
suffering, 101–2, 114, 164, 166, 168,
180, 220–21; divination, 170–81; exorcism, 187–92, 194–200; magic,
186–87, 192–94

Sumerian language, ix, 13, 14, 23, 209; ancestors of the gods, 73–74; creation myths, 83; exorcism/magic, 187; gods listed in catalogues, 48–50; myths of human existence, 98–103; names of gods, 45–46; personal names, 38–39

Sumerian people, 8–13, 19, 27–28, 205, 219; clerical tradition, 121; descriptions of the gods, 47; female gods, 108; nudity of priests, 125; number of gods, 48, 54; origins of the gods, 52–53; pantheon, 46; prayer, 137; sacred marriage, 154–58; transcendence, 61

sun, 212, 216

sun god, 33–34, 44, 46, 49, 68, 91, 226n.6 (chap. 4)

superiority of the gods, 58–64, 71

Supersage. See Atraḫasîs

supreme tetrad, 53

Šurpu, 116–17, 199

Šuruppak. *See* Fâra/Šuruppak

sustenance for the dead, 110

symbolism, 64

syncretism, 46–47, 52–54, 210–11, 227n.14; foreign gods, 96–97

Tablet of Destinies, 93, 163

taboos, 168

Tallqvist, K., 45

Tašmêtu, 157, 161, 163; hymns/prayers, 147

Tavern Keeper, 111–12

Tell Abû Ṣalābīkh, 23, 72; catalogs of gods, 48; teachings about life, 112–13

temples, 53, 89, 115–19, 209; activity levels of, 154; dedication, 85, 142–44; dwellings of the priests, 124; Ésagil, 56; exorcism, 200; sacred marriage, 155

Temple of Akîtu, 163

tetrads, 49–50, 53, 57

theocentric cult, 114–70

Theodicy, 60, 87, 191

theogony, 52–55, 72–77, 98–99; cosmogony, 81–83

Theogony of Dunnu, 75–76

Thrice-Greatest Hermes, 215

Tiamat, 75, 79, 87–88, 93, 163, 207

time, 86

Tišpak, 54

tocomancy, 180, 182

tombs, 109

Tower of Babel, 115

transcendence of the gods, 40, 61, 69–71, 192

transcription of documents, ix

transformation of priests, 120

transgender clothing, 123–24

travel of the gods, 133–34

treatises, 179–82, 196, 231n.73

Tree against Reed, 84

Tummal, 134

Ugaritic language, 14

universalism, 96–97

universe, 68, 77–81; temples, 118

Ur, 14, 19, 118; liturgical year, 152; livestock, 127; sacred marriage, 155; *The Visit of Nanna-Sîn to Nippur*, 133–34

Urartians, 96

Uraš, 46

Ur-Ninurta, 139–41

Ursa Major, 150

Uruk, 53, 62, 94, 115, 117–18, 128, 134, 149; New Year celebrations, 158

Utanapištim, 62, 105–6

Utu, 33–34, 44, 46, 49, 216; Larsa and Sippar, 53

Venus, 211

Venus (planet), 216

vociferators, 173–74

wars, 135

washing of the gods, 132

water, 54, 63, 80, 206, 230n.25

Wê, 100–101, 228n.80

weather, 49, 91

will of the gods. *See* fate

women: divination, 172; priests, 120–23, 149–50, 155–57

workers in the temples, 115–19, 124

worship, ix, 4, 5, 23, 154. *See also* religious behavior

writing, 6, 11–12, 19, 23–24, 203; Akkadian, 15; alphabet, 16; authors, 25; cuneiform, x, 12, 17–18, 23–24, 45; divination, 177–79; vs. oral tradition, 24–25; prayers, 148–49; sources, 28–36; Sumerian, ix, 23

Yahweh, 207–8
year, 151

Zababa, 46, 54, 57
Zarpanit/u, 54, 160
Zeus, 211

ziggurats, 116, 229n.1 (chap. 6); liturgy,
    150
Zimri-Lim, 172–73
Ziusudra, 103
zodiac, 212